REVIVE US AGAIN

REVIVE US AGAIN

VISION AND ACTION IN
MORAL ORGANIZING

THE REVEREND DR.
WILLIAM J. BARBER II

WITH THE REVEREND DR. LIZ THEOHARIS
AND THE REVEREND DR. RICK LOWERY

BEACON PRESS
BOSTON

Beacon Press
Boston, Massachusetts
www.beacon.org

Beacon Press books
are published under the auspices of
the Unitarian Universalist Association of Congregations.

Printed in the United States of America
21 20 19 18   8 7 6 5 4 3 2 1

This book is printed on acid-free paper that meets the uncoated paper
ANSI/NISO specifications for permanence as revised in 1992.

Text design and composition by Kim Arney

Library of Congress Cataloging-in-Publication Data

Names: Barber, William J., II | Lowery, R. H. (Richard H.) | Theoharis, Liz.,
   Works. Selections.
Title: Revive us again : vision and action in moral organizing / Rev. Dr. William
   Barber II, with Rev. Dr. Liz Theoharis and Rev. Dr. Rick Lowery.
Description: Boston, Massachusetts : Beacon Press, [2018]
Identifiers: LCCN 2018003599 (print) | LCCN 2018030855 (ebook) |
   ISBN 9780807025611 (ebook) | ISBN 9780807025604 (pbk. : alk. paper)
Subjects: LCSH: Social justice—Religious aspects—Christianity. | Social
   justice—United States.
Classification: LCC BR115.J8 (ebook) | LCC BR115.J8 R48 2018 (print) |
   DDC 201/.7—dc23
LC record available at https://lccn.loc.gov/2018003599

CONTENTS

INTRODUCTION

Preaching and Prophetic Witness in the Public Square

The Reverend Dr. William J. Barber II

XI

PART ONE

Biblical and Theological Foundations for a Moral Movement

CHAPTER ONE

The Prophetic Word Is Political

The Reverend Dr. Rick Lowery

3

CHAPTER TWO

Blessed Are the Rejected for They
Shall Lead the Revival

The Reverend Dr. Liz Theoharis

11

CHAPTER THREE

Organizing and Shaping a Moral Vision
for Justice in the Public Square

The Reverend Dr. William J. Barber II

18

PART TWO

Vision and Action

CHAPTER FOUR

When the Stones Come Together

The Reverend Dr. William J. Barber II

31

RESPONSE

The Door to Life's Defining Moments

The Reverend Dr. Nancy Petty

46

CHAPTER FIVE

Moral March on Raleigh

The Reverend Dr. William J. Barber II

53

RESPONSE

We Are Not Afraid

Al McSurely

60

CHAPTER SIX

The Call to Be Positioned as Powerful
Prisoners of Prophetic Hope

The Reverend Dr. William J. Barber II

66

RESPONSE

Blues, Gospel, and Jazz Visions for God's
Own Prisoner of Hope

Dr. Timothy Tyson

84

CHAPTER SEVEN

Moral Action on Climate Change

The Reverend Dr. William J. Barber II

96

RESPONSE

Rekindle in Us a Fire:
William Barber's Moral Call to Climate Action

Karenna Gore

100

CHAPTER EIGHT

I Wish You a Mourning Christmas

The Reverend Dr. William J. Barber II

109

RESPONSE

A Call to Mourning: Wish and Warning

The Reverend Dr. James Forbes Jr.

119

CHAPTER NINE

The Danger of Misdiagnosing Terrorism

The Reverend Dr. William J. Barber II

124

RESPONSE

Growing a Local Peace Economy

Jodie Evans

137

CHAPTER TEN

You Have a Right to Fight for a Living Wage

The Reverend Dr. William J. Barber II

143

RESPONSE

Fighting Together for $15 and a Union

Mary Kay Henry

149

CHAPTER ELEVEN

Bothered and Baptized by the Blood

The Reverend Dr. William J. Barber II

156

RESPONSE

Cheating to
Win Elections Is a Sin

Penda D. Hair

167

CHAPTER TWELVE

Standing Down Is Not an Option

The Reverend Dr. William J. Barber II

177

RESPONSE

A Moral Agenda for Mercy and Justice

The Reverend Dr. Katharine Rhodes Henderson

186

CHAPTER THIRTEEN

The Need to Know Who We Are in Times Like These

The Reverend Dr. William J. Barber II

194

RESPONSE

Lyrical Connections:
The Music and Message of the Movement

Yara Allen

213

CHAPTER FOURTEEN

We Shall Not Be Moved!

The Reverend Dr. William J. Barber II

217

RESPONSE

Listening to the Heart and Hurt of the People

Charmeine Fletcher

222

PREACHING AND PROPHETIC WITNESS IN THE PUBLIC SQUARE

THE REVEREND DR. WILLIAM J. BARBER II

In the fall of 2017, I traveled to El Paso, Texas, to participate in a Hugs Not Walls action with the Border Network for Human Rights. Early on a Sunday morning, after listening to the stories of families that had been impacted by extreme anti-immigration policies, I waded into the Rio Grande with Maria, a grandmother who has been separated from her husband and children. She had not seen one of her sons in sixteen years. We were up to our knees in muddy water, but Maria's tears rebaptized me as she held the child she'd borne and raised for five precious minutes in the middle of a river.

I thought of James Baldwin's words: "We made the world we're living in and we have to make it over."

Remaking America will require nothing less than a moral revival. Our inhumanity toward families like Maria's is about something deeper than policy difference or economic transition. It is a moral crisis rooted in this nation's original sins of the genocide of indigenous people and race-based slavery. Though this is not the first time we've faced the demons of systemic racism, their capacity to consume us has rarely been more palpable in our common life. To survive, America must be born again.

The fundamental values of our deepest moral and religious traditions are love, truth, grace, justice, care of family, community, and shared prosperity. But these values are under assault. As systemic racism deconstructs our national reality, more and more people are pushed into poverty while the rich get richer. Hard-won voting rights are under constant assault: lawmakers target African Americans "with almost surgical precision" to gain partisan advantage in elections, as the United States Court of Appeals for the Fourth Circuit ruled in overturning a 2013 North Carolina law limiting voting options. Similarly, emergency-manager laws in Michigan and elsewhere are replacing elected leaders with appointed technocrats. The wealthiest get ever greater tax cuts while life-saving social programs are threatened and cut off. Public education is undermined by underfunding, by attacks on teachers' unions, and by the undemocratic influence exercised by wealthy funders.

Growing numbers of people can't go to the doctor or get their medicine because of the cost; supports that do exist are under attack and insurers, drug companies, big hospital chains, and their financiers are making billions in the process. Job training, food security, and community economic development programs are on the chopping block. Women are too often abused and assaulted, while people of color, immigrants, and members of the LGBTQIA community are treated as scapegoats to distract from devastating political and economic policies that keep wages low, employment insecure, and workers unorganized. Our air and water are poisoned by hugely profitable corporations who are almost never held accountable for their actions. Hundreds of billions are spent on a permanent war economy, escalating violence around the world and lining the pockets of military contractors.

The only remedy for our moral crisis is a transformed national heart, a moral movement for families and communities rooted in the constitutional and sacred values of compassion, empathy, and courageous dedication to the common good. This movement must be broad-based and welcoming to all, embracing the great diversity of religious and nonreligious moral traditions of our people. It must be grounded in a fundamental commitment to the general welfare, the basic moral conviction expressed in Leviticus 19's call to "love your neighbor as yourself" and to "love the immigrant worker as yourself." It is rooted in the call of the great Jewish text Isaiah 58 to be "repairers of the breach."

The scope of this moral vision is universal. The common good we promote is not limited by family, ethnicity, political philosophy, or religious belief. It demands a relentless dedication to the flourishing of all.

The basic vision guiding a moral movement is rooted in both religion and the principles articulated in America's founding documents. "We hold these truths to be self-evident, that all [people] are created equal, that they are endowed by their Creator with certain unalienable Rights, that among these are Life, Liberty and the pursuit of Happiness," Thomas Jefferson wrote, announcing the formal independence of the American colonies from British rule. The Virginia Declaration of Rights, adopted shortly before the Declaration of Independence, states the economic dimension more explicitly, defining the "inherent rights" of human beings as "the enjoyment of life and liberty, with the means of acquiring and possessing property, and pursuing and obtaining happiness and safety." For the founders, civil, political, and economic rights were to be tightly bound. The enjoyment of life and liberty depended on the right to share wealth and live in safety.

More than a decade after the Declaration of Independence, a sufficient number of American states ratified the Constitution of the United States to create the federal governmental system that survives to this day. The preamble states the Constitution's rationale:

> We the People of the United States, in Order to form a more perfect Union, establish justice, insure domestic Tranquility, provide for the common defence, promote the general Welfare, and secure the Blessings of Liberty to ourselves and our Posterity do ordain and establish this Constitution for the United States of America.

According to what was written, the American form of government should promote a stronger sense of national identity, a more vigorous national community. It should establish justice, ensure peace and security, and promote the material well-being and liberty of all, including future generations. This is not a random list. These ideals are closely related to and essential to the success of the democratic republic the Constitution establishes. Liberty is rooted in community. Peace is founded on justice. The general well-being of the nation is secured by shared prosperity and principled concern for the well-being of future generations. These core national and international convictions motivate a moral movement for social, economic, and ecological justice today. They lie at the heart of the moral revival we seek.

But, as the Reverend Dr. Martin Luther King Jr. once said, in a speech to the Southern Christian Leadership Conference, "America has suffered from the high blood pressure of creeds and an anemia of deeds." This is the great American contradiction: the leaders of the Revolution meant their lofty ideals only for white, land-owning Americans. They were flawed messengers for these ideals. Many justified chattel slavery, which rendered black slaves as subhuman property and free blacks as not being endowed with the rights of whites. Many of the founders believed slavery was God-ordained, while others tolerated it, though they claimed it was morally abhorrent. These men lived on land taken by genocide, deception, and brutal force from the people who had resided there for centuries before Europeans came. They denied the rights they claimed for themselves to their wives and daughters.

Clearly, many of the men who signed the Declaration of Independence did not believe that every human being had "inherent" and "unalienable" rights. The power of the idea, however, transcends the shortsightedness and hypocrisy of the men who declared independence and founded the United States of America. The words (and contradictions) contained in these founding documents would ultimately inspire American reformers and revolutionaries to lead moral revivals to abolish slavery, build the economic and political power of workers and their families, and win fuller political and civil rights for women and African Americans. The sentiments expressed in the founding documents of the nation served as the cornerstone of the United Nations'

Universal Declaration of Human Rights and subsequent international human rights covenants and declarations, including the UN's Declaration on the Rights of Indigenous Peoples.

So, a fundamental contradiction lies at the heart of American democracy. There is a tension between the ideals of "unalienable" political and economic rights for all and the legacy of racism, sexism, exploitation, poverty, and economic inequality that runs deep in the American experience. In the all-too-frequent dissonance between our ideals and our reality, however, we find prophetic hope. Our ideals expose our flaws and inspire us to repair the breaches and heal the nation. Social and economic progress in America is built on our resolution of this contradiction in the direction of our highest ideals.

On April 4, 1967, just one year to the day before his assassination, Dr. King declared it was time to break the silence about contradictions at the heart of American society. At the historic Riverside Church, he preached, "We as a nation must undergo a radical revolution of values." He proclaimed that silence was betrayal, that the truth must be told. King's charge for a revolution of values echoes the cries of the biblical prophets to stand up for justice, righteousness, and the dignity of all throughout the ages.

> "If you remove the yoke from among you, the pointing of the finger, the speaking of evil, if you offer your food to the hungry and satisfy the needs of the afflicted, then your light shall rise in the darkness and your gloom be like the noonday. The Lord will guide you continually, and satisfy your needs in parched places, and make your bones strong; and you shall be like a watered garden, like a spring of water, whose waters never fail. Your ancient ruins shall be rebuilt; you shall raise up the foundations of many generations; you shall be called the repairer of the breach, the restorer of streets to live in" (Isaiah 58, New Revised Standard Version).

> "The believers, both men and women, are in charge of and responsible for one another; they all enjoin the doing of what is right and forbid the doing of what is wrong" (Qur'an 9:71).

"The Spirit of the Lord is upon me, because he has anointed me to bring good news to the poor. He has sent me to proclaim release to the captives and recovery of sight to the blind, to let the oppressed go free, to proclaim the year of the Lord's favor" (Luke 4:18–19, New Standard Revised Version).

Today, more than fifty years after Dr. King's call to break the silence, inequality in America is worse than it has been since America's Gilded Age. Voting rights and democracy are being trampled; millions of people lack the health care, living-wage jobs, and quality education they need; and racism, hatred, and bigotry are dividing the country at a time of disintegrating possibilities for life, liberty, and the pursuit of happiness for *everyone* in these United States.

Our faith traditions and Constitution are clear: we must stand up for justice and tell the truth. This is why I have joined with my sister the Reverend Dr. Liz Theoharis and her colleagues at the Kairos Center to cochair the Poor People's Campaign: A National Call for Moral Revival. We challenge the position that the preeminent moral issues today are about prayer in public schools, abortion, and homosexuality. Instead, we declare that the deepest public concerns of our faith traditions are with how our society treats the poor, those on the margins, the least of these, including women, children, workers, immigrants, and the sick; with equality and representation under the law; and with the desire for peace, love, and harmony within and among nations.

Together with hundreds of grassroots organizations and millions of impacted people across America, we lift up and defend the sacred moral principles of our faith and constitutional values. We stand for policies that promote these moral and constitutional values and express the right of all to thrive and not merely survive. This moral policy agenda includes:

I. Prolabor, antipoverty policies that build up economic democracy through employment, living wages, the end of discrimination at work, affordable housing, direct cash transfers, and other support for all families struggling to get by, and the challenging of war policies that preempt a real war on poverty that can protect and defend the sanctity of the lives of all peoples in the world;

2. Equality in education by ensuring every child receives a high-quality, well-funded, constitutional, diverse public education, as well as access to community colleges and universities, and by securing equitable funding for minority colleges and universities;

3. Health care for all by expanding Medicaid in every state; ensuring access to Medicare and Social Security; moving decisively toward a universal, transparent, and equitable health-care system; and by protecting the environment and protecting women's health;

4. Fairness in the criminal justice system by addressing the continuing inequalities in the system for black, brown, and poor white people and by fighting the proliferation of guns;

5. Voting rights, women's rights, LGBTQIA rights, labor rights, religious freedom rights, immigrant rights, and the fundamental principle of equal protection under the law.

We believe our moral traditions are a firm foundation upon which to stand against the divide-and-conquer strategies of extremists. We claim a higher ground in partisan debate by returning public discourse to our deepest moral and constitutional values.

Any nation that seeks to take away health care, pit its citizens against people from other places, foster racism, and normalize poverty is in the midst of a profound moral crisis. The fact that religious extremists and Christian nationalists stand for many of these policies, amounts to a kind of theological malpractice. The cooptation of religious language in defense of extremism, whether in the United States or elsewhere, exploits an underlying public crisis of faith: in government, in political parties, in religious institutions, in nongovernmental groups and, most important, in ourselves and one another. In the United States at present, fear has, in large measure, trumped hope.

America needs a moral reset. The structural inequality endemic to the United States today is not preordained and it need not persist. The poor do *not* always have to be with us. Moral abdication in the face of endemic poverty is born out of fear and feeds false ideas of scarcity and a politics of polarization that weakens the heart of our democracy. To restore the legitimacy of our democracy, people of conscience must resist narrow, regressive thinking and reclaim the moral high ground. We need to rebuild public trust, revive the country's faith in its better angels, and reenvision America's public policies through the moral lens of justice and the constitutional principle of the common good.

The good news is that people across the country are already taking to the streets in unprecedented numbers to oppose attacks on the poor and oppose the structural inequality and state violence those attacks too often involve. America appears ripe for a resurgence of "fusion politics"—politics familiar to students of the movements for the abolition of slavery and for civil rights. These new coalitions of unlikely allies help those who have suffered injustice and been divided by race, geography, gender, and religion to see what we have in common.

The Poor People's Campaign: A National Call for Moral Revival is a transformational effort, rooted in moral and constitutional principles, that brings the dispossessed people of this country together across the trumped-up divisions of race, income, gender, and faith. This movement seeks to help us hear one another, radically change the popular understanding of poverty and racism, and build a unified force to reconstruct a society that creates poverty for most of us and great wealth for a small few. This book arises from our campaign and invokes voices of people who have long worked on various aspects of this struggle. A movement to shift the moral narrative and build power among the people in and across states and local communities is rising up to break the chains of poverty, racism, ecological devastation, and the war economy.

The core of this book is a series of sermons I have preached to sketch the contours of the moral revival we seek for our country. Each sermon is paired with a brief response from an activist, theologian, or writer working on the primary issue I've addressed. These responses demonstrate some of the ways that the basic principles of scripture and Constitution are being fleshed out in the public square and in contemporary struggles for justice. They are, in short, sketches on the Word made flesh in America today.

These sermons are introduced by Part One, which discusses biblical and theological foundations for building a moral movement for justice, peace, and shared prosperity for all, and outlines basic principles and practical strategies for organizing and shaping a moral vision for justice that can lead to meaningful change in our time. None of us does this work alone. I'm grateful to my colleagues Rick Lowery and Liz Theoharis for organizing this project and contributing their own voices in these chapters.

This book is an invitation to join a moral movement in America today. It is a call to speak, to march, to work, to repair the breaches in the social and economic fabrics of our nation and world. We walk in the footsteps of moral giants, countless numbers of everyday people whose moral clarity and passionate commitment to justice led them to join together, speak out, and challenge our nation to heed the call of our highest ideals—abolitionists, suffragists, labor activists, civil rights and women's rights advocates, environmentalists, LGBTQIA organizers, and the ancient prophets who inspired them. We draw strength from their courage and profound wisdom. Their vision of justice and their deep commitment to the highest ideals of the American Revolution guide us as we walk boldly toward a better, morally stronger nation and world.

But Martin and Rosa are not coming back to lead this moral revival. Bayard Rustin, Dorothy Day, Ella Baker, and Cesar Chavez carried the torch in their day, but they are not coming back. It's our time now. Maria has led us into the river of Resistance, and thousands have followed her. As the Hebrew children followed Moses into the Red Sea, we are trusting "a way out of no way" to lead us to the America that has not yet been. And we are praying like so many who came before us, "Revive in us a heart that beats for justice. O Spirit of the Universe, Revive Us Again!"

REVIVE US AGAIN

PART ONE

BIBLICAL AND THEOLOGICAL FOUNDATIONS FOR A MORAL MOVEMENT

Throughout American history, the Bible has played an important role in political discourse and in movements for progressive change. Its root conviction that all human beings have inherent value and are worthy of dignity and respect has been and continues to be a moral touchstone for people of all faiths and beliefs. To appreciate fully the power of the biblical witness for the advancement of human rights and social and economic justice today, it is important to understand the circumstances that gave rise to the biblical books, to seek points of contact between the ancient communities that wrote and read them and our own community today, to note differences between their experience and ours, and to discern how they might inform us in struggles for justice today. It is also important to preach these stories in our public square as we build a moral movement modeled after moral movements of the biblical past.

This section contains biblical and theological interpretation from all three authors. It begins with the Hebrew scriptures as a touchstone for social justice work today. It explores how the Old Testament and the people of Israel were products and producers of protest and righteous moral organizing. It continues into the New Testament and argues that the Bible documents stories of poor and oppressed people rising up with God on their side to right the wrongs of society. It asserts that Jesus was a Palestinian Jew living in an occupied territory who personally struggled with poverty and homelessness and led a Poor People's Campaign to challenge poverty, bigotry, military might, and the destruction of the whole world that still has resonance and relevance today. It concludes with a section on preaching, anointing, and the work that it takes to make justice and peace in the midst of oppression and despair.

CHAPTER ONE

THE PROPHETIC WORD IS POLITICAL

THE REVEREND DR. RICK LOWERY

The prophetic message at the heart of the Bible calls us to act now to build a more just nation, a better world. Prophetic faith is always grounded in the lived experience of working families, and it continues to be so today. This chapter focuses on the social, economic, and political forces in the ancient world that gave rise to Israel's prophetic movement and the prophetic vision at the heart of the Hebrew scriptures and the gospel witness of Jesus and the early church. We will look especially at the disruptive economic impact of ancient empires that concentrated wealth in the hands of a few while requiring the wealth-producing majority to work harder for less return. The result was declining wages, rising inequality, ecologically risky production practices, and greater insecurity for more and more working people. We will examine the prophets' critique of this unjust social-economic order and their courageous challenge to the ruling powers, giving special attention to Isaiah 58, and explore the prophets' vision of hope for a better world, a vision grounded in their understanding of the nature of Israel's God, the liberator of slaves, the champion of the poor and vulnerable. Though our circumstances today are different in many ways, we believe the core of the Bible's prophetic witness offers a fresh and urgent challenge for us. We think it calls for a moral revival in our nation and all nations, a transformation of the heart, a spiritual awakening so that we may catch God's vision of a better world and act now to build a more just society—a better, fairer life for all.

In ancient Israel, an expanding empire gave rise to a prophetic protest movement, first in the north (as reflected in the Elijah-Elisha stories, circa late 800s BCE, and Hosea, mid-700s) and later in the south (Isaiah and Micah, mid- to late 700s). To understand the connection between the expanding power of the monarchy and the empire and the rise of prophetic protest, we need to know a little about the organization of economic life in the hill country along the eastern slope of the Mediterranean Sea, where the Israelite states emerged. This part of the world underwent a series of major changes in the decades after 1,200 BCE.

In the centuries before, the Egyptians had established a series of walled city-states along the coastal plains, connected politically to the Egyptian empire as de facto colonies. The growth in population density in and around the coastal cities coincided with a noticeable migration into the hill country farther east. Though similar migrations had occurred from time to time in earlier centuries, technological innovations made the settlement of the hill country particularly feasible in this period. Most important, the region developed the ability to forge strong iron plows that could turn the rockier soil of the hill country without breaking. The introduction of agricultural terracing and reliable cisterns made agriculture possible on land that once could not be well farmed. These developments prompted surplus populations in and around the coastal and valley walled cities to move into the highlands and establish farms.

Careful reading of some of the narratives that describe "Israelite" and "Canaanite" cities and regions after the "conquest" shows that Israelites tended to settle in the high country and other areas outside the orbit of the Canaanite cities in the lowlands and coastal plains, where Canaanites continued to live. This, combined with the fact that there is no discernible distinction between Canaanite and Israelite material culture—tools, artwork, pottery, et cetera—has led many scholars to conclude that Israelites were in fact "surplus," disempowered, economically marginal Canaanites who rejected the political, economic, and military domination of the walled city-states of the low country. They disavowed the political and religious authority of their kings who claimed to represent the local gods who "owned" the land and demanded rent from those who farmed it. The Israelites' rallying cry was, "The land belongs to YHWH," the God who liberates slaves from the power of Egypt. What the Bible describes as the "conquest" of Canaan was, at least in part, a peasant revolt. Out of this boiling cauldron of change, the people—"Israel"—emerged in Canaan with a revolutionary understanding of a God who sides with peasants and slaves against the abusive power of royal-imperial elites.

A distinctive set of moral values undergirded the social-economic system of the Israelites. Just as every able-bodied member of the household was morally committed to support and safeguard the overall well-being of the family through time, so, too, households in a given region were morally obligated to provide mutual support to one another. This was especially true in the case of vulnerable households: families without an able-bodied senior male, immigrant workers who were cut off from their own kinship networks, or travelers who were passing through, for example. This moral code of support and particular care for vulnerable households (in biblical shorthand, "widows, orphans, and immigrant workers") was mutually beneficial. Collapsed households left rootless, often hungry and desperate individuals who posed a potential threat to the broader community. So, everyone had a very practical interest in ensuring the strength and viability of farm households in their region. This practical value of mutual support and special care for the poor and vulnerable lies at the heart of the basic moral vision of the Torah and the prophets.

The emergence of strong monarchies in the north and the south, coinciding with the rising influence of Assyrian imperialism in the region, began to undermine this social-economic system and the moral values that supported it. The lifeblood of the ancient royal state and its imperial system was the extraction of agricultural wealth from farmers. This was accomplished through the imposition of taxes and the confiscation of household labor in the form of a military draft and forced labor on state building and agricultural projects.

Needless to say, taxes, the military draft, and forced labor subverted subsistence agriculture. Farmers had no choice but to shift toward surplus production, which normally meant planting a less diversified mix of crops. That, in turn, left families more vulnerable to drought, blight, pestilence, and crop failure. Since able-bodied sons and daughters were subject to the military draft and forced state labor, farm families had to increase production with fewer workers. All of these factors led to a rise in debt, as farm families were increasingly unable to produce enough to pay their taxes and still feed their families. Creditors often charged exorbitant interest rates on subsistence loans—loans that under the old moral code were given interest free as part of the obligation to provide support for vulnerable households. Of course, the people who had money to loan were those associated with the crown, and the money and grain they had to loan had passed to them through royal coffers filled by tax revenues from the very farm families who had sought the loans. This system of double extraction created a downward spiral of debt as families were forced to offer clothing, tools, labor, the labor or marriage value of children, and even the family farm itself as collateral for high-interest loans they would never be able to repay. The result was widespread consolidation of land in the hands of crown-connected elites and the impoverishment of farmers who now worked as debt slaves on what had been their own families' land.

The Hebrew prophetic movement rose as a response to this economic and moral deterioration. Isaiah's "Song of the Vineyard" is typical of the prophetic message: "Ah, you who join house to house and field to field, until there is room left for no one but you, and you are left to live alone in the midst of the land" (Isaiah 5:8; New Revised Standard Version).

Although we know little about the lives of many of the biblical prophets, we do know that many—certainly the three "major" prophets,

Isaiah, Ezekiel, and Jeremiah—were familiar with the customs of the court and were willing to speak openly and honestly to kings and high-ranking officials. Their candor, as Jeremiah learned, sometimes put them at risk. They refused, however, to remain silent in the face of injustice and violence toward the vulnerable poor. The anonymous prophet whom scholars usually call "Third Isaiah" described the prophetic mandate this way: "Shout out! Don't hold back! Lift your voice like a trumpet! Announce to my people their rebellion, to the house of Jacob their sins!" (Isaiah 58:1).

Several prophets have particularly strong words to say about religiously pious people who ignore the poor and refuse to confront injustice: "You serve your own interest on your fast day and oppress all your workers!" This is followed by an injunction "to loosen the bonds of injustice, to untie the straps of the yoke, to set those who are oppressed free" (Isaiah 58:3–7).

The prophetic word is inherently political. Prophetic witness makes noise! The prophets spoke their messages in the halls of the palace, in the presence of kings and the high-ranking officials of the court. Their words address both the "private" actions of individuals who harm others or take unfair advantage of them and the public actions and policies of the government that hurt or neglect the poor. At the heart of the prophetic critique is the conviction that the health of the nation and the land it inhabits depends on establishing and maintaining justice, which means adequate food, clothing, housing, and respect for everyone. The prophetic word is, therefore, also inherently economic.

The economic and political dimensions of biblical prophecy are deeply grounded in the nature of God. God liberates slaves, heals the sick, rescues the poor, comforts those who despair. God is, therefore, fundamentally gracious, a champion of justice, the wellspring of life and hope for a better world. The God of the biblical prophets is not detached and distant, the "impassible" God of classical philosophers unaffected by the world. The prophets' God is moved by suffering, passionate for justice, and deeply in love with creation and humanity.

All of the books of the Torah also share the basic moral convictions of mutual support and special care for the vulnerable poor that shaped the culture of the first Israelites. The core values of economic justice, mutual support, and special responsibility toward the poor that shape the prophetic message stand at the heart of the Deuteronomic code. These values are seen in the radical limitations Deuteronomy places on kings and on their ability to extract wealth from farm families or to enter into subservient political-economic relationships with foreign empires (Deuteronomy 17:14–20), and in the stunning restrictions on a king's ability to divert resources into military ventures (17:16; 20:1–20). Prophetic values are reflected in Deuteronomic rules governing debt forgiveness and manumission of debt slaves, the disposition of temple tithes, and policies to promote food security for vulnerable families. Charging interest on subsistence loans is forbidden (23:19–20) and credit practices must be humane (24:6, 10–13, 17). Wage theft is outlawed (24:14–15). All of these laws are grounded in the identity of YHWH as the God who liberates slaves from bondage (24:22 and other chapters).

The moral heart of the Torah and the prophets is grounded in the very nature of Israel's God and in the community's experience of liberation from bondage, an act of divine justice and love. Love, of course, begins with self and extends naturally to family. The Torah and the prophets invite the people of God to have an even more expansive view of love, to include in the family circle the native-born neighbor and immigrant worker as well. Leviticus instructs, "You must love the immigrant worker as yourself, for you were immigrants in the land of Egypt. I am YHWH!" (34).

The truly universal scope of this vision is portrayed with particular power in the shockingly radical proposal of Genesis 1, the introduction to the entire Bible and the lens through which the narratives that follow are now focused. Probably added to Genesis during one of the final stages of the book's production, this story of the world's creation borrows liberally from the imperial creation myths of Mesopotamia and dramatically flips their meaning to make a powerful point about the nature of God, of creation, and of human beings. The climax of the story comes when God rests for a day, blessing and consecrating that day each week. Later in the biblical narrative, God instructs the Israelites to observe sabbath rest as a testimony to God's rest at the end of creation (Exodus 20:8–11) and to God's rescue of slaves from bondage (Deuteronomy 5:12–15). There is a double significance to sabbath. First, it underlines the broader message of the creation narrative that God creates a world of abundance, where there is enough for everyone to survive and thrive. We get seven days of wealth for six days of work. This abundance frees us to share, to live lives of generosity, unconstrained by fear and obsessive acquisition. Second, it completes the radical proposal a few verses earlier in the story that all human beings are created "as the image of God" in the world (1:26–27).

Uniquely among the creatures of earth, human beings, the narrative says, are created "in" or "as" "the image of God." Also, for the first time in the story, the heavenly court is called to bear witness to the creation of a creature. The story thus underlines the "royal" character of the human being, male and female. We are the "image of God" and therefore empowered by God to govern on earth as the divine beings govern in the universe. In this way, Genesis 1 radically democratizes political power and elevates the status of all people. We are created not to be slaves, but to govern! As the image of God, we are worthy of dignity and respect, and we are empowered.

The very high view of human life expressed in the creation/sabbath story of Genesis 1 has ecological and social-economic implications. Leviticus 25 makes those connections explicit, extrapolating from sabbath day a regular cycle of "sabbath years" for the land, when fields are allowed to "rest" from planting (1–7). The idea is expanded even further to a "sabbath of sabbath years," a year of "jubilee" (10–15) when "liberty" is declared for land and people alike. Like sabbath year, jubilee includes rest for farmland, but it goes further, requiring a national redistribution of land ownership to correct the economic inequities that accrue over the decades (13–17). It also moves well beyond the seventh-year man-umission of debt slaves we see in Deuteronomy 15, abolishing slavery altogether, at least when it comes to fellow Israelites (39–46).

Obviously, the economic and political circumstances of the people changed over the centuries of the Bible's production. The admonitions of the prophets and instructions of the Torah adapted and evolved as circumstances shifted. The moral core, though, remained the same: God is the one who liberates slaves, who rescues from bondage, who desires the flourishing of all creation, the freedom and prosperity of all people. As God's people we are called to love God as God loves us. The Torah and the prophets point the way: we must love our neighbor and love the immigrant in our midst even as we love ourselves.

CHAPTER TWO

BLESSED ARE THE REJECTED FOR THEY SHALL LEAD THE REVIVAL

THE REVEREND DR. LIZ THEOHARIS

The New Testament documents a moral movement of the poor and rejected. It portrays the survival struggles of the marginalized, the solidarity and mutuality among different communities, and the critique of a social, political, and economic system that oppresses the vast majority of people. Given his leadership in that movement, it is not surprising that the main theme of many of Jesus's teachings and his ministry in general is bringing good news to the poor and marginalized, standing up for righteousness, and ending all forms of discrimination and oppression. Nor is it surprising that Jesus was recognized by Rome as a threat to the status quo and crucified, the punishment reserved for revolutionaries and those deemed insurrectionists.

Jim Wallis, an evangelical leader and the founder of *Sojourners* magazine, has written that one in every four stories in the Bible is about poverty, making it far and away the most common theme. Certainly, stories about poverty are much more numerous and prominent than those that pertain to issues such as marriage or sexuality or prayer in schools. At the very beginning of his ministry, in Luke 4, Jesus reads from the scroll of the prophet Isaiah and announces that he has come to fulfill the mission laid out in it—to proclaim release to the captives and bring good news to those who have been made poor by systems of oppression. In passages such as Matthew 25, Jesus reminds us that what we do to the least of these, we do unto him. The Apostle Paul, following his revelation of Jesus, started a collection for the poor of Jerusalem.

Jesus's teachings and actions around poverty, wealth, and power create a picture of him as a leader of a social, political, economic, and spiritual movement calling for a world without poverty, want, or oppression. The Sermon on the Mount, the parables, and his other lessons show him to be a "New Moses": a liberator and freedom fighter who brings instruction about how to treat the poor, the stranger, the widow, and the marginalized. Jesus was a teacher too. Contemporary and historical stories, prophetic instruction, and moral guidance were central to his revolutionary work. His was a ministry in which he educated while he organized, taught as he fought, walked as he talked, learned as he led. He admonished his followers and other movement leaders to morally resist the authorities as they built an order of justice and equality in the here and now. The purpose of his education and leadership-development practices was to reveal the lies enshrined in the status quo and to wake people up to the possibility of another way— what he named the Kingdom or Empire of God.

This revolutionary Jesus and the instruction left for his followers, as summarized by the books of the New Testament, follow the prophetic teachings of the Hebrew scriptures. The revolutionary teaching of the early Jesus movement is found not only in the sermons and parables, but also in the lives and community practices of Jesus's followers. The many references to material poverty and simplicity, especially that of Jesus and the disciples, have an important relationship to the lived experience of the poor, who made up the base of that movement during the Roman Empire. The asceticism of the Jesus movement followers, given the economic and debt practices of the empire, can be seen as both a necessary response to the reality of their poverty and resistance to the established order. Rather than romanticizing a simple life, one should read passages such as "Do not worry about your life, what you will eat" (Matthew 6, Luke 12) as comfort for people who are facing serious chronic financial difficulty. These passages tell the poor and rejected that they matter to God, that they can lead a powerful movement even if they own nothing themselves, and that by seeking God's justice together they can build a world without want. In that context, it is possible to interpret Jesus's instructions on how to be disciples—going out with no staff or money or bread, asking for meals to be provided—as a necessity of their economic situation, rather than as a voluntary decision to be poor. In this way, Jesus's teachings can be seen as a declaration of justice over charity and the conviction that poor and oppressed people are agents of change who do not have to wait for religious leaders or those with more resources to fix society's problems. Having heroes and leaders from the ranks of the poor and among those who have been rejected and marginalized for who they are is important for any moral movement. Jesus's own poverty and homelessness (beginning with his humble birth) and Paul's emphasis on his own personal struggles show that the early church was made up of people who did not have much and required a commitment to prosperity through community survival rather than individual accumulation and greed.

In Jesus's time, like our own, the leisure of the wealthy and powerful was held in high esteem. The common sense of those societies said that to work was to be low, dirty, and marginalized. But the people of the Jesus movement, drawing on a tradition stretching back to the Hebrew prophets, challenged that common sense and instead emphasized the value and dignity of labor. They announced that God's desire is for people to benefit from the fruits of their labor. The examples of Jesus, James, Paul, and other leaders of the Jesus movement working for a living—as carpenters, tent-makers, and fishers—affirm the dignity and worth of people who have to work in order to survive. It affirms that the intention in the Kingdom of God is to have community flourishing and prosperity for all, from the bottom up. Living wages are an important theme throughout the Bible for this very reason.

In addition to the reality of poverty and oppression among the leaders of the early Jesus movement, there are examples throughout the New Testament of communal practices of economic redistribution, antipoverty measures, and support for a social, spiritual, economic, and political movement opposed to Rome. Paul's concept of the collection is a central example. He suggested that the best way to spread the Jesus movement throughout the Roman world, to Jews and Greeks, was through this act of solidarity in which the poor of many diverse nations could support the lives and actions of the poor in Jerusalem (rather than the imperial center in Rome). This ancient act of solidarity and protest against the Roman Empire is also a survival strategy of sharing resources. It makes it possible for poor people not just to feed, house, and clothe themselves, but also to develop a movement with other poor people who want to build a different world. Today, we do not hear much mention of the collection for the poor. When we do hear about it, it is in reference to Christian giving (to the church and through charity). The collection, however, is not about giving to the church, nor is it a big Christian charity program (like the Salvation Army). It is about forging relationships of mutuality among diverse poor people to meet their needs. The collection for the poor is an example of the kind of practice called for in Acts 2:44–47 (New Revised Standard Version): "All who believed were together and had all things in common; they would sell their possessions and goods and distribute the proceeds to all, as any had need." In Paul's epistles, we hear that the resolution to disputes about who could be counted as part of the Christian community is participation in the collection for the poor; that one can demonstrate allegiance to the Jesus movement by offering material resources in support of its mission. And through these practices of the poor, a community where everyone prospers is possible.

There are other economic practices present throughout the New Testament that emphasize justice over charity and abundant life for all over riches for a very few. References to Exodus, Deuteronomy, Leviticus, Jeremiah, Hosea, Isaiah, and other Hebrew scriptures emphasize the ideas of liberation, forgiveness of debts, and economic justice. While the early Christians could have chosen any parts of the Old Testament for their New Testament references, the texts related to the elimination of poverty, the exodus from slavery, and the critique of the domination of power and empire resonated most closely with the lived experience of the early Christians. Freedom and liberation and the end of bondage and debt are mentioned throughout the New Testament. Indeed, the New Testament reappropriates liberatory themes from Hebrew scriptures, and this reappropriation is focused on poverty, love, and justice issues in particular.

Although we do not know extensively about the communities that documented the stories of Jesus, we know that they were communities of poor people and prophetic leaders who stood up for justice and peace. We know that they developed communal practices to survive, to spread their movement, and to challenge the theology, ideology, and practices of the empire. The Gospel of John was written by an ostracized and oppressed community. Mark was written by a community of followers from shortly after the destruction of the Temple, facing escalating imperial taxes and debts. Paul points out to the Galatians that they welcomed him, shared what they had with him, and healed him when he first arrived, rather than killing him as an outsider. It's important to see how all of these Jesus followers and communities, especially those from the bottom of society, created communal strategies for sharing and living cooperatively. Several of the New Testament stories, from the feeding of the five thousand to the messages of many of the parables to the community of goods in Acts 2 and 4, fit into this type of collective survival through mutual support and organization.

The New Testament contains numerous critiques of the disparity between the rich and the poor, and the way that systemic greed gets in the way of loving and honoring God and the neighbor. The other side of these critiques is the call to move from hierarchy to mutuality. Some of the passages that are most explicit include the teaching that one cannot worship God and Mammon, James's condemnation of the oppression of the poor by the rich (especially using the courts), and the parable of the rich young man who is told by Jesus that to have eternal life he must give what he has to the poor.

Many New Testament books explicitly critique the wealthy. This includes passages such as "It is easier for a camel to go through the eye of a needle than for someone who is rich to enter the kingdom of God" (Matthew 19); "The first shall be last, and the last first" (Mark 10); "Command [those who are rich] to do good, to be rich in good deeds" (1 Timothy 6); the story of the rich man and Lazarus (Luke 16); and the critique of slavery and the selling of bodies and souls like commodities on the market (Revelation 18). In addition to the more implicit discussions of poverty throughout the gospels and the rest of the New Testament, the existence of these more explicit critiques of wealth make it harder to dismiss the other themes and concepts mentioned above as merely allegorical. These critiques show that poverty is a main concern of the New Testament and that it is a Christian duty to end poverty.

The Greek word for "Kingdom of God" or "Empire of God," *basilea*, has much to do with the economic order that Jesus advocated. Few would disagree that the Kingdom of God is central to the teachings of Jesus and the New Testament. However, many understand this kingdom as otherworldly and immaterial. But if we look at both the prevalence of the concept and the specific references to it in the New Testament, we can see that God's kingdom is a real, material order, with a moral agenda different from and opposed to the reigning order of the day. The *basilea* is particularly present in the parables that describe how the reign of God functions differently from the Roman Empire: in God's kingdom, there is no poverty or fear, and mutuality exists among all. Throughout the New Testament, Jesus's parables and stories paint a picture of a reign in which the poor and marginalized are lifted up and their needs are met, rather than being despised or ignored by those in control. There are many references to *basilea*—particularly where this kingdom is associated with the poor and marginalized, children, and other vulnerable people. From these passages and others, we can see that the Kingdom of God is not ruled by force and coercion; that on earth, God's followers are asked to model a community of mutuality and solidarity; that the poor and oppressed are held up and cared for in the Kingdom of God and that there is no room for oppressors and oppression.

The New Testament is one of the few forms of mass media that has anything good to say about poor and marginalized people. Centuries of interpretation have attempted to spiritualize or minimize this good news for the poor, hiding the reality that the Bible is a book by, about, and for poor and marginalized people. It not only says that God blesses and loves the poor, but also that the poor are God's agents and leaders in rejecting and dismantling kingdoms built upon oppression and in-equality. In the place of the old injustice they build the Kingdom of God, a kingdom without poverty. It is the vision of society the early Christians sought to create on earth, and that we who follow Jesus to-day are commanded to strive for as well.

CHAPTER THREE

ORGANIZING AND SHAPING A MORAL VISION FOR JUSTICE IN THE PUBLIC SQUARE

THE REVEREND DR. WILLIAM J. BARBER II

If we pattern our preaching after Jesus, we learn that proclamation, which begins in a space designated for worship, necessarily moves into the public square. The message of Jesus does not only instruct; it also initiates and invigorates a movement to transform the world that *is* into the world that *ought to be*. This is why preaching in the public square is not extraordinary or unusual preaching; it is normative preaching in the way of Jesus.

We see this pattern throughout the life and ministry of Jesus, but nowhere is it clearer than in his inaugural sermon in his hometown of Nazareth. Jesus does not employ fancy new technology or suggest any methodological novelty in his practice of the craft of preaching. He is a preacher in the tradition of those who preached before him. In Luke 4, mentioned in the previous chapter, he takes up the text assigned for reading in the synagogue that day. It is a reading from the prophet Isaiah:

> The Spirit of the Lord is upon me, because he hath anointed me to preach the gospel to the poor; he hath sent me to heal the brokenhearted, to preach deliverance to the captives, and recovering of sight to the blind, to set at liberty them that are bruised. To preach the acceptable year of the Lord.

As biblical scholar Philip Esler comments in *Community and Gospel in Luke–Acts*, what is significant in this programmatic function is the pride of place in the inaugural preaching of Jesus given to the "poor" and others who are at risk and vulnerable in the world.

The "anointing" that the Spirit brings comes with its own intents and purposes that are rooted in developing a movement for the liberation of humanity. Evangelical, Pentecostal, and other charismatic movements in American Christianity have said a great deal about "the anointing." But careful examination of the Isaiah 61 text reveals that when the word "anointing" is used, it is with specific characteristics that always have to do with someone becoming an agent of a higher calling. One word for "anointing" in Hebrew is *mashach*. It appears 140 times in the Old Testament but is most often connected to vessels in the temple being set apart for specific use within the tabernacle or temple. When used in Isaiah 61 the word shifts slightly to *moshach*, which means separated for service. It means we are to be restricted from certain things for purposes more noble than ourselves.

The anointing for prophetic proclamation, then, is more than feeling. The word suggests consecration for God's purposes in the world. *Moshach* is so forceful and overwhelming that it restricts that which is anointed from doing anything else but that for which it is called. This means that the anointing in Luke is not about a momentary feeling; it is about a way of life, "a call to service for my Lord," as an old hymn puts it. We are anointed to become agents of God, but not merely for personal edification. The anointing creates a guidance system by which our work for God's kingdom is focused. It keeps us when we can't keep ourselves.

The primary evidence of the anointing has to do with action that promotes justice and the power to show uncommon grace. This anointing produces an ability to address the death of our times. It produces prophets who will not merely serve the culture but will call for a counterculture; it saves the church from being a mere consecrated club and transforms it into a prophetic community. The Spirit's anointing moves prophetic proclamation from the pulpit into the public square.

In the text of the prophet that Jesus takes up at Nazareth, he proclaims, "The Spirit of LORD is upon me." "Upon" in Luke's Greek is *epelthontos*, "from above." This Spirit runs counter to that which is of this world; she brings both a power and a process that is counter to the normal ways of ordering and seeing the world. The Spirit joins us to the work of God in the world. Isaiah 61:1–2 places Jesus squarely in line with Israel's prophetic tradition. In effect, he takes the mantle of the servant of God and calls all who would follow him to do likewise. The anointing produces both assurance and commitment to the way of God and to acts of liberation. In the life of Jesus, two elements meet: the power of God to affect the liberation of humanity and the commitment of a life to fully move in that power.

A Christian tradition that is captive to empire has made serious attempts to move away from any interpretation of Luke 4:18 that demands a call to ministries of liberation. Esler notes that many biblical scholars argue against analyzing the social context in which Luke was written. However, Esler and others believe that it is relevant to ask, "What was it like to be poor in the time of Luke? Who were the rich and the poor in Luke 4:18?" Such basic questions save us from "spiritual" interpretations that fail to address Luke's social implications.

Luke/Acts was written in a city of the Roman Empire in the first century CE. In Roman society, there was a clear system of social stratification. British historian A. H. M. Jones notes, "Common to virtually all cities of the Empire was the general pattern of elective annual magistrates, a council and a popular assembly. The members of the council were called 'decurions.' There were normally 100 members of a council. Decurions and magistrates were comprised of the local aristocracy. Additionally, there were senators and equites, who comprised the upper and lower strata of Roman nobility. Only a tiny portion of the population was within these official categories of citizens. Of the fifty million or so in the Roman population, less than 1 percent were in these categories. To be a senator, one had to possess two hundred fifty thousand denari, and to be an eques, half that amount. To be a decurion, one needed twenty-five thousand denari. The average daily wage for a laborer was one denarius. Therefore, to be a senator with political power one had to possess two hundred fifty thousand times what a laborer made in one day!"

The Roman Cicero described the majority of Roman society as "*sodes urbis et faex,*" the filth and dregs of the city. Among this group were several categories of people: merchants and traders, artisans, unskilled workers, debt bondsmen, and beggars. Careful examination of Luke 4:18 in the original Greek language reveals that the word from which we translate "poor" is *ptochos*. This word means poverty to the point of destitution— the poverty of a beggar. Significantly, other words, such as *pentichros*, were available to denote poverty without destitution, but Luke did not choose them. The word he did choose comes from one meaning: "to crouch or cower." He was speaking of those forced to crawl and beg for the very basic necessities of life. The research of A. R. Hands, a social historian and the author of *Charities and Social Aid in Greece and Rome*, reveals that in Roman society this word was applied to the vast majority of the people in the cities who had no claim to income or independence of the ruling elite.

This word study shows that the English translation "poor" does not carry the same force and implications of the original rendering of the word in Greek. Other passages throughout Luke use this same word when Jesus is calling for compassion for the poor or antipathy for the rich. The poor are all those who have to endure acts of violence and injustice without being able to defend themselves, as Jurgen Moltmann points out in *From Christ to the World*. In light of this understanding of the word, Jesus's inaugural message in Luke is a major affront to Roman society. Again, Esler is helpful: "In light of the stratification which characterized Hellenistic society, how extraordinary it must have sounded to an audience in a Greco-Roman city for the Lucan Jesus to begin his public ministry by specifying beggars and a number of other groups at the very bottom of the social register as the primary recipients of the gospel . . . such a perspective entailed a radical upheaval in the prevailing realities."

If we continue to examine Luke 4:18 with an eye for the social context, the implications of other phrases become clearer. "To proclaim freedom for the captives" seems to rely on the Old Testament idea of the year of jubilee, as does the phrase "the Lord's year of favor." The year of jubilee was a time denoted in the Book of Leviticus when, in the fiftieth year, all debts were forgiven and slaves set free. The Greek rendering of the word "captives" speaks to literal captivity by human forces. Within Luke's social context, the captivity spoken of may carry the thought of forgiveness of sin, but spiritual bondage does not carry the full weight of Luke's meaning. Luke understands the work of the Holy Spirit in Jesus as producing a gospel, which relates to both spiritual and physical aspects of bondage. Thus, Esler show us that the liberation promised in the programmatic verse 4:18 must be interpreted so as to cover salvation at a physical level, which commences with the ministry of Jesus.

While Luke's gospel brings good news to the poor, it is sobering news for the rich and influential. Their status, wealth, and power become liabilities unless they are released and used to further the carrying out of the gospel mandate to the poor.

As Moltmann sums up, "The rich will only be helped when they recognize their own poverty and enter the fellowship of the poor, especially the poor who have been made more poor through violence." Preaching in the way of Jesus is preaching in this Spirit. Jesus's example makes it our burden—our calling—to be mindful of the poor, the weak, those on the sidelines of life, and we can't escape the call.

The atmosphere in which Jesus was born and lived was one of oppression caused by the rule of Rome. It was a social situation Jesus could not ignore and still give meaning to life. There was a demand upon Jesus to respond to the political, social, and economic issues of his day. In *Jesus and the Disinherited*, Howard Thurman declares, "This is the position of the disinherited in every age. What must be the attitude toward the rulers, the controllers of political, social, and economic life?" This spirituality calls us to be suspicious of concentrations of wealth and privilege and power, and to mistrust any ideology that justifies subordinating persons.

We cannot be seduced into considering people as the world considers people. Salvation in Luke 4:18 is God's initiative to bring wholeness back into the created order. It is meant to save humanity from its inhumanity. God desires to save us from anything that oppresses us—including economic injustice and anything that works against the solidarity of the human community. The contemporary church has become so accommodative of capitalism that its theology is often viewed as a justification of economic injustice. In order for preaching to seriously confront the economic philosophy of our society, it must unmask the claim that God is the developer of the market economy by showing that the values of God are not rooted in domination.

Preaching in the Spirit cannot accept things the way they are. The anointing makes us aware and concerned about all people's personhood. When I studied economics, our professor informed us that most economic theories write off 5 to 10 percent of the population. The value system of the anointing of the Holy Spirit won't allow you to do that. Our addiction to materialism must be healed. When we preach in the Spirit, Thurman said:

> We can be freed from the falsehood that the accumulation and the consumption of things are the substance and measure of human life. Our alienation from the rest of creation can be overcome. We can be converted from the idea that the earth belongs to us; we can live as if we are a part of a creation that belongs to God. Our ethic of profit can be transformed into an ethic of community as the foundation of our economic system.

We who would preach in the Spirit must ask, "Who are the brokenhearted, captive, blind, bruised, poor in our midst?"; "What are the conditions that create their realities?"; and "What are we doing to address these conditions?" This is the call of the Spirit that leads us into the public square, for these are not simply matters of personal, spiritual concern. The preaching of Jesus demands an account of the principalities and powers. Those who hear it become part of a movement that is political, offering a real and viable alternative to the existing partisan options.

When we have had what Dr. William Turner, professor of preaching and theology at Duke University, calls a "crisis experience of conversion," our active orientation to life is shifted. In other words, "When the Spirit moves and we are saved, born again, changed, filled, however you describe it, what follows is a challenge to the way things are." Being moved by the Spirit necessitates a "quarrel with the way things are in the world." Reliance on the Spirit produces not only a praise that is fervent, or a reliance on God that is ultimate, but also a commitment to a mission and ministry of life struggling against oppression, fighting for the poor, and seeking relief and justice for the weak. Preaching in the way of Jesus calls people to join a moral movement in the world.

A great deal of time and resources have been invested in misleading Christian communities on this basic point. Because God's movement threatens the existing political and economic systems of any society, its truth is resisted by the powerful. As in Jesus's day, many who resist most fervently are themselves religionists, twisting the very message of liberation to justify bondage and injustice. We must beware of popular piety that restricts the call of the faith to merely personal salvation and prosperity. The spirit that wants to keep the good news of Jesus out of the public square is an unholy spirit.

The preacher must preach in such a way that the primary conversation about the Spirit is not about this gift or that gift on the individual level, but about how the movement is using its collective gifts to effect righteous change for those toward whom the concern of God is directed. No matter how much people use the language of faith—"trusting in God," "born again," "filled with the Spirit"—if they speak of Jesus but defend the powerful and do nothing about the forces that ravage people's lives, then their claims of being "in the Spirit" remain suspect.

Preaching has the potential to unleash God's power—the most powerful force in the universe, the Word by which the world was spoken into existence. But this power must be used in exactly opposite the way power is so often used in our world. Human beings often use power to get above and stay above others: creating brokenness, captivity, and poverty. This demonic use of power dismisses those who have no strength of their own. But where God's anointing occurs, something different happens. Anointed power is used to move into situations where the ministry of healing, restoration, liberation, and redemption is needed. The power of the anointing is to cut across the grain and to go where the normative power of this world abandons us. With the anointing of the Spirit, a new age appears.

The anointing of the Holy Spirit that rests upon Christ enters human affairs with a specific agenda: to engage in the messianic activity of liberation and justice. The suffering of humanity becomes his suffering and his focus and the focus of those who would follow him. In the power of the Spirit, those oppressed are offered the freedom to rebel against all who subjugate their humanity. The anointing breaks the yokes of selfishness and power-grabbing. By the Spirit, our collective efforts are reconcentrated on being involved in the ministry of liberation and deliverance.

American Christianity, as a whole, has never taken this understanding of the prophetic/liberation ministry of Jesus seriously. Though Jesus rooted his preaching in the prophetic tradition, much of American preaching refuses to preach the prophets in this manner. This malpractice has its roots in the theological and philosophical strategies employed to justify slavery in America. If you take Luke 4:18 in its intended meaning, you can't be Christian and own slaves. But popular American Christianity attempted to suggest that what Jesus was talking about here was spiritual poverty, spiritual captivity. Therefore, our concern as the people of God should be private soul-saving, private devotion, private praise, and private morality that address issues of the "inner-man" only.

Slavery occurred without a major outcry from the church because liberation was deemed outside of the reach of the gospel.

The same malpractice was evidenced when the Reverend Billy Graham told the Reverend Dr. Martin Luther King Jr. that he couldn't join the civil rights movement because he was a New Testament preacher and not an Old Testament prophet. Preaching in the Spirit cannot be limited in this way. Privatized, society-ducking religion is not Christian, prophetic, or anointed. Preaching in the way of Jesus confronts every system and ideology that holds people captive.

Jesus's preaching is necessarily public. His very first sermon cannot stay within the confines of the synagogue. By the power of the Spirit, the preaching of Jesus confronts the world as it is. Those who are committed to demonic power rise up in resistance, determined to throw him off a cliff at the edge of town. But those who hear and believe the good news join the movement for God's justice and peace in the public square. They cannot be confined by church walls or religious segmentation.

The Christianity of this land, which Frederick Douglass castigated as the polar opposite of the Christianity of Christ, is confined to the private lives and sacred spaces of Sunday mornings, Christian TV, Christian radio, and corporately sponsored Christian "festivals" in public spaces for private religion. Even when this faith mobilizes to pray for a governor or president, it does not challenge the principalities and powers that be or question systemic injustice. Those who would preach in the way of Jesus must choose to abandon the compromised Christianity of this land in favor of the Christianity of Christ.

We cannot shy away from Spirit-filled preaching in the public square. It is, in fact, the only language strong enough to challenge the prevailing unjust powers. Partisan rhetoric is too puny and social justice movements are too fragmented by single-issue organizing. We need the language of faith and morality to mobilize a faithful resistance movement, which will empower people to see through deception.

Prophetic preaching speaks order into the chaos of our contentious public square, offering the possibility of healing. Politics need not be a zero-sum game in which some have to lose for others to win. The same power that spoke creation out of nothing is able to speak life into spaces of social death, giving rise to unexpected friendships and fusion coalitions for the common good. This is not simply wishful thinking. It is, in fact, how moral movements inspired abolitionism, women's suffrage, labor protections for children, and civil rights for minorities in our society. Preaching in the public square has always been an essential part of social transformation in America's public life.

Finally, prophetic preaching in the public square is a necessary discipline to inspire subversive hope as we work and wait for justice to come. We who believe in freedom cannot rest until it comes, but we also know that the race is not given to the swift but to those who endure until the end. Jesus met resistance to his first sermon, and the resistance grew as his movement for justice grew. Yes, Luke's gospel points to miracles and mobilizations of as many as five thousand people. In his Acts, Luke describes the movement by saying, "Daily there were added to their number those who were being saved." But at the same time, the Pharisees organized to subvert Jesus, his disciples betrayed him, the Roman authorities executed him for a capital crime, and the movement was scattered by persecution. Prophetic preaching cannot expect or promise a smooth transition from the injustice we face to the great jubilee when all flesh shall witness the glory of God's justice together. But it can and must instill in its devotees the truth that weeping may endure for a night, but joy comes in the morning. Good Fridays are hard and long but we who stand with the Savior through the darkest of nights will also experience the power of resurrection.

PART TWO

VISION AND ACTION

At a time when political, economic, and social systems are breaking down and inequality, injustice, conflict, and repression are on the rise; and at a time when people are increasingly and necessarily grappling with the power of religion, the Forward Together Moral Mondays Movement in North Carolina and the Poor People's Campaign: A National Call for Moral Revival have become sources of moral and social consciousness, inspiring action and analysis in states across the country. The strong popular response to religious voices like that of Pope Francis demonstrates what a powerful force preaching in the public square really is. Very often leaders of social change efforts, both historic and current—William Wilberforce, Fannie Lou Hamer, Oscar Romero, Mahatma Gandhi, Cory Aquino, Lech Walesa, Desmond Tutu, Shirin Ebadi, Martin Luther King Jr., and Aung San Suu Kyi, to name only a few—express and ground their actions and beliefs in deep religious convictions and in strong moral terms. Many of these leaders have left the confines of houses of worship and the ivory tower to preach social transformation and organize a liberation movement in the public square.

The sermons and speeches included in Part Two cover years of Reverend Barber's organizing and educating as the architect of the Forward Together Moral Mondays Movement, president of the North Carolina State Chapter of the NAACP, senior lecturer for Repairers of the Breach, visiting professor at Union Theological Seminary, pastor of Greenleaf Christian Church in Goldsboro, North Carolina, and cochair of the Poor People's Campaign: A National Call for Moral Revival. They are paired with responses from important thought leaders, theologians, and activists who have been involved in a fusion movement and who are building the Poor People's Campaign: A National Call for Moral Revival.

The purpose of the sermons and responses is to inspire, prod, press, and inform moral organizing and action for social change in our times. They break out of the left-right and progressive-conservative dichotomy that can dominate popular theology and biblical studies as well as social theory and analysis. They take on the very relevant and urgent topics of police brutality; ecological devastation; the war economy and militarism; racial and religiously motivated violence; attacks on voting rights; attacks on reproductive choice, immigrants, and LGBTQIA communities; increasing economic insecurity and poverty; and draconian and mean-spirited social program cuts across the nation and weave them together into a larger framework for a morally based social movement to address mounting dispossession and inequality in our world. In a moment when morality has been defined as personal responsibility over social responsibility, when poor people are called sinners rather than poverty being described as a sin, the moral witness of the Forward Together Moral Mondays Movement and the Poor People's Campaign is inspirational, encouraging, and necessary in order to catalyze action and reflection that can transform society.

CHAPTER FOUR

WHEN THE STONES COME TOGETHER

EQUALITY NORTH CAROLINA
AWARD CEREMONY, NOVEMBER 17, 2012

Raleigh, North Carolina

THE REVEREND DR. WILLIAM J. BARBER II

Every time I go to jail, I pray. And when I pray, I ask God, "What would you have me to do?" Twice I went to jail with the Reverend Nancy Petty, whom I believe is an angel in disguise as a Baptist preacher. Two and a half years ago, I was getting ready for bed around 11:30 p.m. and was quite despondent because we could not seem to get people, some clergy, to rally in support of children in Wake County. I picked up the paper late that night before going to bed and I read a beautiful letter to the editor of the Raleigh *News & Observer* and it was signed simply "Nancy Petty." She wrote that she was the mother of two kids in Wake County schools and that "we must speak now with one voice on the issues facing public education in Wake County: black and white; male and female; Republican and Democrat; Muslim, Christian, Jew, and Catholic; CEO and unemployed; educated and uneducated." I had said something similar at one of our mass meetings protesting the Far Right's efforts to resegregate Wake's nationally acclaimed, diverse school-assignment policies. I don't know what lead me to read her letter, pick that paper up at 11:30 that night, but I can remember clearly that it revived my spirit and made my heart overflow. I had the crazy idea in the middle of the night that I would call Ms. Petty and tell her how much her letter meant to me. And so that night I called Nancy, and we had a wonderful talk, and we set up a meeting to talk some more. Soon.

You need to hear this story in order to understand the Amendment I fight against homophobia in North Carolina and the many fights beyond. It turned out that Ms. Petty had left out of her letter two other important facts about herself. Besides being a mother, she was the *Reverend* Nancy Petty. And that night we did not talk about sexuality; we talked children and what mattered for all children. Only later, when someone was trying to be ugly and criticizing us for standing together, did I learn that she was the first openly gay minister at the historic Pullen Memorial Baptist Church and that she had been a great advocate of civil rights down through the years.

We became close friends and jailbirds. We went to jail together, not based on politics but based on the soul and the kind of camaraderie that forms when you fight for justice together. Her directness, her honesty, and her steadfast support of the antiracism, antipoverty movement we call Historic Thousands on Jones Street (HKonJ), which we had been building for six years, has been a great source of strength to me and our movement. I invited her to speak to the Historic Thousands on Jones Street Moral March on Raleigh. She asked me to come and preach at Pullen, and then I invited her to preach at Greenleaf Christian Church.

When national and local Far Right millionaires came up with their scheme of buying four Wake County school-board seats in 2009 and promoting Ron Margiotta to be its chair, the NAACP asked him several times to meet. Mr. Margiotta did not answer our requests. Finally, Reverend Petty, Dr. Tim Tyson, the famed gospel singer Mary Williams, and I decided that if Margiotta would not meet with us, we would go meet with him at a public hearing to petition him and his extremist ideologues for redress of our grievances. We looked into his eyes. He had that look of fear, that look of hatred toward diversity. He spun his chair around and rather than listen or look at us, he stood up and walked out of the room, and when he returned he said, "Arrest them."

When we got out of jail, all of us were told that we could not go on school grounds until our trial. Nancy Petty and Mary Williams both had kids in Wake schools and they wanted to ask that Margiotta's order be amended to allow them to take their kids to school and meet with their teachers. We drove to the edge of the board's big building to hand a written request to an officer to deliver to Margiotta and learned that he had told his police to arrest Petty and myself. Also there that day was the Reverend Greg Moss, the leader of about half a million black Baptists in North Carolina at the time. When people inside heard that we had been arrested, about twenty young people and their elders—intergenerational, different races, different creeds, different sexualities—sang freedom songs, prayed, and held hands. And sure enough, they were also arrested and joined us in jail.

Nancy Petty and I went through these epiphanies together. While we were building a movement, the five-term conservative Republican senator Jesse Helms's political machine tapped the national right-wing forces for millions of dollars to pay for openly racist and homophobic television and mail ads to attack centrist Democrats for being Barack Obama supporters and NAACP allies. North Carolina businessman Art Pope, with money and organizational support from the Koch brothers, paid for the ads and targeted House and Senate districts that showed me, NAACP president Ben Jealous, and a black man in a prison jumpsuit sneaking around a white suburban neighborhood with the message that we wanted to let convicted killers and rapists off death row to threaten housewives. When we went to Republican headquarters in North Carolina to request that the GOP denounce the ads, the chair ducked into the back room and refused to meet with us. They continued the vicious, bigoted, and untruthful ads and managed to win majorities in both houses of the North Carolina legislature. When the Republicans took office in January 2011, they made their agenda clear: use wedge issues, abortion and gay rights, to divide and distract us, and hope that while we were chasing those rabbits they would sneak through their reverse–Robin Hood budget after midnight.

Until the extremists took over the North Carolina General Assembly, the NAACP was always welcome to meet with the leaders of both parties. But like Margiotta, House Speaker Thom Tillis had three times ignored and played games with our traditional request for meeting at the start of the session. He refused to sit down with our HKonJ coalition. So, we reserved a large room at the legislature and put together an afternoon public education session about critical issues the great majority of North Carolinians were facing. And then a group of us, black and white ministers, some with the Council of Churches, some with the AME Zion Church, and some with the Baptist Church, entered the balcony of the people's house to invite the legislators to attend the large assembly next door to the House chamber. I stood up in that chamber and asked a simple question: why were they passing a budget that would devastate educational funding and safety nets for the poor? It was not a rhetorical question. It was a question I thought they were familiar with since all of them had put their hands on a Bible and been sworn into office. The question was simply: "What doth the Lord require?" And the other ministers responded, "to do justice and to love mercy." Before I could invite him, Speaker Tillis shouted, "Arrest him, arrest him!"

When a member of the media asked the Speaker that afternoon why he had ordered our arrests, he said we had disrupted "his" house. I give you this background, this story, to say that the struggle we're in is a long one. It demands grace; it demands courage. It will have ebbs and flows. Later, when the Amendment I fight began, we didn't have to find one another and come together, as some have wrongly said in the media. We were already together. That's the point.

In the summer of 2011, we learned the Tea Party Republicans had decided to put a bill up to vote that had been drafted by some national Republican advisers to pass Amendment I and make same-sex marriage unconstitutional in North Carolina. Because we were already together through our past and shared struggles, we were able to stand. I counseled and prayed with my sister Nancy. Speaker Tillis allowed one hour for debate before they quick-voted to put Amendment I on the May 8,

2012, primary ballot. As Equality North Carolina and its many friends geared up for what they believed was going to be a unilateral fight, I was invited as the NAACP president to preach the ideas and share an open letter to this annual convention last year. I shall never forget the electricity that shot through the crowd as I spoke. I shall never forget the young man who came and cried on my shoulder to thank me that a minister would even see him as a fellow human being. I saw the waves of hope and love and relief and laughter and joy as we realized there was new hope in the room, swept over all of us, black and white, gay and straight, a new movement of young folk and a movement of old warriors. All of us knew, I think, that we might lose the battle, but we'd already won the war. What seemed like a complicated knot that had tied up the progressive movement in California and other places came apart easily for us just by pulling the right strings of justice, love, and humility.

As the story continues, the national Far Right sent its paid organizers to North Carolina to stir up votes in favor of Amendment I. They were sent to both black and white churches, where their Tea Party cadre had been working, using the time-tested tactic of fear-mongering. They paid a few black ministers, some of them friends and colleagues of mine, to make radio and TV ads and to preach on the sins of homosexuality. But the NAACP stuck to our argument that matters of conscience and private morality were matters for the church and that America must make a firm separation between matters of conscience and matters of civil society, and that no member of any minority can afford to permit a majority vote to allow the government to decide our fundamental human rights. Since we had seen it happen many times in our struggle, we had faith that if we worked hard and stuck to our strong moral constitution and scientific positions, we could reach the minds and the hearts of thousands of voters with our radio announcements, our newspaper ads, and thousands of voter mailings.

I know many of us were devastated the night of May 8, 2012, when Amendment I passed. I know that young people who had been fed the illusion that North Carolina is a reasonable and progressive state were disillusioned with the buckets of ice-cold waters of fear and hate and hypocrisy. However, African Americans and our Latino brothers and sisters have always known that even in North Carolina, where in time we have progressed, the Tar Heel soil is fertile ground for hate and fear. And we've always known and can never be deluded about the fact that the fight will be long and that there are no shortcuts. We must reduce fear through public education, in the streets, in the courts, and in electoral campaigns. We must dare to struggle and dare to win. And from my religious tradition, I view defeat as merely a prelude to a season of hope.

Our opponents' campaign was built on hypocrisy and cynicism. Ours was built on truth and hope. The day before the May vote, seven of us who had dared ask the House Speaker what the Lord required stood trial in Raleigh. And while waiting for the judge to decide what our sentences would be, I prayed in that courtroom and thought about the fact that in less than two weeks the national NAACP board would meet in Florida. While in that courtroom I thought, wouldn't it be something if we could come up with a resolution to pass at that meeting that would give hope to people and untie another knot in the people's movement. The judge interrupted my thoughts, finding my friend and brother the Reverend Curtis Gatewood and me guilty of disorderly conduct, which I wear as a proud badge of service to justice.

I'm sure that in that courtroom the same angels who brought me the paper that night to read Nancy Petty's letter led me to think about taking North Carolina's decision to the national stage. I was firmly convinced it was the right thing to do, and after talking to scores of disappointed, disillusioned, fearful people, I could feel their isolation, their fear. I talked it over with our national board member Carolyn Q. Coleman, and on May 19, 2012, Chairman Brooks asked me, as president of the North Carolina NAACP and chair of the National Political Action Committee, to present in closed session to the NAACP board the lessons learned in our recent struggle in North Carolina. With my sister Nancy in mind, and many others, I said the following to the board:

"The question regarding the equality of rights for the LGBT community, and our citizens, and same-sex couples, is not a question for black America; it is a question for America itself. When we say, 'we the people' and 'equal protection under the law for all people,' does that mean only those who we agree with personally and religiously? Do we mean some people and not others? If this is the case, we render the noble sentiments of our democracy and the lofty language of inclusion to be painfully hypocritical." I went on, "Theologically and from a Bible-centric perspective of a Judeo-Christian faith, the issues that should dominate the public square ought to pertain to how we treat the poor, the sick, children, and women, and those on the margins, and those unaccepted."

I said to them, "The reality is that when you examine the voting records and public policy positions carefully, the same forces fighting us on voting rights and educational equality and economic injustice and addressing racial disparities in the criminal justice system are the same ones behind the attacks on the LGBT community." I asked the board to consider with me that the forces advocating to hurt the LGBT community also advocate to reduce taxes on the wealthy and increase the burdens on the poor and strengthen laws while ignoring racial disparities in the criminal justice system. They support policies rooted in a philosophy of Jim Crow and the new, credentialed iteration, James Crow, Esquire, through voter ID laws and race-based redistricting. I told them that in our recent fight here in North Carolina against the discriminatory Amendment I, we learned that once the NAACP and our allies properly framed and contextualized the issue, the people quickly grasped how the treatment of LGBT citizens is an issue of civil rights and human rights.

I said to them that in each of North Carolina's five largest cities, voters in majority-black precincts—regardless of what the media reported—rejected the measure: Charlotte, 52 percent; Raleigh, 51 percent; Greensboro, 54 percent; Winston-Salem, 55 percent; Durham, 65 percent. Somebody ought to tell the truth! Not one single majority-black precinct supported the amendment. Several crushed it by margins of three to one, and even four to one. And yes, even in rural North Carolina, where we have seen islands of resistance, the amendment failed two to one on the African American side of Scotland Neck. I noted to the board that within our democracy, because of the First Amendment, we have a right to disagree or agree on issues of personal and religious morality. However, because of the Fourteenth Amendment, we do not have the license to enact laws that, because of our religious or private conviction, remove equal protection of the law from any citizen.

I reminded them that this was not a new position for us. The NAACP has always opposed any custom, tradition, practice, law, or constitutional amendment that denies any right to any person. I asked them to stop for a minute and remember the history of amending the US Constitution. Our nation had to fight a long and bloody civil war in order to amend the Constitution and to begin to expand its protections to all persons. The Thirteenth Amendment abolished slavery, the Fourteenth guaranteed equal protection, the Fifteenth provided voting rights to men of all races, the Nineteenth guaranteed voting rights for women, the Twenty-Third provided voting rights in presidential elections to residents of Washington, DC, the Twenty-Fourth eliminated discriminatory poll taxes in federal elections, and the Twenty-Sixth provided voting rights to those eighteen or older. No other amendment had ever restricted the rights of any person except the two established and then repealed. And when we look at the history of the US, there has never been an amendment to narrow protections, but rather only ones to expand protections to all persons and to remedy past injustice.

I said to the board, "Those who think the sons and daughters of the civil rights movement can't see through their Trojan-horse trick, when they try to use wedge issues to seduce us to be part of their scheme to deny LGBT citizens fundamental rights, must be crazy. And we cannot let them do it on our watch!" And, finally, at that closed session, I said from a moral perspective that my reading of the Bible says Jesus commanded us to love one another, no exceptions. He made this clear by setting an example of going out of his way to show love for people who had been excluded and marginalized. And after thirty minutes in closed session, late on the afternoon of May 19, the sixty-four-member board of the national NAACP debated and passed a strong resolution supporting equal rights for gay marriages. I wrote it, so I know what's in it.

And not only did I write it, I had the privilege of conferring with Julian Bond and making the motion that

> The NAACP Constitution affirmatively states our objective to ensure political, educational, social, and economic equality of all people; therefore, the NAACP has opposed and will continue to oppose any national, state, local policy or legislative initiative that seeks to codify discrimination or hatred into the law, or to remove the constitutional right of the LGBT citizen. We support marriage equality, consistent with equal protection under the law provided under the Fourteenth Amendment of the United States Constitution. Further, we strongly affirm the religious freedom of all people as protected by the First Amendment.

And when the vote was taken, and when it was passed, I felt a great joy. I knew it was a historical moment for America. I knew we had done the right thing. I flew home to Goldsboro and unwound at my Greenleaf Christian Church, preaching the next morning, and, finally, at home with my family that afternoon after months of traveling, preaching, teaching, writing, texting, emailing, and responding to the challenge that the Lord sends to all of us daily. I recalled the wonderful events of the past few years, ever since I read that letter from Nancy Petty one late night. There are some lessons, as I conclude, that we must learn. One of them is that we cannot buy into the regressive, ultra-right strategy that intends to build a wedge between the African American community and the LGBT community.

And we have to be careful of our own description of the politics. I had to challenge some of my friends, my white friends, my liberal friends during the marriage-amendment fight who would say that it was on the backs of black people whether the amendment passed or failed. Don't ever repeat that! Because black folks have had enough put on their backs without this one being added too. First, it's not empirically true. According to the voting statistics, as the disappointing votes were counted last May, two facts leaked out. Over half the black voters who voted against the amendment had changed their position once we came in coalition and dealt with it as a civil rights issue. And the percentage who voted against the amendment was larger than the percentage of whites. To blame any one community is a waste of time and creates unnecessary division. Instead, we should spend our energy seeking to organize and find allies in every community.

Another lesson we must learn, particularly progressives and liberals, is not to throw away the high moral ground and walk away from religious discourse. We cannot assume that the majority of people who confess faith do so along the same lines of the ultraconservative, so-called religious-right evangelicals. The truth is, and some of you might be shocked when I say it tonight, I'm a Christian evangelical conservative. You can't buy their rhetoric and accept it willy-nilly. You have to unpack it. You have got to exegete it. I'm a Christian evangelical conservative. I want to conserve what's at the heart of faith, and what's at the heart of faith is love; what's at the heart of faith is justice; and what's at the heart of faith is fairness for all people. So, go tell Franklin Graham and all those who call themselves conservatives that you met a *real* conservative, one who knows Jesus, and we have a question: why do you say so much about what God says so little, and so little about what God says so much?

Furthermore, if we are to broaden and deepen the electorate, particularly on this issue, we must recognize that there are friends and allies of the LGBT community who may not endorse a particular lifestyle— listen to me now—religiously or culturally, but their nonendorsement is not rooted in the meanness and hatred of the ultraconservatives, but another theological base, another exegetical perspective that professes love and justice for all. When the issue is framed along the lines and requirements of loving all humanity, seeing all people as brothers and sisters, and as a fundamental or constitutional right guaranteed to every person regardless of their race, creed, class, gender, or sexuality, we're left with persons who may not necessarily agree with a particular life-style but who will stand beside and defend the LGBT community every day and every time. We've got to work there too.

Thirdly, we must have a deep commitment to building and strengthening what I call twenty-first-century fusion politics. As my sister Nancy and I have shown, we can't just wait until my issue is being attacked and then start to rally the people. She was with the NAACP on educational equality long before the marriage equality fight began. And we must have a twenty-first-century form of fusion politics where we stay together not sometimes but all the time. And that agenda must be broad. The NAACP and North Carolina Equality need to stay together on economic sustainability; addressing systematic poverty and the lack of jobs; insuring the wealthy pay their fair share; providing living wages and labor rights; guaranteeing every child a high-quality diverse education; ensuring health care; protecting Medicaid, Medicare, and Social Security; addressing the disparity in our criminal justice system; enforcing equal protection under the law regardless of race or creed or class or gender or sexual orientation; securing equal rights and full citizenship for our Latino and other immigrant brothers and sisters; and protecting and expanding voting rights. If our agenda is big enough, we can stay together, and if we stay together long enough and strong enough, then we will win.

If I was at my church, I would say, "Touch your neighbor and tell 'em we need more than sporadic unity!" Remember the fusion politics in 1868, right after the Civil War, where blacks and whites fused together, created a new electorate in the South, and rewrote state constitutions. Together they guaranteed voting rights and equal protection under the law and expanded labor rights and pushed progressive tax reform to address the economic injustices created by slavery. And again, in the 1960s, there was fusion politics throughout the South, including in this city. Our movement parents took on Jim Crow and segregation. Blacks and whites, Jews and Protestants and Catholics, students and labor unions created a new kind of politics with a deep moral center and commitment to nonviolence, antiracism, and antipoverty. They had hope and faith in the possibility of reconstructing the nation toward what she had promised on paper: to build a more perfect union, to establish justice, to insure domestic tranquility, to provide for the common defense, to promote the general welfare. The energy and ethics of that fusion tore down Jim Crow in the face of viciousness that some thought couldn't be overcome. Each of our movements has faced a vicious, mean backlash. But my point is that every time this fusion happens in America, our country becomes a little more beautiful, and this fusion helps this country mend the flaws of injustice and inequality.

In 2006, we embarked upon a journey to build a twenty-first-century fusion movement led by the NAACP called the HKonJ People's Assembly Coalition. Many of us had already walked together. We came together around a fourteen-point agenda including the goal of ending all forms of discrimination. Five years before the Amendment I fight, we said it was time to inject a new politics into the veins of North Carolina's public square. We were 60 organizations then. Now we're 140, and we've seen the fruit of this fusion. Winning same-day registration and early voting in North Carolina. Being able to stand up against voter ID and give a southern white female governor the backbone to do what no other southern governor did: veto voter ID laws. That's a part of the fruit of this fusion. We took on the General Assembly when the regressives passed a budget that in just one line item hurt sixty-four thousand poor children who were eligible for a program. Winning that fight in the courts is a fruit of that fusion. NAACP, Democracy North Carolina, the League of Women Voters, and the A. Philip Randolph Institute are taking on the race-based redistricting plan passed by the General Assembly that could set back political representation for twenty years. But our coming together is the fruit of fusion, and we're going to win.

Our Truth and Hope Poverty Tour demands that we address the fact that in North Carolina there are 1.6 million poor people, 600,000 children, 751,000 living in deep poverty. Putting a face on poverty, telling the truth about poverty is fruit of this fusion. We lost against Amendment 1. But being able to mount a campaign in North Carolina, being able to change the dialogue in the nation, moving the NAACP nationally, and inspiring winning coalition work in Maryland . . . that's fruit that comes from fusion!

Last year, more than 15,000 people gathered in front of the General Assembly, the most diverse coalition of its type seen in the South in recent years, from over 140 organizations: black, white, labor, gay, straight, all holding hands together. This is the fruit of fusion! And that's why there's been so much money spent in North Carolina to push us back. That's why there's been so much energy to divide us. Because a tree is known by the fruit it bears and the forces of regression can see the fruit of this fusion. They're betting we're going to become despondent because of the way the elections turned out here in North Carolina, but I challenge you in this room tonight that this is no time to be despondent in North Carolina or in America. There's too much evidence that things are changing.

My friends, this is no time to be despondent and wring our hands. It's time to keep building, to keep strengthening and building the ties that bind. They pushed back. We must push forward. We must believe that in the work of justice, defeats are only temporary. Right never ultimately loses. Weeping may endure for a night, but joy always comes in the morning. The fact and truth of the matter is that I come from a faith tradition that believes that life can be resurrected out of death. Pain can produce power and deeper camaraderie. Mountains of despair can be molded into stones of hope and life. The truth is, truth outweighs lies, and love is still more powerful than hate. So, this is no time to be despondent! It's a time to believe a little deeper, to dig the foundation of our coalitions a little deeper, to love one another a little deeper, to become more than political allies, but brothers and sisters.

Fifteen thousand of us stood together last year at HKonJ in front of the legislature. We need thirty thousand this year.

Now we must lobby like never before and fight in the courts like never before. I have an idea I've been sharing around the country and I need some of you all to help me share it with those with money. They spent $50 million in Wisconsin and lost the recall. Why don't they give us 10 percent of that $50 million; give us $5 million and let us hire four organizers per electoral vote for the next four years in North Carolina. That's sixty organizers. Let's turn them loose in the African American community, in the Latino community, in the white community, in the LGBT community, in the labor community, and in the faith community, and let's see what would happen if we had four years of continuous organizing. We can reshape politics in North Carolina. Can we break open the solid South? Can we turn this nation around?

And so, as my grandmamma said, it's time to dig a little deeper down in your soul. It's time to steady your spine and declare, "I ain't gon' let nobody turn us around." I often think about the challenge of when I was born. August 30, 1963, two days after the March on Washington. Bayard Rustin, who was openly gay, organized the March on Washington in the face of the president's opposition, the opposition of vicious racists who didn't want them to march, some in his own community who didn't believe it could make a difference. Despite all the odds they came together. Fusion politics took place and changed America. And echoing the words some of you heard that day, I still have a dream. I still believe. They did it then; we can do it now.

One of my favorite passages of scripture is "The stone that the builders rejected has now become the chief cornerstone." In other words, God can use the rejected to produce revival, and I know in this room there are some who have known rejection: rejection because of sexuality, rejection because of who you love, rejection because of how you were born, rejection because somebody needed somebody to hate to try to feel good about themselves. There's folk in this room that have known rejection: rejection because of income, rejection because of faith, rejection because of race, rejection because of lack of faith, rejection because somebody decided in their own ideology that they had a right—a false mandate—to demean your humanity and my humanity, given to us only by God. But I want you to know tonight that the stones that the builders rejected are now the cornerstones of this experiment called America. I want you to know tonight that when the rejected get together, we can in fact redeem America from hate and discrimination. I want you to know tonight that when hands that once picked cotton join the hands of Latinos, join the hands of progressive whites, join faith hands, join labor hands, join Asian hands, and join Native American hands, and join poor hands, and join wealthy hands, and join gay hands, and join straight hands, and trans hands—when all those hands get together, when the rejected join hands, our togetherness becomes the instrument of redemption.

And when we join hands we can revive and make sure that the promise of life, liberty, and the pursuit of happiness and equal protection under the law and care for the common good will never be taken away or forfeited for anybody, anytime, anywhere. So together the rejected will revive a promise that this land is your land, this land is my land. Together we will make sure that hope, not hate, has the last word in the State House, in the White House, and even at the ballot box. Together we will ensure that all of God's children are respected and treated with dignity. Together the rejected will redeem the heart of America and we will make sure that this nation lives out its promise: one nation under God, indivisible, with liberty and justice for all.

THE DOOR TO LIFE'S DEFINING MOMENTS

THE REVEREND DR. NANCY PETTY

Senior Pastor, Pullen Memorial Baptist Church

There are moments which mark your life. Moments when you realize nothing will ever be the same and time is divided into two
parts—before this, and after this.

—From the film *Fallen* (1998)

In Joshua 24:1–18 of the Hebrew scriptures the prophet reminds the
Israelites of the defining moments that have marked their journey as
God's people to that moment at Shechem. When I read this text, I
marvel at the writers' ability to so profoundly and concisely recall the
defining moments of the Israelites' journey—the moments that truly
marked the "befores and afters" of their life together. I think: If I had
only eighteen verses to write of the defining moments in my life, which
moments would I include? For certain the late-night phone call with
the Reverend Dr. William Barber in January 2010 would become one
of the most significant moments in my life. From that moment on,
nothing would ever be the same. It was in that moment that a relationship formed. A relationship and partnership that focused on a common goal: justice and equality for *all* people. This partnership would
twice take me to jail for civil disobedience, send me out marching in the
streets of Raleigh to protest unjust legislation, and beat a path for me
time and again to the North Carolina General Assembly to speak out
against laws and policies that target the most vulnerable in our communities. But most of all, this relationship marked the defining moment
in my life when I woke up to the realities of racism and the hate and

violence that my black and brown brothers and sisters experience day in and day out. It was a waking up to America's institutional and political systems of power and privilege that lift up the wealthy and beat down the poor and vulnerable. My relationship with Reverend Dr. Barber woke me up on that January night in 2010 and nothing has been the same since, nor will it ever be the same again.

It was that phone call that led to a relationship rooted firmly in fighting for *justice for all*. It was a defining moment in my life personally and professionally. Whether fighting for high-quality, well-funded education; or basic health care; or voting rights; or human rights for LGBTQ people and immigrants and refugees—the fight is for *justice for all people*. When justice depends on the color of our skin, or where we live, or how much money we make, or the name by which we call the Holy One, or whom we choose to marry, or what religion we practice, or whether we practice a religion, it is not justice. Justice is justice when it is rooted in the truth that "all [people] are created equal, that they are endowed by their Creator with certain unalienable Rights, that among these are Life, Liberty, and the Pursuit of Happiness."

When Reverend Dr. Barber and I first met, we knew nothing about each other's lives. I had no idea of the struggles he had lived or of the accomplishments he had enjoyed. He had no idea that I grew up in western North Carolina watching the Ku Klux Klan burn crosses along the rural road that my family traveled daily, or that I was pastor of Pullen Memorial Baptist Church, or that I was a lesbian. None of that mattered in that defining moment when individually we saw an injustice and reached out to each other to stand together.

There are moments that mark our lives. In those moments, we make manifest the values and principles by which we will live and to what or whom we will give our lives in service. In the presence of Joshua's words, we must ask ourselves: Will our lives be marked and defined by moments of self-indulgence or by moments of shared experiences with others? Will our lives be marked and defined by moments of scarcity or moments of generosity? Will our lives be marked and defined by moments of forgiveness or by grudges tightly held? Will our lives be marked and defined by loving power or by the power of loving? Will our lives be marked and defined by guilt and shame or by the grace and mercy of God? Will our lives be marked and defined by our communal sins of commission or our communal sins of omission? Will our lives be marked and defined by what we risk for the sake of sharing God's radically inclusive love or by how safe we play it when it comes to taking a risk for the sake of establishing God's commonwealth here on earth? What and whom we will serve are decided in moments—the big defining moments, and the everyday moments, that show us who we truly are.

My work with the Forward Together Moral Movement has reaffirmed for me the principles and values that I want to define my life. In those days when Reverend Dr. Barber and I were fighting the regressive policies of the Wake County School Board, when they were trying to resegregate our school system by dismantling our nationally recognized diversity policy, the fight that I was in personally for my own rights as a gay person never came up—not because it wasn't important, but because it wasn't an obstacle. The fight for justice can never be about one issue. We cannot simply fight for our own personal rights and ignore the rights of others. In the moral movement, we don't get to pick and choose whose rights we are fighting for. We must fight for the human rights of *all* people and for the common good of humanity. We cannot afford to draw circles that shut people out based on the color of their skin, or their gender/gender identity, or their economic status, or their education, or whom they choose to marry, or their religion. This justice-love work of the moral movement is about drawing the circle wider and wider to include all people and demand that all people are ensured their constitutional rights.

Reverend Dr. Barber woke me up to my responsibility as a pastor to be a prophetic voice in these most challenging times. I knew what my faith required of me. I knew my responsibility as a person of faith when I wrote an op-ed piece for the Raleigh *News & Observer* calling out the racism in the actions of the Wake County School Board. But it was that phone call from William Barber that was the defining moment. It was that phone call and the conversations that followed that gave me the courage and the grounding to speak truth to power; to partner with Reverend Dr. Barber and other clergy and laypeople to shine a light on the injustices being perpetrated in our communities by our elected leaders. As a pastor who represents the institutional church, silence was no longer an option. The proclamations of mercy and justice, of caring for your neighbor and doing unto others as you would have them do unto you could no longer be contained in the pulpit of my church. Such proclamations were needed in the public square.

In 1963, as he sat in the Birmingham jail, Martin Luther King Jr. wrote to eight Alabama clergymen: "If today's church does not recapture the sacrificial spirit of the early church, it will . . . be dismissed as an irrelevant social club with no meaning for the twentieth century." King's words serve as the foundation for the essential questions "What is the role of the church today?" and "What is the role of the clergy today?"

When I met William Barber, King's words came alive for me. And my role as a member of the clergy and the role of the church became clear for me. No more silence. No more playing it safe. No more leaving it up to someone else to do. Now was the time to act, to speak, to march, to protest, to go to jail for the sake of justice. It was the defining moment of my life when I said yes to waking up to life. It was the defining moment when I said yes to taking a risk for something that I believed in. It was the defining moment in which I understood that my freedom and my dignity and my basic human rights are bound to the freedom and dignity and human rights of my black and brown sisters and brothers, and the freedom and dignity and human rights of immigrants and refugees, and the freedom and dignity and human rights of my Muslim and Jewish brothers and sisters, and the freedom and dignity and human rights of *all* people. And it all started with one late-night phone call from the Reverend Dr. William Barber. I will forever be grateful to him for waking me up to life!

The Buddhist teacher Thich Nhat Hanh said, "The present moment is the only moment available to us, and it is the door to all moments." Each defining moment that we face calls us to live faithfully in the *present* moment. I would submit to you that if we look back on history, both individually and collectively as a nation, we can see how each defining moment was indeed the door to the next defining moment. It is the way life works. Defining moments that mark our lives are just that—moments in which we lean forward into the next.

The quote that opened this section ends this way: "There are moments which mark your life. Moments when you realize nothing will ever be the same and time is divided into two parts—before this, and after this. Sometimes you can feel such a moment coming. That's the test, or so I tell myself. I tell myself that, at times like that, strong people keep moving forward anyway [and always breaking forth], no matter what they're going to find."

In the months that followed our fight against the Wake County School Board, our state would engage in another battle over equality and justice for all. The people who brought to North Carolina the same regressive politics that tried to resegregate our school system would also introduce Amendment I, a measure that defines marriage in the state constitution as between one man and one woman and bans any other type of "domestic legal union," such as civil unions and domestic partnerships. Again, Reverend Dr. Barber and I would join together to fight Amendment I based on equality and justice for *all* people. It was because of watching him step outside of what was familiar to him to fight for my rights as a gay person that I had the courage to preach a sermon asking my congregation to relieve me of my duties to legally perform marriages until marriage equality was the law of the land.

If you know or research my church, you will question why I call that sermon a risk. Pullen Memorial Baptist Church voted in early 1992 to become a welcoming and affirming congregation to the LGBTQ community and to bless same-gender covenants. In 2002, ten years after I served as associate pastor, they called me, an out lesbian, to be their pastor. And yet the debate around Amendment 1 sparked a new level of conversation about equal rights. When I asked to be relieved of my duties to legally perform marriage until marriage equality was the law of the land, I wasn't sure what the congregation would say. I had imagined and hoped that they would grant my request. But I could never have imagined their response: at a congregational meeting on November 20, 2011, members of Pullen Memorial Baptist Church voted unanimously to affirm that marriages between same-sex and opposite-sex couples will be treated equally and, because of that, *no* marriages would take place in our church until marriage equality.

This is one example of what I have learned from William Barber, and it is a witness to what his boldness to seek justice has called forth in the world. When we take a risk for justice-love, when we ground ourselves in a moral response to hatred and bigotry and greed, when we live and have our being from a place of compassion and kindness and generosity, things that we never imagine open up to us. Movements are built. Thousands choose to go to jail based on the dictates of their conscience. Hundreds of thousands join weekly, driving from as far as five hours away to protest regressive politics. Dozens of justice-oriented organizations ban together to create a Forward Together Moral Movement that draws eighty thousand–plus people to Raleigh in one day to march for justice and equality. These are the moments when you realize nothing will ever be the same and time is divided into two parts: before this and after this.

THE REVEREND DR. NANCY PETTY has served since 1992 on the staff of Pullen Memorial Baptist Church, where she has been pastor since 2002. She has been a leader in the Moral Monday Movement started by Reverend Barber and was active in the formation of Repairers of the

Breach. The North Carolina NAACP named Petty the 2014 Minister of the Year. The Wake County branch of the ACLU recognized her with the W. W. Finlator Award in 2011, and in 2015 she was honored as the individual recipient of the Human Relations Award from the city of Raleigh.

CHAPTER FIVE

MORAL MARCH ON RALEIGH

HISTORIC THOUSANDS ON JONES STREET
SEVENTH ANNUAL MARCH, FEBRUARY 8, 2014

Raleigh, North Carolina

THE REVEREND DR. WILLIAM J. BARBER II

Today is 146 years since black and white progressive Lincoln Republicans such as the Reverend J. W. Hood and Samuel Ashley came together and led our state forward in voting rights and educational rights. It is fifty-four years since students from North Carolina A&T in Greensboro sat down at Woolworth's and caused a nation to stand up against segregation. Soon after that, at Shaw University in Raleigh, students of all colors and classes formed the Student Nonviolent Coordinating Committee, led and nurtured by that champion of organizing, Ella Baker. SNCC joined with NAACP youth chapters all over the country to fight for change. And we here in the Old North State have heard the call of the Spirit of Justice to come together yet again.

The idea of the kind of coalition we see here today is as old as the fusion politics that tried to wrest the South free from slavery during the First Reconstruction. It is as recent as the civil rights movement of the 1960s. In North Carolina, this Forward Together Movement builds on the work of the Historic Thousands on Jones Street People's Assembly (HKonJ), which has gathered thousands of people in front of the State Legislative Building every February since 2007. Standing on deep and historic constitutional principles and sound values of faith, we have challenged Democrats and Republicans alike. But this year—after an avalanche of cruel and extremist Tea Party policies and more than thirty Moral Monday rallies—we return to Raleigh with renewed strength and a sense of urgency.

This year's Moral March makes five fundamental demands of our elected leaders:

1. Secure prolabor, antipoverty policies that ensure economic sustainability
2. Provide well-funded, quality public education for all
3. Promote health care for all, including affordable access, the expansion of Medicaid, protections for women's health, and the assurance of environmental justice in every community
4. Address the continuing inequalities in the criminal justice system and ensure equality under the law for every person, regardless of race, class, creed, documentation, or sexual orientation
5. Protect and expand voting rights for people of color, women, immigrants, the elderly, and students

To promote these principles and to challenge the premeditated attacks on them by extremists, this Moral March kicks off a year of grassroots empowerment and voter education, litigation, and nonviolent direct action. The North Carolina NAACP and the Forward Together Movement will fight extremism, defend the ballot, encourage voter turnout regardless of party, and sue to restore voting rights in our state.

We call on all people of goodwill to resist attacks on the poor and working families of North Carolina. The Reverend Dr. Martin Luther King Jr. once said, "In the end, we will remember not the words of our enemies, but the silence of our friends." In this moment, we cannot be silent. We must speak up! We must become the "trumpets of conscience" that we are called to be, echoing the God of our mothers and fathers in the faith. Now is the time. Here is the place. We are the people. And we will be heard. We have come today to raise our moral dissent at the path down which our elected leaders are pushing the people of North Carolina. We are called to high standards in our civic life. The Word of God set a high standard for how we should live as people and conduct ourselves as nations.

And what does the Lord require of you? To act justly and to love mercy and to walk humbly with your God (Micah 6:8).

Woe unto those who legislate evil, write oppressive decrees that rob the poor of their rights (Isaiah 10).

For I was hungry and you gave me something to eat, I was thirsty and you gave me something to drink, I was a stranger and you invited me in, I needed clothes and you clothed me, I was sick and you looked after me, I was in prison and you came to visit me (Matthew 25).

Every major faith tradition lifts up the high standard of justice. The Constitution of the United States also sets a high standard of how we should conduct ourselves as a democracy and a nation. And when we look at these standards for North Carolina and for America, we must declare there are those who have chosen to live, govern, and act mighty low.

In policy and politics we face two choices: one is the pathway to destruction and the other is the pathway to higher ground. One way is a road filled with greed and the other is a path full of grace. One is a road of hate and the other is a path of love. One road is built of chaos and meanness and the other is built on caring and kindness.

In North Carolina, we have come together to fight against a dangerous agenda of extremist laws by the ultraconservative right wing—policies that are constitutionally inconsistent, morally indefensible, and economically insane. It's extreme and mighty low to cut Medicaid for more than five hundred thousand people, many of them children. It's extreme and mighty low to raise taxes on nine hundred thousand poor and middle-class citizens in order to cut taxes for the twenty-three wealthiest families in North Carolina. It's extreme to end unemployment benefits for one hundred seventy thousand people who have lost jobs through no fault of their own. It's extreme to resegregate our schools and to eliminate preschool for more than thirty thousand poor children. These legislators cut so much money from public education that we are now forty-eighth in the US in teacher pay; and then they remove $10 million from public schools and give that money to a private voucher scheme. It's mighty low to raise taxes on 89 percent of North Carolina's people so you can give the richest 11 percent a tax break, knowing that this transfer to the top will drain a sorely needed $650 million from the budget of our state. It's mighty low for us to sing "America, America, God shed His grace on you" with one breath and with another deny workers the grace of labor rights and union rights, to cut safety nets to the needy and raise taxes on the poor and working poor, to deny immigrants fair immigration policies, and to undermine the rights of women and the LGBTQ community.

We have to look at policy through the moral lens of justice for all and through the constitutional principle of the common good. Kicking hardworking people is not just bad policy, it's against the common good. We have come to say to the extremists who ignore the common good: your actions will not discourage us! The more you push to go back, the more we will fight to go forward. Your actions will not discourage us! Instead, they inspire us to mobilize more. This is no mere hyperventilation; this is a fight for the future and soul of our state. It doesn't matter what the critics call us. They deride us and deflect because they can't debate on the issues. They can't make their case on moral and constitutional grounds.

We know who we are. We are black, white, Latino, Native American. We are Democrat, Republican, third-party-affiliated, and independent. We are people of all faiths and no faith who believe in a moral universe. We are natives and immigrants; business leaders and workers; doctors and the uninsured; gay, straight, and trans; students and retirees. We stand here—a quilt of many colors, faiths, and creeds. We stand united in our full color against our state government's current attack on the most vulnerable. We stand together to lift up the most sacred principles of our democracy.

And we know who you are. We refuse to even call you Republicans. We know progressive, sensible Republicans. Abraham Lincoln, who stood for equality and justice. Black and white Republicans who in the 1800s expanded voting rights and educational opportunities to those who had been enslaved. Teddy Roosevelt, who called for health care for all and a minimum wage. Dwight Eisenhower, who right after the *Brown v. Board of Education* case said that public education was a matter of national security. He invested more money in public education than any other president before him. Republicans and Democrats alike signed off on the Civil Rights Acts of 1964 and 1965 and the Voting Rights Act of 1965. Black Republicans such as Edward Brooke, Ralph Bunche, and Benjamin Hooks—a past president of the NAACP—championed the cause of justice and freedom and stood up to the extremists of their time. Ronald Reagan supported the Earned Income Tax Credit. In North Carolina, there was a history of Republicans and Democrats working together for the common good in education and rural economic development. But no more.

No matter how you extremists tried to twist things, this is not about Republicans versus Democrats. It's not about liberals versus conservatives. It's about right versus wrong. It's about extremism versus the more noble vision of our Constitution. It is about policy that is immoral versus policy that is moral.

When we leave here today, we will motivate every citizen to be involved by maintaining our appeal to people's deepest moral and constitutional values. We will meet every challenge to suppress the right to vote. We will mobilize people in North Carolina to get educated on issues and to get to the polls and vote. We will fight in the courts against all efforts to undermine the vote. We will fight to restore Section 4 of the Voting Rights Act. We are people who see and seek the higher ground. There is a higher ground where we can pay hard workers living wages and ensure their basic human right to form unions and collectively bargain for fairness on the job. There is higher ground where we can use global technology, a green economy, and targeted tax cuts for economic and infrastructure investment in underserved communities. We are on higher ground when we reject hate and division and mean attempts to write people out of their due constitutional protections because of their race, their creed, or their sexual orientation. We are on higher ground when we support education and job-creation programs that fully address the ugly realities of poverty. If we see the poor as our neighbors and if we remember we are our brother's keeper, then we shall put the poor, rather than the wealthy, at the center of our agenda. We who believe in freedom can't settle for anything less than higher ground! No matter which governor is in office, what the Congress does, or what the Tea Party says, we can't be silent anymore.

The extremists didn't have enough political power to vote us away, enough insults to talk us away, or enough money to buy us away. We are still here. We are the children who have been born for such a time as this, and there is no way we will ever abdicate our birthright. We want a democracy that protects the rights of everyone, where we are truly one nation under God with liberty and justice for all. One where all of God's children are seen as special and loved and important.

We deserve higher ground. Is there anybody here that still believes in higher ground? Too many tears have been cried, and too many people have sacrificed, bled, and died for us to settle for anything less than higher ground. Weeping may endure for a night but joy comes in the morning! The hymn writer said,

> I'm pressing on the upward way,
> New heights I'm gaining every day;
> Still praying as I onward bound,
> Lord, plant my feet on higher ground.

My heart has no desire to stay
Where doubts arise and fears dismay;
Though some may dwell where these abound,
My prayer, my aim, is higher ground.

Lord, lift me up, and let me stand
By faith on Canaan's tableland;
A higher plane than I have found,
Lord, plant my feet on higher ground.

Plant North Carolina. Lord, plant this nation. Plant America. Plant our politics on higher ground!

WE ARE NOT AFRAID

AL McSURELY

Lawyer, North Carolina NAACP

Upwards of eighty thousand Hispanic Americans, African Americans, Native Americans, Asian Americans, European Americans, Muslim Americans, Jewish Americans, and other Americans from North Carolina and other states gathered for the annual People's Assembly of the Moral Fusion Movement on a cold Saturday morning in February 2014.

The weather prediction was "cloudy, cold, with rain." Veteran organizers, responsible for getting tens of thousands of people and thousands of buses in and out of downtown Raleigh, were hopeful—but not overly confident—that the rain would hold off. One year we had to postpone the Historic Thousands on Jones Street Assembly (HKonJ) for two weeks because of a blizzard. A couple of other Saturday mornings had been bitterly cold, wet, or both. But all things considered, we had been blessed with good weather for the Saturday closest to the birthday of the NAACP and Abraham Lincoln, which we chose for our annual People's Assembly.

Two nights before the assembly, scores of clergy from virtually every organized religion in North Carolina—Hindus, Buddhists, Methodists, Baptists, Catholics, Jews, Presbyterians, African Methodist Episcopal Zions, Christian Methodist Episcopals, Unitarians, Ethical Culturists, Muslims, and more—had gathered at a special interfaith service to bless Saturday's Moral March. They represented different ways of worshiping the creation of our shared universe, meditating, praying, thinking, and praising the righteous paths of justice, peace, and grace. All perspectives were united against the extremist backlash that had spewed from the North Carolina Legislature.

All present recognized Reverend Dr. Barber's special presence and insights. He told me, "I was overwhelmed that night. I knew many tenets of the different faiths in the room. But I learned their faiths on a deeper level when I looked in the eyes of my sisters and brothers with us that evening and associated them with my knowledge of the holy teachers and histories of their personal faiths. When I preached my social justice theology, we were all smiling and moving forward together."

The night before the assembly, we gathered to pray and sing at a large African American church. A powerful choir led us in song after song that reminded us of the long-term hope and faith of black mothers and fathers who have taught their children to persevere since the holocaust of slavery and Jim Crow. The songs were beacons of warmth and light during a long cold and dark journey.

Early Saturday morning it was cold, damp, and dark. Virtually all the clergy who had gathered two evenings earlier circled the Great Seal of North Carolina in front of our People's House on Jones Street. The seal proclaims North Carolina's creed: "To Be, Not to Seem," a perpetual reminder of the lies, hypocrisy, euphemisms, and pretexts that have long leached out of Jones Street, like Duke Energy's coal ash leaches into our rivers.

Rabbis across the state had invited their members to take part in the Moral March instead of worshiping at their synagogues that Saturday. They brought the traveling altar of the Torah, the scroll of five Old Testament books, to the historic Shaw University Chapel. This is the same chapel where, fifty-three years earlier, Dr. King and his associate, Ms. Ella Baker, blessed the formation of the Student Nonviolent Coordinating Committee. These young people would test out a prophetic theology and theory of fundamental radical transformation of the segregated South by intentionally disobeying the immoral and unconstitutional system of Jim Crow. Ms. Baker, Ms. Rosa Parks, and scores of old NAACP warriors and white progressives across the South helped give life to the holy teachings of Justice, Grace, Love, and Peace. They followed the movement tactics developed by unions of sleeping-car porters, steel workers, and millions of peasants in far-off India, all against the systems of racism and poverty that had subjugated the great majority of the world's people in the southern region of the United States—and the Southern Hemisphere more broadly.

I knew this march was going to be special when the rabbis prayed with the family of three Muslims who had been assassinated by a hate-filled man in Chapel Hill a few weeks before. They were joined by the family of Lennon Lacy, a young man who had walked down the streets of 2014 Bladenboro holding hands with a white woman and was found hanging on a morning designated by the Ku Klux Klan as a date to remind people of white supremacy. It was the anniversary of the day Emmett Till was murdered for allegedly saying something nice to a white woman in Mississippi in 1955.

Imams, rabbis, and ministers prayed for the Chapel Hill martyrs and for Lennon Lacy. Then, lifting high the ram's-horn trumpet, they sent its mournful melody into the cloudy sky. The vast and noisy crowd silenced itself instantly. A rabbi wrapped her forty-pound Torah in a holy cloth and held it tightly. She walked in the center of the first row of the marchers. Reverend Dr. Barber grabbed the hands of his old and new clergy friends and walked up behind the Torah. Every person of faith, and some with no faith, knew there was a special spirit taking hold of the largest civil rights march in southern history. The Torah was a reminder of Moses, afraid yet full of faith, walking resolutely toward the raging sea.

We walked north two blocks on Wilmington Street, went west two blocks, and then entered the Fayetteville Street Mall arena. Hundreds climbed concrete stairwells to find perches in the parking decks lining the mall. Hundreds packed the doorways of the stores on the mall. When you stood on the stage and looked south, all you could see was a sea of humans jammed into the mall, with more still squeezing themselves into the packed crowd.

We were so packed that the warmth we generated helped ward off the drizzle and cold. But it was a cloudy day. The sunless day had a haunting darkness. We had cut the program in the hope of ending it by 12:30 so the thousands of marchers from our new Appalachian Branches and our older Atlantic Coast Branches could get home by nightfall.

By noon, the river of humanity was still stepping off from the march's starting point. People were still squeezing into the penned-in mall crowd. Our 2013 Moral Monday organizing against the backlash of extremists, and our work to greet extremists when they came back with their racist agenda for the 2014 legislative session, had led to more than a thousand arrests by the white extremist caucus. They seemed to get a thrill from ordering their personal police department to arrest North Carolina citizens rather than talk with us. Thousands were at their first Moral March on Raleigh, and we wanted it to be a memorable experience for them.

People from Sylva, from Mitchell County, from Boone and Rockingham Counties, from Elizabeth City and Kitty Hawk, had to leave home at 5 a.m. to get there. Many had done that every Moral Monday. When they were arrested and then released from jail at 2 or 3 a.m., they had to drive home to go to work the next morning. Some of these warriors from the mountains and the Atlantic Coast were still pouring into the mall to catch a glimpse of the speakers and musicians on the giant Jumbotrons a patron had helped us pay for (he had not been able to see the stage very well the year before, so he donated money for the Jumbotrons!).

Reverend Dr. Barber began his address at 12:15, as promised. He took a few minutes to acknowledge the warm and resounding support for the overwhelming numbers and the glorious diversity of the crowd. His assessment that truth was the best antidote to arrogant power was ratified by the crowd's enthusiasm. Reverend Dr. Barber, like all mortals, always experiences some doubts when he addresses crowds like this, knowing he will not meet everyone's expectations. If you watch and listen to him carefully, in person or in videos, you can see him become an instrument of justice and love. On this rainy, cloudy, chilly day, he was trying to share his vision of an uncloudy sky. Of a sky of hope and light. He talked about moving to higher ground. He lined out the old hymn. Then, he called on the movement singer Yara Allen and her sister Sauuda. He wanted the massive crowd to sing together. What better song than the civil rights movement anthem "We Shall Overcome"? Bernice Reagon, Guy Carawan, Zilphia Horton, Ella Baker, Pete Seeger, and other movement giants who had a hand in simplifying this old gospel and union song for mass singing all did it for an occasion such as this. The gigantic crowd took a moment to join in. But by the time we got to the third line, *We shall overcome, someday*, Yara and Sauuda had the largest mass choir ever assembled in the South feeling and singing with movement spirit.

They took us directly to the second verse, my favorite: *We are not afraid. We are not afraid, today*—with the emphasis on *today!* Not someday. *Today!* Upwards of eighty thousand people, some just coming into the mall and looking up at the Jumbotron, sang with great spirit, *We are not afraid, TODAY! HERE! NOW!*

From the stage, Reverend Dr. Barber saw the bright sun first. Over the heads of the massive crowd, behind the sea of human beings, the dark clouds that had shielded the sun's warmth and light split wide open, like the sea did for Moses and those who kept the faith. Reverend Dr. Barber pointed to the sun. Everyone turned and cheered and cried at the same time. We sang the second verse again. "We are not afraid. We are not afraid, *today.*" We are part of something much bigger than ourselves.

AL McSURELY joined the Moral Fusion movement in 1962 in Virginia CORE, the short-lived war on poverty in Metro Washington and Appalachia, and the Southern Christian Education Fund, the Southern Christian Leadership Conference, and the first Poor People's Campaign through December 13, 1968. That night, white terrorists dynamited his family home, just a month after Richard Nixon was elected president. For seventeen years of popular education and zealous legal advocacy, he and Margaret Herring apprenticed themselves to Mort Stavis, Bill Kunstler, and Arthur Kinoy to beat bogus charges of sedition and contempt of Congress. McSurely used his legal earnings and learnings to get a law license in North Carolina in 1988, built an effective civil rights law practice, and volunteered twenty years with the North Carolina NAACP and Moral Fusion Movement with Reverend Barber.

CHAPTER SIX

THE CALL TO BE POSITIONED AS POWERFUL PRISONERS OF PROPHETIC HOPE

MARTIN LUTHER KING JR. COMMEMORATION, JANUARY 15, 2015

Duke University, Durham, North Carolina

THE REVEREND DR. WILLIAM J. BARBER II

I'm reminded today of the words of John Hope Franklin, who said, "One might argue the historian is the conscience of the nation." He said, "Knowing one's history leads one to act in a more enlightened fashion. I cannot imagine how knowing one's history would not urge one to be an activist." So, I am humbly trying to fulfill my small role in the world as a scholar, activist, and really as a Christian. I don't know how to be a Christian and not be concerned deeply about love and justice. I am thankful for the gracious invitation to step into this beautiful sanctuary, climb these hallowed stairs where people of ebony hue were not always welcome, to be in a place that has been graced by so many speakers of truth, prophets of their time, and historians of their era. It is a humbling privilege.

Today I want to wrestle with the theme from Zechariah 9, verses 11 and 12, which read, "As for you, because of the blood of My covenant with you, I will free your prisoners from the waterless pit. Return to your fortresses, you prisoners of hope. Even now, I announce that I will restore twice as much to you."

I want to talk about the call to be positioned as powerful prisoners of prophetic hope.

Zechariah is a short book, unfamiliar to most, tucked away close to the end of the Old Testament. The message of the prophet Zechariah in the scripture was addressed to those he described as prisoners of hope. The Jews from Babylon had begun to move back to Jerusalem, their homeland, but they were ill-equipped to restore the temple. They'd come out of slavery—up from slavery, if you will—and were back home. But there was work to be done. They looked for a completion. Instead, the text before this passage says that their enemies were challenging them. Obstacles were in their way. Something on every hand was trying to stop them from completion.

Now, the prophet Zechariah, speaking for God, does not deny their continuing challenges or offer them some cute optimism. In fact, in verse 11, he owns where they are. They are in waterless pits. It is the metaphorical description of their despair. And this, interestingly, is a crucial step to prophetic hope: publicly owning despair. Old Testament scholar Walter Brueggemann helps us with texts like this, when he notes in his book *Prophetic Imagination* that "counteracting the numbness of empire requires recognition of humanity's passion: the capacity and readiness to care, to suffer, to die in order to recognize the conditions that breed new worlds. To stoke such fires, the prophet must be fluent in the language of both grief and hope." Prophets must be multilingual. They must know how to speak in tongues that the people can understand, that they might open their ears, for Isaiah said, "Awake my ear every morning, O Lord, that I might have the tongue of the learned and know how to speak to those that are weary." They must be able to talk about human suffering and liberation.

Brueggemann goes on to say that "tears are a way of solidarity in pain where no other form of solidarity remains." Matthew, chapter five, verse four, says only those who mourn can be comforted. If you know nothing about mourning, you will never know anything about prophetic hope. There is a kind of truthful touching of pain that is the only way to find the power of prophetic hope. In other words, owning the despair caused by domination and oppression in the public square opens us up for a new movement toward community rooted in the strength of prophetic hope.

And, finally, Brueggemann says, "The prophet does not ask first if the vision can be implemented, for questions of implementation are of no consequence until the vision can be imagined." The imagination must come before the implementation. So, hope, in this sense, is the refusal to accept the reading of reality that is the majority opinion. Therefore, this hope is subversive. That's why if you dare to say, "I have a dream" to the wrong people in the wrong place, it can get you hunted. It can cause you to be tracked. Because prophetic hope is subversive. It limits the grandiose pretention of the present. It dares to announce that the present, to which we have all made commitments, is now being called into question. Dr. King was a prophet. And as such, he called us to be like Zechariah, prisoners of the kind of prophetic hope that dares to say and act in the face of the nightmarish visions of injustice, "I have a dream"; not a plan, but a dream of another reality.

Today, I want to lift some of the words from some of the sermons of Dr. King which, like Zechariah's, we hardly hear in this season. I want to lift some sermons from 1967 and '68. King was wrestling heavily with the reality of the desperate situation, yet surrendering to the power of prophetic hope; he was lifting it, believing it, preaching it, and marching as a prisoner of prophetic hope. On December 10, 1967, Dr. King said something that grabbed me. He opened one of his last sermons, titled "The Meaning of Hope," saying, "I'm worried about America." He preached this in the season of Advent, just five months before he was killed. This was after the passage of the '64 Civil Rights Act and the '65 Voting Rights Act. Many people, from preachers to presidents, were telling him enough had been done. They said, in time, things would just get better. They told him to hold out. But he said, "I'm worried about America," a country founded on the principle that people were created equal by God, yet still wrestling with whether the color of the skin determines the content of the character. He posed that he was worried about America, a nation sick with militarism, a nation where at that time the gross national product was $800 billion and there were still fifty million poor people within its borders. Something was wrong.

At first, it doesn't sound like a message on the meaning of hope. But the truth is, there is no real dealing with prophetic hope without knowing clearly the sources of despair. King said because there is something wrong, we must continue. And in the sermon, he began to announce the initial strategies that would lead toward the Poor People's Campaign. In the sermon he defined prophetic hope not as optimism, nor desire, nor magic, nor inevitability, but as the willingness to risk defeat. The kind of hope that cares about "we" and not "I." The kind of hope that is contagious. It is a hope rooted in the power of love and the strength of faith, a hope that believes there are moral laws in the universe. The moral arc of the universe may be long but it bends toward justice. Hope that believes that right will eventually break the chains of injustice and the foundation of evil. Hope that never gives up the call for justice but sings in every battle for justice when the odds are against it. I've seen the lightning flash. I've heard the thunder roll. It's sent breakers breaking, trying to conquer my soul. But I heard the voice of Jesus say to still fight on, for he promised never to leave me alone.

This kind of prophetic hope, as Dr. King would say in another place, was a call for a worldwide fellowship that lifts neighborly concern above one's tribe, race, class, nationality. It was a hopeful call for an all-embracing and unconditional love for all human beings. And it's right that I would say this in this pulpit today. Dr. King spoke to the basic Hindu, Muslim, Christian, Jewish, and Buddhist belief about ultimate reality that is beautifully summed up in the first epistle of Saint John: "Let us love one another, for love is God and everyone that loveth is born of God and knoweth God."

This hope is our ability to recapture the revolutionary spirit and go out into a sometimes-hostile world, he said, declaring our eternal hostility to poverty, racism, and militarism. I want to suggest today that we need to make contemporary Dr. King's legitimate anxiety. I want to suggest today that we still ought to be worried about North Carolina. I want to suggest today that we still ought to be worried about America. And we ought to recognize that we, even now, need the witness and the power of prisoners of prophetic hope once again in our country and in our world. Because prophetic hope demands that we tell the truth.

Now, I'll tell you a little story. I once was invited to speak at an MLK event where the theme was "Chaos and Community," so I chose to address contemporary issues of chaos that were keeping us from community. Afterward I received a letter saying that I had offended some of the funders and caused division. They said I had been invited to talk about Dr. King's peaceful activities, not to address contemporary political and social issues. Preachers are not supposed to do that. But truth-telling is critical to the mandate of prophetic hope. Only the truth can set us free.

For so many of us, morality is merely group consensus. In our modern social lingo, war is accepted as the right way. We have unconsciously come to believe that right is discovered by a Gallup poll. The reality is that truth is messy. Truth-telling is messy. And it will mess with us. It will mess with the systems around us, which is what makes it so troubling and sometimes dangerous. I know there are those who say our concern as the people of God should be private soul-saving, private devotion, private praying, private morality that addresses the issues of the inner person only. I'm not against pastoral inner healing, but I am against limiting the moral voice of the faithful to the categories of abortion, homosexuality, and prayer in the schools. There are those who espouse some kind of weird theology that places God on the side of private ownership, rugged individuality, mass gun ownership, the death penalty, and war at the expense of the poor, claiming these are divinely sanctioned. That's why I'm worried about America.

They say the church faithful should have no real voice in social justice and liberation, but I want to say this form of pharisaical hypocrisy dismisses too liberally the weightier matters of faith. To be a true conservative is to conserve love and justice and mercy, which are at the heart of the gospel. True spirituality calls us to be suspicious of concentrations of wealth and privilege and power and to mistrust the kind of rationalism that justifies subordinating another person to our own benefit. We are called to be sensitive to the poor, the disenfranchised, the stranger, and the outsider.

I had a professor here who used to mark my papers up quite red. His name is Dr. William Turner. He was not only my professor of preaching here at Duke Divinity School but also my mentor. Dr. Turner speaks about the crisis experience of conversion. He says that when you're converted, when you're called, when you become prisoner to this hope, our active orientation to life is shifted. In other words, when the spirit moves, we are saved, born again, changed, and filled. However you describe it, what follows is a challenge to the way things are. He says being moved by the spirit necessitates a quarrel with the way things are, and if there is not a quarrel with the way things are, particularly as it relates to injustice, then our claim to be filled with the spirit is suspect.

Dr. Turner said to us in a sermon that it wasn't King's message about love and truth that was the problem. The problem was the way he chose to preach it, whom he chose to say it to, and the systems that he chose to critique through the lens of love and justice. That's what made him a threat to the power structure. And so, to honor that legacy, let's speak some truth. Truth is, in North Carolina and America, we still need to deal with the realities of poverty. Dr. King warned us in 1968 that there are two Americas. One America is beautiful. Millions of people have milk—the milk of prosperity and the honey of equality. But there's also another America. This America has daily ugliness about it. It transforms the buoyancy of hope into the fatigue of despair.

My friends over at the North Carolina Poverty Research Fund, formerly the University of North Carolina's Center on Poverty, Work, and Opportunity, will tell you we are the richest nation ever and yet we have more poor people than at any other moment in our country's history. Our poverty numbers, especially child poverty numbers, are far higher than in any other advanced Western democracy. We add to that now the greatest gaps between the rich and the poor since we began collecting data five decades ago. We began a War on Poverty in the '60s. It began to drive the numbers down. And then we shut it down. It was the quickest war we've ever fought. And our income inequality now is documented to be the highest in the so-called advanced world. We have also become the least economically mobile advanced country, so if you're born poor, you're more apt to stay that way.

The Poverty Research Fund knows, further, that the South—North Carolina, Alabama, Georgia, Tennessee, Virginia, Mississippi, Louisiana, and South Carolina—is the native home of American poverty, and we have more poor people and more political leaders who are utterly untroubled by it. In fact, they are against any programs to help the poor. Ten of the country's twelve poorest states are southern. In North Carolina, more than 1.6 million people live in poverty and that's just using the limited poverty standard and not the living-wage standard. Six hundred thousand of them are children and more than 35 percent of those children are African American. And the poorest counties in America are in so-called red states led by and represented by politicians who are the most ardent opponents of the program that would help the poor right in their own districts.

In North Carolina, we have seen an active disdain for programs that empower the poor by many state and elected leaders, even though Article 11, Section 4 of the state constitution, which every North Carolina governor and legislator swears to uphold, says that beneficent provisions for the poor, the unfortunate, and the orphan are the first duties of a civilized and Christian state. That means we are constitutionally out of order.

A Harvard University study asked Americans what they believe the pay gap is between the average US worker and the average CEO. Most people said 30 percent. The study found that the CEO's pay was thirty times greater in the 1960s but is 350 times greater today. Half the jobs in this nation pay less than $34,000 a year, according to the Economic

Policy Institute; a quarter pay below the poverty line for a family of four, less than $23,000 annually. And we have people who don't even want to raise the minimum wage.

Another study, by Stanford sociologist Sean Reardon and published by the Russell Sage Foundation in a report called *Whither Opportunity?*, noted that children born into low- and high-income families often have the same abilities, but they have very different educational opportunities. By some estimates, the gap today is twice as large as it was two decades ago. And rising income inequality breeds more inequality in educational opportunity, which in turn translates into a waste of human talent, a less educated workforce, slower economic growth, and even greater income inequality. In other words, it costs us more *not* to address poverty than it does to address poverty.

You know opportunists will try to blame this situation on one politician or another. The truth is, we need a contemporary moral vision that's committed to economic sustainability and ending poverty by fighting for full employment, living wages, the alleviation of despair and unemployment, a green economy, labor rights, affordable housing, targeted empowerment zones, strong safety nets for the poor, fair policies for immigrants, infrastructure development, and fair tax reform. We must tell the truth.

We must tell the truth about mass incarceration and the brokenness of the criminal justice system. Not just the flash points. Sure, we know Ferguson. Been there, marched there. We know about New York and Eric Garner. Been there, marched there. We know about Jonathan Ferrell. We know about the situations right here in Durham. But we must tell the truth about the whole system. In his book *Punishment and Inequality in America*, sociologist Bruce Western shows that prison is the dominant and most formative institution in the lives of poor black men in the United States. That's just wrong. Crime among young black men has plunged while incarceration has increased. Today, less than 5 percent of the world population is in the United States, but we have almost 25 percent of the world's prisoners. China has a billion more people than us and we have a million more prisoners than China. African Americans now constitute 1 million of the total incarcerated population of 2.3 million. If you add brown people, that figure is even higher. African Americans are incarcerated at nearly six times the rate of whites, according to United for a Fair Economy's 2009 report *The State of the Dream*. Together, African Americans and Hispanics made up 58 percent of all US prisoners in 2008, yet they make up only about 25 percent of the population.

According to the NAACP Criminal Justice Fact Sheet, in drug centers, about 14 million whites and 2.6 million African Americans report using an illicit drug. Five times as many whites are using drugs as African Americans, yet African Americans are sent to prison for drug offenses at ten times the rate of whites. African Americans represent 12 percent of the total population of drug users, but 38 percent of those arrested for drug offenses and 59 percent of those in state prisons for drug offenses—and the issue is even broader than that. It's not that we want more white people arrested for drug offenses. What we want is for those with addictions to be treated for their disease and not just arrested for nonviolent crimes.

Right here in North Carolina, we've seen black and white men exonerated while on death row. Think about it. These are men who would have been killed in your name, in your name, in *your name*, in my name. They would have been killed. And we've had more than any other state in the country, while we have legislators repealing the Racial Justice Act, which prevents seeking or imposing the death penalty on the basis of race. Legal scholar Michelle Alexander calls the prison-industrial complex "the New Jim Crow." Theologian James Cone is more explicit. He calls it "the lynching tree." Addressing the continuing inequalities in the criminal justice system and providing equal protection under the law for black, brown, and poor white people must be a part of our vision.

We must tell the truth about this continuing reality of racism. I want to drill down a little bit here, because we've got to make a few modern adjustments in how we talk about racism. I saw the other night a white man arguing that there was racism in America and a black person saying there wasn't. And Dr. King always advocated that people look deeper into the well of racial discrepancy with an analysis that goes beyond surface explanation and symbolic remedies. This is truer today than it was in the 1960s, because we don't have the signs and the signatures up. Sometimes we believe racism has shown itself only when we catch somebody using the n-word. We wonder if race is a factor only when an unarmed black man is killed by the police and protests rise. That's often the only time the media even wants to talk about race. In fact, I've almost stopped answering interviews about that. Call me when you want to talk about the budget. Call me when you want to talk about health care and public education.

There's a book titled *Racism Without Racists*, and its conclusion must become part of our critique. The author, Eduardo Bonilla-Silva, notes that we have virtually run out of racists today. He says even self-proclaimed white supremacists deny being racists. They say that they are merely extolling white pride the same way that African Americans celebrate theirs. But if we look deeper, what we are seeing is the transformation of the Southern Strategy with a twenty-first-century twist. It's the strategy of Richard Nixon and George Wallace, which they bequeathed to those that came after them. You remember Lee Atwater in a taped interview said that George Wallace advised nearly fifty years ago that his followers stop using racial epithets. He said, don't do it anymore. He said, instead, use words like "socialism," "law and order," "neighborhood schools," "social engineering," "welfare," "food stamps," "cutting taxes," and "forced busing." He said, do this so your policies will sound race-neutral but their impact will still be race-specific.

And so today you have many saying there's no real racism, and some on a certain sly-as-a-Fox television channel who purport to be fair and balanced spend hours attempting to deny systemic racism with a smile. But despite denial and the abundant willful blindness toward racial disparities, sociologist Glenn Loury teaches us that we can clearly see racial disparities whether or not people say racialized words; in wages, unemployment rates, income and wealth levels, prison enrollment and crime victimization rates, and health and mortality. Loury goes on to explain that some try to say there are no racists, and yet only the willfully deaf do not hear the dog-whistle politics calling President Obama the food stamp president and a juvenile, which is what they called slaves. That's why we've got to take care of these people, because they're childish. They call Obama unfit. They don't call him a liar, but a lie. Listen to the language. Not "you are a liar" but "you are a lie." Your existence is a lie. This is not supposed to be.

No racists, yet only the willfully indifferent can ignore the studies that prove young black men are imprisoned at a greater rate than their white counterparts, and now the United States is at a point where we are imprisoning a larger percentage of the black population than South Africa did at the height of apartheid. No racists, yet our public schools are in the process of resegregation sixty years after *Brown*. No racists to be seen, and yet we willfully forget how federal housing policies and red-lining by banks created home-owning for white middle-class people while walling off blacks into overcrowded ghettos, where a home could never be the stepping-stone to the middle class—while mortgage markets, the cost of home loans, residential segregation, and the way families accumulate wealth through home appreciation all continue to systemically disadvantage black and brown families.

No racists, and yet activist and author Tim Wise notes that there is little doubt that there was a growing opposition to social safety net efforts, unemployment, Social Security, housing finance programs, food assistance, and health care among whites from the 1930s through the 1960s. And the dislike of these programs mirrors almost perfectly the time period during which black and brown folk began to gain access to them. So, he says in large part the critique of entitlement programs has been bound up with a racialized narrative of who constitutes the deserving and the undeserving.

The truth is, we have an extreme agenda afoot in America. I'm worried. I'm worried about North Carolina's extreme agenda. We have to know the greatest myth of our time is the notion that these extreme policies hurt just a small set of people. Not only must we tell the truth, but prophetic hope demands secondly that we refuse to believe that misguided politicians and mean money have the last word. Dr. King said we are called to be thermostats that change the temperature, not thermometers that merely measure the temperature. Gandhi said first they ignore you, then they ridicule you, then they fight you, and then you win. And the truth is, every movement that has ever changed America began when electoral politics, the majority, and even the law were antagonistic. The abolition movement didn't have the majority with it, or the politics, when it began. The women's suffrage movement didn't have the majority when it began. The fight against legalized lynching didn't have it. The fight for Social Security, the battle to end segregation and Jim Crow, the campaign in Birmingham, the Greensboro sit-ins, Selma, the 1964 Civil Rights Act, the 1965 Voting Rights Act, none of these efforts was popular. None of these efforts had the Gallup poll with them. None of these efforts had the political sway with them. But what changes the country and what changes the world is not just electoral politics, but moral movements that change the atmosphere in which electoral politics have to exist.

That's why as prisoners of hope our greatest temptation is to turn, cop a plea, and sell out as slaves to fear. That's what happened to Ancient Israel in biblical times. That's what happened to Josephus Daniels, the early-twentieth-century progressive populist who caved in to the Redeemers and incited the racist riots and attacks on black wealth and white politicians in Wilmington. It is what happened to so many well-meaning liberal people who turned their backs on King when J. Edgar Hoover moved to assassinate his character.

We've seen the extremists. We know who they are. They are petty, they are mean, they are irrationally sure of themselves. But the mean-spirited extremists, Dr. King told us, are not our greatest enemy. Our greatest enemy is the temptation to give in to fear: fear of terrorism, fear of losing donors, fear of offending, fear of staying true to what we know is right. And sometimes the fear we have to fight is the fear that if we stay true, our enemies might be transformed and become our allies.

Our role is not to put a finger in the wind and measure the wind. Our role is to change the wind. Our role is to do like Isaiah 10 and say, "Woe unto those who make unjust laws and issue oppressive decrees that deprive the poor of their right." Our role is to do what God said to Jeremiah:

> Go down to the palace of the king of Judah and proclaim this message there: Hear ye the word of the Lord, King of Judah, you who sit on the throne of David, you and your officials and your people who come through these gates. This is what the Lord says. Do what is just. Do what is right. Wrest you from the hand of your oppressor, the one who has been robbed. Do no wrong to the foreigner. Do no wrong to the stranger. Do no wrong to the fatherless. And do not shed innocent blood.

Our role is to say the spirit of the Lord is upon me, for he has anointed us to preach good news to the poor. He sent us to proclaim freedom to the prisoner, recover sight to the blind.

Our job is to say to North Carolina and America, "You said on paper that the establishment of justice was the foundation of all your claims of freedom. North Carolina, you said on paper that the good of the whole is what is supposed to be the preface of all political power, and since you said it, we're going to hold you accountable to it."

Somebody must stand and say that it doesn't matter what party is in power. There are some things that transcend political majorities, mere majority politics. There are some things that transcend narrow categories of liberal versus conservative. There are some things that must be challenged because they're wrong, they're extreme, and they're immoral. And there is a longing for a deep moral movement that says it's time to challenge those things that are morally indefensible, constitutionally inconsistent, and economically insane. We have to raise our dissent.

We must raise our dissent knowing that whether it is heard now or later, history has shown that moral dissent sows the seeds of change and justice that eventually blossom on the landscape of our democracy. We must raise our moral dissent because it is our calling to do it. We must raise our dissent because to live life without standing for justice is a waste of air, breath, and precious time. So, I'm glad today to be part of a generation of moral dissenters. I'm glad to be among those who give voice and spirit and body to the cause of justice. I'm glad it's our turn now. It's our time and our turn to declare and act and live as though we are prisoners of hope who believe in a better way. Not only must we tell the truth, not only must we say that electoral politics and mean money don't have the last word, but prophetic prisoners of hope understand we must stay together. Because when we do stay together, change happens. The Forward Together Moral Movement is a model of fusion politics rooted in a deeply moral, indigenously led, constitutionally antiracist, antipoverty, projustice framework. We have come together. We have come together. And we've seen change. They're not really acknowledging it yet, but we know what's happening.

When we started out more than 50 percent of North Carolinians believed we ought to use public money to fund private school. But now, more than 61 percent say no. When we started out, we had some lower numbers, but now 58 percent of North Carolinians would rather see taxes raised than teachers' pay cut. When we started out, our opponents had a majority, but now 58 percent of North Carolinians believe we should expand Medicaid and provide health care for a half million uninsured people. And I could go on down the list. Oh, something's happening. We've been able to organize in places like Mitchell County, where in 1920 every black person was run out of town. And now, using this moral framework, blacks and whites and Republicans and Democrats have dropped partisanship and picked up their humanity and consciousness afresh. And I get regular invitations to Mitchell County. Only problem is, they want to march at night, and I tell them black folk don't march at night.

By staying together, we've seen people become inspired in marvelous ways. I got this letter a few days ago that had gotten hid away in the mail. Maybe it was God's reasoning that I wouldn't get it when it came and I would get it before I came to talk to you. Because sometimes I do get worried, even about where we are. The letter says: "Reverend Barber, I know you get a lot of mail from a lot of people. You have no reason to remember me. Therefore, I thought that this picture might help. I'm the bald woman on the oxygen machine. I have fond memories of you and the movement and the work of Moral Mondays, because you all made a profound impression on me last summer, so much so that I decided to practice civil disobedience. I want to thank the movement for that. During this postelection season, I've marveled at the ability of the movement to maintain hope for a better world. I know there are times when you must get discouraged. I know I do. Please know that you and the work and the work of the movement are making a difference. You are important and an example of the teachings of our Lord. Before long, I'll be entering hospice care and I probably won't see you again. But I'm grateful that I lived long enough to be a small part of the Moral Monday movement. And I take hope from the words of Dr. King that indeed, in time the moral arc of the universe will bend toward justice."

And so, my friends, let's heed Zechariah. Let's heed Dr. King. I believe we are possibly in the embryonic stages of a Third Reconstruction in America. If we come together even more, if we return to our fortresses as prisoners of hope, there's no telling what God's going to do. But we come not as individuals but as collective prisoners.

And I stopped by to tell you that the Forward Together movement is no ways tired. Since we left Raleigh, we've been up moving all over the state and even in other states, and right here we're getting ready to march and protest again and litigate again and raise our dissent again on St. Valentine's Day, when we remember the love that is always at the heart of justice. Our fusion coalition will gather in Raleigh for another Mass Moral March and People's Assembly. Our agenda is clear. Our partner organizations are more committed than ever. We are black, we are brown, we are young, we are white, we are old, we are rich, we are poor, we are Republican, we are Democrat, we are Independent, we are Christian, we are Jews, we are Muslims, we are Hindus, we are people of faith, people not of faith, business owners, leaders, doctors, the sick, and we are coming back to Raleigh in the dead of winter to say we will still be here together.

Together, as prisoners of hope, we're not going to give up. Together we're going to say to this state, reverse your attacks on voting rights. Together, receive federally funded Medicaid. Together, raise the minimum wage and index it with inflation. Repeal regressive taxes that hurt the poor and working people. Restore cuts to public education and raise teachers' salaries. Reject the voucher system that drains millions from our already strapped public schools. Reject the attack on women's health and environmental protection. Repeal the death penalty and restore the Racial Justice Act. Reform the criminal justice system, as well as policing, to ensure fair treatment for African Americans, poor whites, and other minorities. Realize just and fair immigration reform. Respect the constitutional rights of all humanity regardless of their race and class and sexuality. We are no ways tired.

And . . . we will have a pray-in and teach-in led by statewide clergy who will deliver our agenda to every legislator on both sides and to the governor. And if during any part of this agenda folk decide they want to come to their epiphany, we'll stand with them. So, Governor, let me make it clear. If you decide you want to expand Medicaid with no frills, without trying to be funny, but just to do what should have been done in the first place, we don't care if you're Republican. We have no permanent friends or permanent enemies, only permanent interests. We'll stand with you. Because we are prisoners of hope, we'll pray together, we'll work together, and we'll raise our moral voice together for the soul of this nation.

I'll conclude by saying I know the power of staying together. I know it biblically. I know the power of staying together, because when Moses and his people and that rod came together, Pharaoh came down and the Red Sea opened up. When Esther and her uncle Mordecai came together, they were able to stop the plots of destruction against the Jewish people and Esther got the courage to say, "If I perish I perish, but I'm going to see the king." When David and his rock and his sling-shot and his faith came together on a battlefield, Goliath fell, and they tell me the next day the headline read "The Bigger They Come, the Harder They Fall." Oh, my God, I know the power of staying together. When Shadrach, Meshach, and who in the black church we call "that bad Negro" (Abednego) stayed together, went down in the pyre and burned, then God cooled the fire down and somebody said they saw a fourth person come in to stand with them, right there in the middle of the flames. Can I get a witness? When the disciples got together in the Upper Room, God gave them power to come out publicly and stand against domination.

I know what staying together does biblically but I also know what staying together has done historically. The truth is, when you hold onto truth and hope, justice never loses. I didn't say justice hasn't been fought. I didn't say justice hasn't been beat up. But justice has never lost. During slavery it looked like justice had lost, but when Harriet Tubman and Frederick Douglass and some Quakers and white evangelicals and Henry David Thoreau got together, they formed a fusion movement that brought about abolition. Women didn't have the right to vote, but when former slave Sojourner Truth and Quaker Lucretia Mott got to-gether, they won the right to vote. *Plessy v. Ferguson* looked like it would carry the day, but when Thurgood Marshall got white lawyers and black lawyers and Jewish lawyers together, an all-white Supreme Court, with one member who had been part of the KKK, voted unanimously to tear down "separate but equal." It looked like Jim Crow had beaten down justice and was going to win, but when Rosa Parks got together with Martin King and Bayard Rustin and all of the other people, white and black, they tore down the system of Jim Crow.

I know what staying together does biblically, I know what staying to-gether does historically, but I've got to tell you one more thing: I know what it does personally. Because several years ago some said I might never walk again. They said I might never get out of a wheelchair again. I was thirty years old and had always depended on my legs. But I woke up one morning here in Durham and I couldn't move. They rushed me to the emergency room. I spent three months in bed not knowing if I would ever get up again. For twelve years, I was in a wheelchair or on a walker. But over those twelve years, something happened. My mind got together. And then my doctors here at Duke got together. And my swim coach got together. And the therapists got together. And my nutritionists got together. Then the church got together. My families got together. And we became prisoners of hope. I can jump now. I can walk now.

Because when the prisoners of hope all get together, what a day. What a day when we all get together. What a day of rejoicing it will be. We need those who know the power of being prisoners of prophetic hope led by the spirit. We need you to stand up again, to speak up again, to come together again until justice is realized, love is actualized, hate is demoralized, war is neutralized, racism, classism, and religious bigotry are marginalized, and the beloved community is actualized. Until then, you who are the prisoners of prophetic hope, return to your fortresses and stand up again and again and again.

BLUES, GOSPEL, AND JAZZ VISIONS FOR GOD'S OWN PRISONER OF HOPE

DR. TIMOTHY TYSON

*Senior Research Scholar, Center for Documentary Studies, and Visiting Professor
of American Christianity and Southern Culture, Duke University*

Karl Marx and Thomas Jefferson may or may not have possessed genius, but they agree on one thing: our ancestors are a burden. "The earth belongs to the living," Jefferson insists. He paints the ancestors as an imperial army of a foreign power, gripping the present with "the dead hand of the past." Marx agrees: "The tradition of all dead generations weighs like a nightmare on the brains of the living." American progressives likewise imagine that genius becomes visible when its avatar shakes off history's shackles and streaks across the human sky, its brilliance embodied in this bold rupture with the past.

This vision of meteoric genius will not illuminate Reverend Dr. William J. Barber II, from 2005 to 2017 the builder of the largest state NAACP in the South and second largest in the nation; this advocate of an Emancipation proclaimed but not completed; this herald of a Third Reconstruction; this gospel poet and blues shouter of what Dorothy Day, founder of the Catholic Worker Movement, called "a revolution of the heart." Barber is surely singular but far from purely prodigal. To understand Reverend Dr. Barber, we do well to turn to English-American poet T. S. Eliot and African American novelist and essayist Ralph Ellison, an unlikely pair whose visions of genius and culture regard the rhythms of the ancestors as the wellspring of creativity.

For Eliot, tradition is not a lifeless museum piece but instead the blood-stained banner of the past that we carry forward to produce something new. Rather than Jefferson's "dead hand of the past," the cultural legacy of our ancestors is the citadel where past and present abide together to birth and to battle for the new day. The spirituals, for examples, are not dead incantations of the dusky past but a fresh blast of Joshua's horn at our never-ending siege against the walls of Jericho.

The work of the visionary poet, preacher, artist, politician, or prophet, Eliot insists, cannot be separated from its historical dimension or from the traditions she or he represents and reinterprets. Those traditions "cannot [simply] be inherited" but "must be obtained by great labor." Reverend Dr. Barber engages those labors as both legatee and scholar of the revolutionary faith of his enslaved ancestors. Those traditions of struggle cannot be protected by preserving them in amber but only by making them speak to the new day. What a deeply rooted and transformative figure like Barber does is to make the old world preach liberation to the new. Ironically, the most striking and original expressions of Reverend Dr. Barber's life—of cultural striving generally, in Eliot's framework—"may be those in which [the] ancestors assert themselves most vigorously."

Ralph Ellison defines three ancestral inflections of African American culture as the blues, gospel, and jazz "impulses." Ellison's impulses animate the distinctive Afro-Christianity of the black South embodied in this sermon by Reverend Dr. William Barber, "The Call to Be Positioned as Powerful Prisoners of Prophetic Hope." His theological and constitutional embrace of what Dorothy Day calls "a revolution of the heart" carries us beyond the politics of domination toward a social vision grounded in love. It is no real paradox that Barber's theological vision springs upon us newly minted as the morning and yet that the black church in slavery is its wellspring.

That "invisible institution," as religious scholar Albert Raboteau terms it, spat out the polluted Christianity poured upon it by the European American slave masters. But, a smattering of literate intellectuals among enslaved communities in the South drew their water straight from its home in that rock of the gospel; that is, from the sacred texts of the people who had enslaved them. These subversive theologians and the generations of mostly illiterate preachers who subsequently absorbed their interpretations of scripture discerned in the narrative elements, particularly the Exodus of the Israelites out of bondage in Egypt and the crucifixion of Jesus—this ultimate identification with the despised and downtrodden. These stories bespoke a moral vision resonant with their own brutal saga. Not surprisingly, at the heart of this triumphant story of good over evil was a rejection of the notion that a person can be a thing; that is, a repudiation of the very idea of slavery. Its chained adherents were America's first abolitionists. In time, the victories of their theology of liberation would become the only developments that might have lifted the Declaration of Independence and the Constitution of the United States to their full meaning, a project that Barber implores us to complete.

This potent Afro-Christianity of the black South represented more a *discovery* of what Howard Thurman terms "the religion of Jesus" than an adaptation, let alone adoption, of the embalmed and unresurrected Christianity of the slave traders and flesh dealers. This can be proven by asking two questions. Why is the central narrative of the enslaved the Exodus of the Israelites out of bondage in Egypt? And are we to suppose that white southerners, possessed as they were by the rampant fear that the enslaved would rise up and slaughter them in their beds, taught the enslaved this story? They did not paint the vision of Pharaoh's legions sinking beneath the Red Sea. They knew they were Pharaoh. They didn't tell the story about a little shepherd boy bringing down Goliath with a handful of stones from the creek. They knew they were Goliath.

The masters carefully taught the slaves a highly selective version of Christianity, which stressed obedience and long suffering. In the 1840s, the Reverend Alexander Glennie, of All Saints Parish on the coast of South Carolina, offered this instructive verse to white preachers who might address slave congregations: "Servants, be obedient to them that are your masters according to the flesh, with fear and trembling, in singleness of your heart, as unto Christ; not with eye service as men pleasers; but as the servants of Christ, doing the will of God from the heart: with good will doing service, as to the Lord and not to men; knowing that whatsoever good thing any man doeth, the same shall he receive of the Lord, whether he be bond or free." This passage, Reverend Glennie told the enslaved, would help them "to do your duty in that state of life unto which it has pleased God to call you (Ephesians 6:5)." One slave complained: "Church was what they called it, but all that preacher talked 'bout was for us slaves to obey our masters and not to lie and steal. Nothing about Jesus was ever said, and the overseer stood there to see the preacher talked as he wanted him to talk."

Reverend Dr. Barber stands in a prophetic tradition that knows in its bones that neither Pharaoh's army nor Goliath stands a chance. This is the faith that the nameless and numberless authors of the spirituals turned into a theology in song. Its gospel vision still challenges the powers of this world with the eternally radical assertion that a person is not a thing. It burns with the democratic moral vision that still demands to know: "Didn't my lord deliver Daniel? And why not every man?" Barber's exegetical genius seems to strike fire at its most creative and compelling when the ancestors speak through him most powerfully. It comes as no surprise, then, to find Ellison's blues, gospel, and jazz impulses reflected in those same ancestors and gleaming in the prophetic pearls of Reverend Dr. Barber.

To understand how Barber resonates within Ellison's framework of blues, gospel, and jazz, one must think far beyond mere bins at the music store or categories on your iPod. These are three cultural impulses, expressed in as many forms as African American culture might take—in art and oratory, slang and style, literature and scholarship, through James Baldwin and James Brown, through the poet and the preacher. In fact, Ellison's blues, gospel, and jazz impulses are not merely approaches to the saxophone or the sermon but interpretations of the human and the divine.

Ellison's definition of the blues in *Living with Music: Jazz Writings* remains classic: "The blues is an impulse to keep the painful details and episodes of a brutal experience alive in one's aching consciousness, to finger its jagged grain, and to transcend it, not through the consolation of philosophy but by squeezing from it a near-tragic, near-comic lyricism. As a form, the blues is an autobiographical chronicle of personal catastrophe expressed lyrically."

The blues, gospel, and jazz impulses all begin in a brutal historical experience—in the blues realities of black lives and all of our lives—and hence the blues forms the foundation for all three. It addresses the grittiest realities of human life: sex, money, violence, mortality, and the lack of practically everything. The blues encompasses but goes beyond the heartbreak songs of Zora Neale Hurston: "Love made and unmade." It goes deeper even than Muddy Waters's earthy lament: "There's another mule kicking in my stall." Cultural historian Craig Werner writes in *A Change Is Gonna Come: Music, Race & the Soul of America*, "By a conservative count, 180 percent of blues deal with sex or money. The extra 80 percent accounts for the times sex and money are the same damn thing." Those blues grip you the evening when your beloved goes to visit her sainted mother in the nursing home and then you notice that her dancing shoes, her favorite red dress, and the contents of your wallet all went with her. That kind of sorrow could give you the blues, and blues humor, "laughing to keep from crying," remains crucial to our survival. But the deep-blues sea runs still deeper than simply out of money and unlucky in love. The blues impulse knows that we don't just have a problem, we *are* a problem.

A blues world offers no good choices. Both victim and executioner, sometimes our only question seems to be who to kill next; oneself is generally the first nominee. Sure, we had our reasons, but there is a body on the floor, a gun in our hand, and a cop on the way: damned if we fight and damned if we flee. "It's hard to win when you always lose," as Tom Waits frames it in "Fumblin' with the Blues," adding, "Two dead ends and you still got to choose." Counting the chief culprit in the mirror, a quick exegesis of the blues precinct confirms Bessie Smith, a conservative theologian not unlike Reverend Dr. Barber: "Nineteen men living in my neighborhood / Eighteen of them fools and the one ain't no damn good."

Deeper still, writes Albert Murray in *Stomping the Blues*, the blues confronts Hamlet's eternal question, "To be or not to be?" This predicament prods humanity in the gray, friendless morning of our shame and isolation. It bespeaks Bessie Smith's inquiry in "Empty Bed Blues"— what do you do when you wake up once again with the blues not only all around your bed but all in your head? With all that trouble in mind, I might "lay my head on some lonesome railroad line / And let the 2:19 train pacify my mind." A few lines later, though, I might instead "lay my head on that lonesome railroad track / But when I hear that whistle, Lord, I'm gonna pull it back." Because the heart of the blues impulse is to look the brutal truth in the eye, to deny nothing, and endure, saying, in the words of Willie Dixon, "I'm here, everybody knows I'm here." In other words, Hamlet, damn good question, but since you put it that way, yeah, I'm gonna be, and since I am going to be, I may as well roll high or roll home.

And so the blues isn't about twelve-bar structures, Ma Rainey's piano player, or a guitar B. B. King named "Lucille." It resonates, however, in Reverend Dr. Barber's rendition of the prophet Zechariah, speaking with the voice of God, who does not deny the brutal history of his people or the dilemmas they continue to confront, nor, as Barber puts it, "offer them some cute optimism." Unflinching, Barber "fingers the jagged grain" of history and calls us to change it, though familiar with the odds that we face as human beings.

Reverend Dr. Barber, the people's prophet, owns our long odds and dicey predicaments and shortchanges none of them. He notes how Zechariah traces our despair in harsh candor and dispiriting metaphor, calling brokenhearted humanity "waterless pits." Likewise, Barber the blues historian sees the Reverend Dr. Martin Luther King Jr. "wrestling heavy with the reality of the despairing situation while yet lifting it, believing it, preaching it, marching as a prisoner," as Barber asserts, "surrendering to and in the power of prophetic hope." One cannot mistake this for garden-variety optimism; Barber's blues carries as much lamentation as liberation. As he points out, the latter is not possible without the former. If liberation happens, Barber knows, it must happen in human history; the light must rise right here in the broken world where, generally speaking, as Flannery O'Connor puts it, "The blind don't see and the lame don't walk and what's dead stays that way."

Like both a bone-deep bluesman and any of the unnamed authors of the spirituals, Barber understands that crucifixions precede resurrections but that nothing in the fallen world precludes catastrophe. Barber battles "the numbness of empire," in Walter Brueggemann's phrase, by being "fluent in the language of both grief and hope."

Barber's translation of the blues, however, is not bilingual but trilingual; his mastery of the dialects of lamentation and hope are matched by his mastery of the dialectics of blues humor. In a sardonic invitation to his own murder, Barber calls himself the follower of "a brown-skinned Palestinian Jew." While his devotion to the divine vision of love and liberation outweighs most any other concern, Barber speaks of grave matters in blues-inflected banter and tongue-in-cheek braggadocio. "When David and his rock and his slingshot and his faith came together on a battlefield," he writes, "Goliath fell and they tell me the next day that the headline read 'The Bigger They Come, the Harder They Fall.'"

As the conservative theologian he rightly claims to be, Barber does not believe the moral universe bends toward justice by way of some sunny cosmic weather report. His sermons evince no spirit of evasion with respect to our history of genocide, slavery, oppression, and violence against the vulnerable. He does not hesitate to note our nation's failure to extend democracy to all of our citizens; our devastation of the natural environment; our repression of the citizenship rights and full humanity of women; our wholehearted embrace of greed.

"Our poverty numbers, especially child poverty numbers, are far higher than any other advanced Western democracy," Barber observes. He comments on the 1960s War on Poverty, which made significant success before Congress forced President Lyndon Johnson to choose between the poverty war and the Vietnam War. "We shut it down," says Barber. "It was the quickest war we'd ever fought." This is standard blues "laughing to keep from crying." Like Ellison's blues artist, Barber confronts the world by means of existential honesty, prophetic clarity, and hard-won laughter. Barber's foundational blues theology rests upon endurance, not innocence or triumph, and its barbaric yawp heralds our humanity.

Though the blues holler is a first language for Barber, he is both inheritor and interpreter of the African American freedom struggle. At its best, that historic movement distilled Ellison's "gospel impulse" and moved multicolored America together toward higher ground. Its most ecumenical visions, however, evaporated like spilt lemonade on hot pavement in the wake of tragedy after murderous tragedy during the 1950s and 1960s and more recently as well. But the movement continues to struggle, and the blues is part of that resistance. The blues impulse, rather than sipping the weak tea of optimism or praying for divine intervention, braces itself with the straight whiskey of a fatalism and finitude, confessing its isolation and despair. Rather than succumb to grief, the blues artist narrates these dilemmas in ways that laugh to keep from crying and cry to keep from dying. Barber's preaching is a case in point. American popular memory, however, clings to sugar-coated clichés that both overstate and understate our actual accomplishments and ignore the nation's obvious failures.

To envision the civil rights movement rising triumphant and redeeming the soul of America, one has to wave away clouds of smoke and wipe up all kinds of blood. The delusionary confections of memory ignore our blues realities of dreams deferred and defeated and rely upon what theologian Willie Jennings calls "the sin of forgetfulness." Whatever his other flaws, the suppression of memory is one sin to which Reverend Dr. Barber appears immune.

To extoll progress while the building burns requires a level of mendacity that Barber cannot muster. He will not simply sing and wash brushes while white America paints Rosa Parks as Mammy. Nor can

Barber peddle tickets to a pageant in which white America casts Dr. King as Black Santa Claus; a melodrama in which Parks and King remain innocuous vessels for whatever vacant sentiments the occasion might dictate. This saccharine insistence on a bright, shining lie remains one of white America's hoariest racial impulses. "The country's appetite for facts on the Negro question," W. E. B. Du Bois wrote in 1912, "has been spoiled by sweets."

Having been drafted by his father on at least one occasion in his early teens to stand in the kitchen with a .12-gauge shotgun trained on the back door, waiting for a Ku Klux Klan attack, Reverend Dr. Barber has never been possessed of a simplistic understanding of nonviolent direct action, even as he has become one of its leading exponents and practitioners. Barber's devotion to nonviolent direct action reflects not just the blues impulse that makes it necessary but the gospel impulse that resonates outward from every testimony for justice.

Like the blues impulse, the gospel impulse at the heart of Reverend Dr. Barber's ministry begins by testifying about a brutal history, asking: "Were you there when they crucified my Lord?" Gospel testifies to the same burdens that the blues carries, makes its honest case, but it also seeks to transcend those burdens by expressing itself in relation to others and to God. The gospel impulse reaches out and reaches up and moves toward higher ground. It bears witness to the burden and upholds the tradition, but it extends a hand to humanity and to God and works toward redemption. Where the blues endures, the gospel transcends. This is the essence of the gospel impulse, taking up the cross of history and reaching beyond it through powers larger than our own.

Barber's fiery gospel impulse sings "How I Got Over." The blues makes no claim for transcendence, except in the sense that telling the truth about our lives and the conditions we battle has value and integrity on its own terms. This carries more a spirit of defiance than optimism. The blues endures. But the gospel transcends through its ministers and its sense of the divine. The gospel impulse is about hope and transcendence. The blues makes no claim for transcendence—it is more about defiance than healing—but the gospel addresses the isolation and cruelty of human life and calls a congregation into being. It holds out the hope for a better tomorrow. At its best moments, the African American freedom struggle distilled the gospel impulse, but simplistic histories and popular memories cling only to those, ignoring the blues realities of dreams deferred, defeated, and unfinished.

The jazz impulse addresses the same brutal history, the same isolation and despair that gospel and the blues confront, but it is more about finding new ways to express them. Blues and gospel both ground themselves in the way things are, while jazz imagines how they could be. Listen to jazz, and you hear tradition on the one hand and innovation on the other. Jazz keeps one foot on the main melody, the old standard, the traditional form, but then it reaches out with the other foot and tries to find forever-new ways of saying it. A jazz artist keeps one hand wrapped in what Ellison calls "the chain of tradition" and yet improvises outward, finding new ways of phrasing the problem and innovative means of dealing with it. Louis Armstrong said that "jazz is music that is never played the same way once." The jazz impulse is a means of rethinking the human condition, not just an approach to the saxophone.

Jazz says we don't have to do it the way we have always done it. Jazz imagines the transitions of understanding to a world beyond white supremacy. It traces the brutal origins of a historical moment but leaves us open to the possibility that history "could have been much better if human beings had acted differently." It violates narrative boundaries of history, memoir, and folklore, leaving us laid open to radical retellings of all of our stories. It may not offer an easy add-water-and-stir redemption, but it opens a history in which we can see the faces of flawed, well-meaning people like ourselves who might do much better—especially if we remember that we have the capacity to do much worse. Nothing here is inevitable except trouble and even "trouble don't last always."

As president of the North Carolina NAACP, Reverend Barber organized a statewide "fusion" coalition of progressive organizations that has fought for public education; equality for lesbian, gay, bisexual, transgender, and queer citizens; voting rights; criminal justice reform; labor rights; environmental protection; Medicaid expansion and health care for all; immigrant rights; living wages; and women's control of their own bodies. The Moral Monday movement practices transformative rather than transactional coalition politics—working toward an understanding that we have not only common enemies but shared values. When we meet others on that higher ground, in the name of our most deeply held beliefs, it lifts all of us up. We see that we are not alone and we see our best selves in the eyes of our compatriots. We find not only a sense of belonging, but one that holds us to the highest that we know.

Reverend Barber resists divisive ideology and partisan politics. "If you think this is just a left-versus-right movement," he says, "you're missing the point. This is about the moral center. This is about our humanity." His approach sets aside the politics of domination for a social vision grounded in love—in respect for the dignity of human personality, the needs of the poor and the sick, the well-being of all our children, equality before God and the law, and the health of our democracy.

This is the moral vision that has made Reverend Dr. William J. Barber; that defiant love that refused to see a person as a thing; that declined to call love that which folded its hands before hunger and human need; that demanded a social vision grounded in love, the dignity of ordinary people, the equality of humanity as children of a loving God, a people defined not by their color but by their humanity. When you see him, see this. When you hear him, hear this. This is his rock in a weary land. This is his balm in Gilead. This is what guides and guards his step and ensures that he will not run this race in vain. It is something new entirely, never before seen in the world. And it is the highest wisdom of the ages, distilled from blood and sweat in a weary land, but expressed in the joy of victory beyond the politics of domination.

DR. TIMOTHY B. TYSON is senior research scholar at the Center for Documentary Studies at Duke University and at Duke Divinity School, where he teaches African American and US history, culture, and politics. His books *Radio Free Dixie: Robert F. Williams and the Roots of Black Power* and *Blood Done Sign My Name* won major awards and became critically acclaimed films. His 2017 *New York Times* best seller, *The Blood of Emmett Till*, made the Long List for the National Book Award. Tyson serves on the executive boards of the North Carolina NAACP, the University of North Carolina Center for Civil Rights, and Repairers of the Breach.

CHAPTER SEVEN

MORAL ACTION ON CLIMATE CHANGE

RALLY AROUND THE VISIT OF POPE FRANCIS, SEPTEMBER 24, 2015

National Mall, Washington, DC

THE REVEREND DR. WILLIAM J. BARBER II

We gather here today as one human family to raise our moral voices and to welcome Pope Francis and his message that true faith is not a disengagement from the challenges of the world but an embrace of those very challenges. The truth is, there is no gospel that is not social. There is no gospel that relieves us of our call to love our neighbors as ourselves. There is no gospel that lives outside God's admonition to serve the least of these. Pope Francis has made this clear, and for that we thank him.

In the history of the United States, a moral critique has always been at the center of any challenge to the structural sins of society—slavery, the denial of women's rights, the denial of labor rights, the denial of equal protection under the law, the denial of voting rights, and the promulgation of unchecked militarism. We have never overcome any of these evils without a moral critique that challenged their grip on the heart and imagination of our society. A moral critique is still needed today.

We hear Pope Francis's cry that we cannot love our earthly neighbors and yet sit quietly while the earth herself is made unfit for human habitation. We cannot love humanity and yet give way to forces that derail the very climate that gives us life. As His Holiness has said, we must acknowledge the "very consistent scientific consensus that we are in the presence of an alarming warming of the climactic system." We cannot be silent about a world "devastated by man's predatory relation with nature." The earth is the Lord's and the fullness thereof, the world and they that dwell therein. We must make a moral demand that shifts the energy supply strategy from coal, oil, natural gas, and other fossil fuels to solar, wind, geothermal, and other clean, renewable energy sources.

We must establish policies and programs to modernize the national infrastructure for the twenty-first century, transitioning toward full employment with millions of new green jobs to help build a sustainable economy. We must provide educational and job training programs, transitional financial assistance and job opportunities for the industry workers displaced due to the transition to a renewable-energy-based economy. We must choose community and care of the earth over chaos and greed. Not only must we push to protect the Earth's delicate climate balance, but we must also challenge the social climate in which the poor live.

The pope was right when he said, in 2013, "The times talk to us of so much poverty in the world and this is a scandal. Poverty in the world is a scandal. In a world where there is so much wealth, so many resources to feed everyone, it is unfathomable that there are so many hungry children, that there are so many children without an education, so many poor persons. Poverty today is a cry." Some 4.5 percent of US deaths have been found to be attributable to poverty. That is nearly 120,000 people per year, each of them created in the image of God. Each of their precious lives matters. Their death is the scandal the pope exposes. It is a moral disgrace that, according to the Children's Defense Fund's Poverty Report, there are 14.7 million poor children and 6.5 million extremely poor children in the United States of America, the world's largest economy. We know that nearly half of the world's population—more than three billion people—live in poverty on less than $2.50 a day. One billion children worldwide are living in poverty.

According to UNICEF, 22,000 children worldwide die each day due to poverty; 805 million people do not have enough food to eat.

This is the scandal that a moral critique must expose: the poor are being destroyed, society is destabilized, and our shared humanity is terribly diminished. We can and we must do better. If we focus more on ending poverty than cutting the social safety nets that help the poor, we could do better. If we move beyond the politics of lust for power to the politics of love for people, we can unify around a moral agenda and we can do better. If we secure prolabor, antipoverty policies that insure economic sustainability by fighting for living wages, strong safety nets for the poor, fair policies for immigrants, infrastructure development, and an end to extreme militarism that puts more resources in bombs, missiles, and weaponry than food, jobs, and shelter, we can do better.

God is using Pope Francis to prod our consciousness and push us toward action. By daring to preach the gospel of truth and justice, challenging the sins of economic exploitation, poverty, and climate destruction, he is showing the way to revival, repentance, and redemption. To our ears, the pope's message resonates with the ancient Jewish text that says, "Woe to those who legislate evil and rob the poor of their rights." This pope sounds a lot like Jesus, who said in the Gospel of Matthew that love, mercy, and justice are the weightier matters of the law.

There are some Americans who applaud the pope for his theological orthodoxy when he calls on us to love one another but decry his message as "political" when he points toward inequality and injustice. These are the same voices that grow hoarse touting "morality" with respect to abortion and homosexuality but cannot hear any suggestion that poverty is a moral issue. This deafness to the pontiff's purpose suggests that Jesus himself would not be welcomed by them in America. Their complaints reveal the serious moral crisis we find ourselves in. Somebody must stand and say it doesn't matter which party is in power or who has a political supermajority. There are some things that transcend political majorities, partisan politics, and the narrow categories of liberal versus conservative. There are some things that must be challenged because they are wrong, extreme, and immoral. Destroying the earth is just wrong. Hurting the poor is wrong. Treating corporations like people and people like things is just wrong.

And so, to those who complain that the pontiff is engaging in politics, we say, prophetic voices must rise up and challenge immorality in every age. It's our time now. So, let us join the Holy Father not in the politics of Democrat and Republican, but in God's politics of love and justice. Let our prayer be like the Franciscans': "May God bless us with discomfort at easy answers, half-truths, and superficial relationships, so that we may live from deep within our hearts. May God bless us with righteous moral anger at injustice, oppression, and exploitation of God's creation, so that we may work for justice, freedom, and peace."

Let us fill the whole earth with the song of hope and redemption in this hour and sign with our lives that old hymn that says, "Revive us again; / Fill each heart with thy love; / Let each soul be rekindled / With a fire from above."

Lord, rekindle in us a fire for justice, a fire for truth, and a fire for hope.

REKINDLE IN US A FIRE: WILLIAM BARBER'S MORAL CALL TO CLIMATE ACTION

KARENNA GORE

Director, Center for Earth Ethics, Union Theological Seminary

The sermons of Reverend Dr. William Barber are not dainty, staid affairs. His welcome of Pope Francis at the Moral Action on Climate Change on September 24, 2015, was no exception. Barber stood in his black-and-red vestments on the national mall in Washington, DC, rallying people to join him, framing his remarks with group singing, calling out to the crowd—which responded—and surrounding himself with local folks from all walks of life.

The heart of his sermon could be found in a simple and powerful truth: the ruthless exploitation of people and of nature are linked at the root level. And it is at the root that we must respond. In Barber's words, "We must choose community and care of the earth over chaos and greed."

How refreshing it is, two years later, to read those words again. Unfortunately, we have seen an abundant share of chaos and greed in the intervening time, but Barber gave us hope with his remarks that day. He spoke of the health of the planet as a whole: "We hear Pope Francis's cry that we cannot love our earthly neighbors and yet sit quietly by while the earth herself is made unfit for human habitation." He called for shifting our energy supply strategy "from coal, oil, natural gas, and other fossil fuels to solar, wind, geothermal, and other clean, renewable energy sources." He echoed the pope's acknowledgment of the role of science in helping us to understand the long-term impacts of industrial society on the earth's atmosphere. And he reminded us of the moral mandate to care for future generations of life. But what is truly extraordinary and vital about Barber's call is the way he illuminates and weaves the connections between climate change and poverty, bringing us together and challenging us to see the systemic nature of this crisis.

This sermon has caused me to reflect on four ways of looking at the relationship between poverty and climate change: the harm done by pollution from extractionist industries, the harm done by the impacts of manmade changes to the global climate system, the need for connections between different ways of talking about the ecological crisis, and why this is the moment to join our movements together in a moral call to action.

The truth about fossil fuels is coming to light through the rising voices of people who live on the front lines of pollution. The extraction and burning of fossil fuels generates particulate matter that is highly toxic to those that breathe it in, causing cancer, respiratory diseases, and other illnesses; a study by New York University of four hundred fifty thousand Americans between 1982 and 2004 found that increased exposure to fossil fuel emissions also significantly increased the risk of death from heart disease. More than five million people die from air pollution every year worldwide, according to Global Burden of Disease research, including two hundred thousand in the United States alone.

In the United States the number-one indicator for the location of a toxic facility, such as a coal-fired power plant, is race. The health impacts follow accordingly. African American children are twice as likely to die from asthma as white children, an example of what Coretta Scott King called "slow violence." Theologian Emilie Townes has gone further, labeling the issue of toxic waste in African American communities a "contemporary version of lynching a whole people."

In 2014, at Barber's suggestion, I traveled to North Carolina with the director of the NAACP environmental and climate justice program, Jacqui Patterson, to speak with many who had lost loved ones to the toxic, coal-ash-filled air in their community. Amazingly, some local public health institutions have been reluctant to connect cancer clusters and asthma rates to industries that are seen as providing jobs and other resources for the community. Residents, besieged by grief as well as pollution, were told that cancer "runs in their family." Some of them spoke to us about the connection they were making between the layers of ash on their windowsills and windshields and the health impacts of the harmful substance they were all breathing in. No one in their publicly financed health and education systems had helped them to make that connection—they had to make it themselves.

Afterward, Jacqui and I participated in a press conference at the North Carolina State House to talk about this issue, an event organized by the Moral Mondays Movement. When a reporter asked, "Is this a health event or an environment event?" I thought of the answer Barber gives when he rhetorically poses a question he often gets about poverty: "Is it race or is it class?" The answer is "It *is*." Climate-change pollution harms the health of our most vulnerable brothers and sisters and it harms our shared global environment.

Another immediate impact of extractionist industries comes from spills and leaks. Activist Cherri Foytlin of Louisiana has called attention to the devastating effects of Gulf of Mexico oil spills, not only on health and property, but also on a way of life. People who rely on the gulf for fresh crabs, shrimp, and fish for their livelihoods and their meals have suffered momentous losses. When people have to buy processed food from stores rather than feed their families directly from the ocean, the flawed measurement of "economic growth" known as GDP may go up but everything of real value goes down. "We still have oil in our marshes, fishermen are out of work and it seems like everyone knows someone with cancer," Foytlin told *Rolling Stone* in 2013. "It's time to take the blinders off and see what this industry is doing to us."

It was the threat of an oil pipeline leak into an aquifer that galvanized the Standing Rock Sioux to breathe new life into the climate movement just a couple of years ago. In 2016, First Nations peoples came from around the world and stood in solidarity with Standing Rock against the Dakota Access Pipeline. Facing down militarized police on their own ancestral land, they explained to the world that they were "water protectors" and that the purpose of their nonviolent prayer camp was to protect the water and defend Mother Earth, calling out the cry we will never forget: "*Mni wiconi!*"—water is life.

Of course, the rest of the world also suffers these corporate assaults on their ecosystems, mostly unpublicized in the West. For example, the Niger delta, which supplies a significant percentage of crude oil to the United States, is a world capital of oil pollution. "If this [Deepwater Horizon] Gulf accident had happened in Nigeria, neither the government nor the company would have paid much attention," said Ben Ikari of the Ogoni people, chronicled in Rob Nixon's book *Slow Violence and the Environmentalism of the Poor*. "This kind of spill happens all the time in the Delta." Any moral analysis of climate change must see beyond national borders and confront the depth of exploitation of the so-called "developing" world, as well as the serious flaws in the very way we define and measure development.

After many decades of increasing heat-trapping air pollution, the impacts of climate change are here, and it is those without the resources to evacuate and rebuild who bear the brunt. Hurricane Katrina, Typhoon Haiyan, and Superstorm Sandy all gathered lethal force when they traveled over waters warmed by climate change and hit communities living on the coast. The human cost of these stronger storms is devastating: the final death toll of Hurricane Katrina alone was 1,836, with four hundred thousand people displaced. A 2013 study in the journal *Climactic Change* determined that under the atmospheric conditions of 1900, the storm surge of Katrina would have been significantly less destructive.

Heat waves are also taking a toll, including causing the melting of ice that leads to rising sea levels and massive displacement of people. There is now a greater danger that the West Antarctic ice sheet will melt into the ocean, causing sea levels to rise by five to six feet by the end of the century, twice the increase that we were warned about only a few years ago. If that were to happen, it would wipe many island nations and coastal cities and villages from the map. According to a 2016 report by the National Oceanic and Atmospheric Administration, 13.1 million people would be at risk in the US alone. This trend has already caused evacuation of low-income communities such as the Biloxi-Chitimacha-Choctaw of Isle de Jean Charles, Louisiana. "We're going to lose all our heritage, all our culture," lamented Chief Albert Naquin to the *New York Times* in 2016. "It's all going to be history."

These patterns are threatening to drive millions more into extreme poverty in the years to come. According to estimates by the United Nations University Institute for Environment and Human Security and the International Organization for Migration, between fifty million and two hundred million people—mainly subsistence farmers and fishermen—could be displaced by 2050 because of climate change. "Climate change is already stretching the international humanitarian system," Ertharin Cousin, executive director of the World Food Program, told the *Guardian*. "More than 80 percent of the world's hungry live in areas prone to natural disasters and environmental degradation. Climate change is not waiting—neither can we."

As Barber has reminded us, building solidarity is often a matter of recognizing different language for talking about the same issues. Just because mainstream political dialogue has recognized only one group of people as "environmentalists" does not mean that is an accurate assessment of the dynamic movement afoot. As the activist and scholar Catherine Coleman Flowers, of the Alabama Center for Rural Enterprise, says in *Grist*, "I grew up an Alabama country girl, so I was part of the environmental movement before I even knew what it was. The natural world was my world."

It is worth remembering that the very concept of manmade climate change challenges the widespread assumption that human beings are separate from and superior to the rest of the natural world. Those who hold that assumption often (sometimes subconsciously) draw on

Judeo-Christian concepts of "dominion" and "Imago Dei," making the faith-based words of both Pope Francis and Reverend Barber all the more essential to our ability to see clearly. Sometimes all the jargon of the climate conversation has clouded the simple truth that Barber tells in this sermon: "Destroying the earth is just wrong. Hurting the poor is wrong. Treating corporations like people and people like things is just wrong."

Of course, the colonial presence in this land (now known as the United States) began with a theological argument that built on that sense of separation. It was a distortion of Christianity by the forces of empire. The papal bulls of the late fifteenth century classified the non-Christianized natives of the New World as part of the "flora and fauna" and mandated that they be "conquered," "vanquished," and "subdued." The same theological argument was applied to force the people of Africa into the slave trade. The dehumanization of whole peoples has always gone hand in hand with the exploitation and destruction of nonhuman life.

Barber's call lights the way for the mainstream environmental movement to commit to seeing these connections among racism, poverty, militarism, and ecological destruction. Now is the time to understand the big picture, get behind grassroots community leadership, and break through to another level. Now is the time to listen to voices such as Bobby C. Billie of the Council of the Original Miccosukee Simanolee Nation Aboriginal Peoples, who described climate change this way in an official 2016 statement: "These actions [extractive industries] are changing the Layer of the Earth or Layer of the different Energies of the Earth. . . . [These industries are] creating a so-called economy that is destroying the future." And as Billie and others have consistently pointed out, we humans are also intimately connected with and morally responsible to the other living beings with whom we share this earthly home.

Whether you see the divine in God or in the laws of nature (or both), there is a power greater than ourselves calling us to see the error of our ways. We can see that the richest people in the world drive current systemic destruction, while the most vulnerable are the first to suffer the consequences. We can see that the more we wholly subject our God-given natural resources to the current market system, the more they will be hoarded by those who can afford them and denied to those who can't.

A moral revival is also necessary to point out the false idol in this flawed notion of "economic growth," relentlessly pursued no matter how inequitable or ecologically destructive it is. The simple way we measure growth is gross domestic product (GDP), a crude calculation that does not take into account harmful components of production and consumption over time, such as the depletion of natural resources and the health impacts of pollution. It also disregards inequity and injustice. For example, of all the income generated by global GDP growth between 1999 and 2008, the poorest 60 percent of humanity received only 5 percent, according to the *Guardian*. This pattern is as unsustainable for the planet as a whole as it is unjust for the poor in our own country.

A few months after Reverend Barber's sermon, the world reached an unprecedented agreement on climate change. The accord, negotiated under the United Nations Framework Convention on Climate Change and signed in Paris in December 2015, marked a milestone in which almost all the countries in the world agreed that we must cut (and eventually end) fossil fuel use so that we can keep the global temperature rise to less than two degrees Celsius above preindustrial averages and preferably with a limit of +1.5 C, which is the scientifically determined threshold for climate stability. The commitments each nation made in Paris were not enough to achieve this goal in the first round, but there is a built-in "review and ratchet" process for nations to increase their commitments every five years, as they more fully envision and embrace this challenge—and as costs for renewable energy generation and storage continues to plummet.

The United States committed to the Paris Agreement under President Barack Obama, pledging that we would reduce our greenhouse gas emissions by more than a quarter below 2005 levels by the year 2025. Obama's main strategy for doing this was the Clean Power Plan, which was designed to reduce harm to human health as well as reduce the emissions harming the earth; this plan aims to cut emissions 32 percent below 2005 levels by 2030, which is almost nine hundred million tons a year. As I am writing, President Donald Trump is at the helm, reinforcing the fossil fuel industry's propaganda campaign of misinformation and handing them the reins of government. His policies include pulling out of Paris, revoking the Clean Power Plan, dismantling energy-efficiency standards, and permitting more pollution and extraction, including on public and sacred lands and offshore in our precious ocean waters.

In the face of this assault on decency, common sense, and justice, there is a growing consensus that only a genuine moral revival will save humanity from eventual ecological ruin, and that we must use the intensity of this political moment to make it happen. In a *GQ* interview, Mustafa Ali, the longtime head of the EPA's Environmental Justice Office who resigned in protest when the Trump regime took over, explained, "I think folks will remember this as a flashpoint, when we began to come together and think critically about how to create sustainable change."

The moral call is to see the error in our sense of separation from one another. Although the poor suffer first and foremost from both the extractionist economy and the impacts of climate change, it is the habitability of the planet for all of humanity that is ultimately at stake. Those who ignore the suffering of the poor have a value system so unmoored that it can even lead them to ignore the suffering of future generations of their own families. As Martin Luther King Jr. wrote in his "Letter from Birmingham Jail," we are in an "inescapable network of mutuality, tied in a single garment of destiny." It is that spirit of mutuality that Barber invokes in his sermon calling for Moral Action on Climate Change. It is the best of the prophetic tradition that he brings to the climate movement when he challenges us to see the connections between ecological destruction and poverty and uses clear moral language to talk about it. Reverend William Barber lifts up care for the earth when he declares, "Lord, rekindle in us a fire for justice, a fire for truth, a fire for hope." And I say, Amen!

KARENNA GORE is director of the Center for Earth Ethics at Union Theological Seminary.

CHAPTER EIGHT

I WISH YOU A MOURNING CHRISTMAS

CHRISTMAS DAY, DECEMBER 25, 2015

Union Theological Seminary, New York, New York

THE REVEREND DR. WILLIAM J. BARBER II

I wish you a Mourning Christmas. All over America, you are hearing what was heard at the first Christmas. At that time, extreme poverty and hurt were widespread. Money ruled the political system. Wages were kept low. Workers worked hard. And a religious and political leader named Herod was scared of a changing demographic threatening his power base with an upsurge in protest against those systems of injustice. Herod issued a decree for the systematic killing of black and brown boys through police and judicial abuse. The cumulative pain was so great that the first Christmas was not twinkling lights and cute images of red and white. The first Christmas was filled with the blood of innocent boys; an out-of-control social and political system was issuing unjust decrees. The scripture declares: "A voice is heard in Ramah, weeping and great mourning, Rachel weeping for her children and refusing to be comforted, because they are no more." Could it be that what we are hearing in America is prophetic mourning, the cry of cumulative pain? Could it be the necessary mourning that must occur in order to shame, stun, and wake up the nation and signal the birthing of a new day? Could it be that America can't be blessed until she first mourns?

I believe that deep within our being as a nation there is a longing for a moral movement that plows fully into our souls—a movement that recognizes that we can't, as the scriptures say, be "at ease in Zion." There is a longing that recognizes that the attacks we face today are on our fundamental civil rights—including attacks on the great hallmarks of equal protection under the law and the promise to establish justice, values that are supposed to be at the heart of who we are as a nation. These attacks are not a sign of our weakness. Instead, they are the sign of a worrisome fear by those who hold extremist views and do not welcome a truly united society. It is this longing for a moral movement that explains why today, despite the attacks, we are seeing a merging of the tributaries that run toward the great stream of justice. People are coming together regardless of race, creed, color, gender, sexuality, or class; whether in the Hands Up, Don't Shoot, I Can't Breathe, or Black Lives Matter movements; in the Fight for $15, Raise Up, and minimum wage movements; in the battle for voting rights and the People Over Money movement; in the women's rights and end-rape-culture movements; in LGBTQ rights movements; in immigrants' rights movements; in Not One More and the right-to-health-care movements; in antipoverty, housing, and water rights movements; and in the state-based antiracism, antipoverty, projustice fusion Moral Mondays movement. We are flowing together, because we recognize that the intersectionality of all of these movements is our opportunity to fundamentally redirect America. Together we represent a combined moment of prophetic mourning and a longing for a better country.

If we do not become at ease in Zion and if we recognize that they who mourn shall be comforted, we can continue pushing forward together. This will be the birth of a Third Reconstruction movement in America. It is a movement that will push us closer to our truest hope of a "more perfect union" where peace is established through justice, not fear, and where, in the prescient words of Langston Hughes from his poem "Let America Be America Again," "opportunity is real, and life is free . . . where equality is in the air we breathe."

This is what Dr. King said in essence to America at a speech in Memphis twenty days before he was killed. He challenged America to understand what he was seeing and hearing. America, King said, "has failed to hear that large segments of white society are more concerned about tranquility and the status quo than about justice and humanity." And so, King concluded, in his sermon "The Other America," preached at the Grosse Pointe Historical Society in March 1968, "The question now is whether America is prepared to do something massively, affirmatively, and forthrightly about the great problem we face in the area of race."

This is the question we are still asked today: How will America respond to this season of mourning? Every faith tradition speaks of prophets who know how to mourn. There is a prophetic necessity for weeping, and prophetic mourning must refuse to be comforted. This is what we hear in Isaiah 58:

Shout it aloud, do not hold back.
Raise your voice like a trumpet.

And this is what we hear from James 5:

And a final word to you arrogant rich: Take some lessons in lament. You'll need buckets for the tears when the crash comes upon you. Your money is corrupt and your fine clothes stink. Your greedy luxuries are a cancer in your gut, destroying your life from within. You thought you were piling up wealth. What you've piled up is judgment. All the workers you've exploited and cheated cry out for judgment. The groans of the workers you used and abused are a roar in the ears of the Master Avenger. You've looted the earth and lived it up. But all you'll have to show for it is a fatter than usual corpse. In fact, what you've done is condemn and murder perfectly good persons, who stand there and take it.

I believe that deep within our being as a nation there is a longing for a moral compass. For those of us who are moved by the cries of our sisters and brothers, we know that, like justice, the acts of caring for the vulnerable, embracing the stranger, healing the sick, protecting workers, welcoming and being fair to all members of the human family, and educating all children should never be relegated to the margins of our social consciousness. These are not only policy issues. These are not issues for some left-versus-right debate. These are the centerpieces of our deepest traditions, our faiths, our values, and our sense of morality and righteousness.

MIT senior lecturer Otto Scharmer writes on his blog (blog.otto scharmer.com), we commit "attentional violence" against the poor and working poor. They are a blind spot in our economic philosophy and economic conscience. If you ignore the poor, one day the whole system will implode and collapse. The costs are too high if we don't address systemic racism and poverty. It costs us our soul as a nation. Every time we fail to educate a child on the front side of life, it costs us on the back side—financially and morally. Every time we deny living wages and workers' rights, leaving whole communities impoverished, it costs us on the back side. Every time we fail to provide health care, it costs us on the back side. Every time we attack teachers and undermine public education, it rips not only our nation's economy but our nation's integrity. Every time we attempt to suppress the right to vote, it tears at the heart of our democracy. It crumbles the necessary foundations to establish justice.

Political extremists—whether called the Tea Party, ultraconservatives, or Koch-money puppets—feed the public with an immoral agenda. Sam Dickman, David Himmelstein, Danny McCormick, and Steffie Woolhandler of the Health Affairs Blog, estimate that the number of deaths attributable to the lack of Medicaid expansion in opt-out states is between 7,115 and 17,104. Medicaid expansion in opt-out states would have resulted in 712,037 fewer persons screening positive for depression and 240,700 fewer individuals suffering catastrophic medical expenditures. Medicaid expansion in these states would have resulted in 422,553 more diabetics receiving medication for their illness, in 195,492 more mammograms among women ages fifty to sixty-four, and in 443,677 more Pap smears among women ages twenty-one to sixty-four. Instead they cut taxes for the wealthy and then declare we don't have money for critical investments. And because they know their agenda can't survive if America really votes, they engage in the worst forms of voter suppression since Jim Crow. How do they do it?

We need to unpack why we need a movement. We need to look at how the Koch brothers and other billionaires steal our battle plans. At the 1963 March on Washington, King said, "Go back." In other words, he called on his audience to go build a mourning movement that would engage in deep analysis of structural injustice and cut to the quick of America's consciousness. The billionaires and corporate groups have been remarkably successful in pushing Congress to pass legislation that helps their interests while hurting the rest of us.

The *New York Times* in 2010 ran a story that looked at the origins of the Koch brothers' shadowy network of front groups, think tanks, and other organizations. The key lies in a 1974 speech in which Charles Koch said, "The most effective response was not political action, but investment in pro-capitalist research and educational programs." In other words, they started building institutions that reached the public to tell them about a libertarian, antigovernment philosophy. The *Times* quoted Koch as saying, "The development of a well-financed cadre of sound proponents of the free enterprise philosophy is the most critical need facing us today." The Kochs, other billionaires, and corporations put their money into think tanks, communication outlets, publishers, various media, and schools with a long-term plan to change the way people see things.

This "apparatus" has pounded out corporate/conservative propaganda for decades. You can't get away from it. The conservative movement rewards its friends and punishes, smears, intimidates, bullies, discredits, and neutralizes its opponents. That is how they were able to get Congress to lower taxes on the rich and corporations, break unions, defund schools, defend their interests abroad, and in many other ways enact policies that have made them so much money and wreaked havoc on the rest of us. The money the Kochs and other billionaires give directly to politicians was only part of their strategy. They spend most of their money building organizations to execute long-term strategies to secure what they want tomorrow.

The moral of the story is that the extremists put their resources into long-term movement building. They set up think tanks, radio shows, even an entire TV network to reach the public and convince them that conservative ideas would make their lives better. They infiltrate and take over organizations like the National Rifle Association. They set up rapid-response organizations to pressure politicians. They deliver for their constituents—the billionaires and their giant corporations—and keep "our side" from delivering for ours, the American people. Instead, on our side, we put money, resources, and effort primarily into electoral campaigns. So many of us are looking for a "messiah" candidate who can lead us out of the wilderness and somehow convince the public of the rightness of our cause. But after the campaigns are over, the infrastructure dissolves, the expertise disperses, and we need to rebuild from scratch two or four years later. It is a remarkably ineffective approach.

Some might say the success of our opponents has come about because there is so much more money on the corporate/conservative side. But we have the numbers. Imagine if one hundred million left-of-center Americans gave an average of $100 (27.4 cents a day) each year to build progressive organizations. That adds up to $10 billion a year. Imagine dozens of fully funded, fully staffed progressive organizations reaching out to all corners of America, employing people to write op-eds, speak on the radio, speak to audiences, knock on doors. Imagine TV commercials showing people how progressive values and progressive approaches to issues would do good things for regular people. Imagine our elections after a few years pushing back against the kind of propaganda we constantly have to hear from the extremists. Money put into efforts to build an ongoing information infrastructure today is money put into every single progressive initiative and candidate in every single future election. We should declare today that we will organize and fight for the soul of our democracy.

In 1961, labor's top leaders projected a $2 million campaign to assist grassroots organizing in the South. Dr. King joined them for a union convention and closed his inspirational talk with a simple request: that every union ask its members to tax themselves $1 each to make "democracy real for millions of deprived American citizens. If you would do these two things now in this convention," Dr. King said, in an address delivered at the AFL-CIO's Fourth Constitutional Convention, "resolve to deal effectively with discrimination and provide financial aid for our struggle in the South, this convention will have a glorious moral deed to add to an illustrious history."

Today, I humbly stand on Dr. King's broad shoulders and update his logic and his requests. Labor and civil rights are one and the same. You can't have one without the other. We are all trade unionists. We are all civil rights activists. We can win against extremism. Yes, we are in tough times. But it's not worse than the slavery abolitionists faced. It is not worse than what women faced. It's not worse than apartheid. It's not worse than the legal segregation and violence civil rights leaders faced fifty years ago. That's why we have come together to revive the vision in this moment of moral crisis—and I tell you it works. Fusion politics works. Moral voices coming together works. An indigenously led, state-based, state-government-focused, deeply moral, deeply constitutional, antiracist, antipoverty, projustice, prolabor, transformative fusion movement works. We need language to break through coded words, fear, and the continuing "southern strategy" of dividing people by race.

Let's update Dr. King's request. Let's build a moral movement. Let's find a way to fund labor and civil rights organizers in the former Confederate states for as long as necessary. The Black Belt region is in a state of change. Waves of black remigration and Latino and Asian immigration are infusing Black Belt states with a more diverse, more tolerant, and more progressive population. At the same time, extreme right-wing attacks on women's rights, as well as a rising generation of increasingly tolerant young white voters, have begun to increase the possibilities for successful multiracial voter coalitions to elect candidates of color at the statewide level. The first and most important lesson is that massive voter registration can overcome massive voter suppression. Our analysis shows that registering just 30 percent of eligible unregistered black voters or other voters of color could shift the political calculus in a number of Black Belt states, helping blacks elect candidates who share their concerns and forcing all candidates to pay attention to the community's concerns. Registering 60 percent or 90 percent would change the political calculus in an even greater number of states. As extremists in the "party of Lincoln" take aim at people of color by restricting their right to vote, there is a very clear solution. The antidote to voter suppression, particularly in states south of the Mason-Dixon Line, is voter registration.

New data shows that a progressive future is coming in the South, and despite the actions of the extreme right wing, we can make it come faster. The South is at a moment of great demographic change. Thanks to African American remigration and Latino and Asian immigration, the population of people of color in the South has exploded in recent years. According to the 2010 US Census, from 2000 to 2010, the non-Hispanic white population grew at a rate of 4 percent, while the so-called "minority" population grew by 34 percent. There is evidence this trend will continue. In 2000, the South was 34.2 percent people of color, and that number jumped to 40 percent by 2010. Extremists on the right are aware of these facts, and more important, they are intimidated by them. They understand that African Americans have for some time now been the backbone of the progressive vote in the United States. They have witnessed how increases in the African American vote, boosted by increases in the Latino vote, have made southern states such as Florida, Virginia, and even North Carolina competitive every four years. They know that states like South Carolina and Georgia are not far behind. It is up to us to double down on the one rule of politics that has always worked and will continue to work. The extreme right wing's response has been to attack the most basic civil rights of people of color. Of the thirteen southern states historically considered part of the "Black Belt," nine have passed strict photo-based voter ID laws and eleven have passed restrictions meant to limit the power of the African American and Latino vote. These have included curtailing early voting, making it harder to register to vote, and introducing voter ID laws that have a disproportionate impact on African Americans, students, poor people, and people of color generally.

We must build deep state-based moral fusions across the country around an agenda that does the following:

1. Engages in indigenously led grassroots organizing across the state and nation
2. Uses moral language to frame and critique public policy, based on our deepest moral and constitutional values, regardless of who is in power
3. Demonstrates a commitment to civil disobedience that follows the steps of the movement and that is designed to change the public conversation and consciousness
4. Builds a stage from which to lift the voices of everyday people affected by immoral, extremist policies—not a stage for partisan politics
5. Builds a coalition of moral and religious leaders of all faiths
6. Intentionally diversify the movement with the goal of winning unlikely allies
7. Builds transformative, long-term coalition relationships rooted in a clear agenda that doesn't measure success just by electoral outcomes and that destroys the myth of extremism
8. Makes a serious commitment to academic and empirical analysis of policy
9. Uses social media coordination in all forms: video, text, Twitter, Facebook, etc.

10. Pursues a strong legal strategy
11. Resists the "One Moment Mentality." We are building a movement!

If we engage in voter registration and education, we can unite the voices of prophetic mourning in a way that will shake the core conscience of this nation. And if we mourn right, comfort will come. Change will come. Like Rachel, we cannot not stop wailing and protesting. We cannot be comforted. We must say to this nation, you cannot and will not turn a deaf ear to what is being said. In forensic science, we are taught that wounds talk.

And that's why God's people cannot be comforted. We cannot be satisfied until justice comes and everyone's life is valued. We cannot and will not be comforted until then. And, so, we need to wish America a Mourning Christmas, because blessed are they that mourn, for they shall be comforted. My grandmother was a mourner, and she used to say, "When you mourn, the devil doesn't know what to do with you." Mourning doesn't make you weak. It brings you to power.

A CALL TO MOURNING: WISH AND WARNING

THE REVEREND DR. JAMES FORBES JR.

Pastor Emeritus, Riverside Church; President, Healing of the Nations

Members of the Greenleaf Christian Church should help America digest the Christmas sermon preached by their pastor in 2015. In that sermon, Reverend Barber wished America a "Mourning Christmas." That is not a title one expects to hear during the season when neighbors are wishing each other "Merry Christmas" and "Happy New Year." However, people who have listened regularly to messages from a pastor with a prophetic proclivity learn to extract grace from judgment. They patiently endure divine critique in confident expectation that hope and healing are the ultimate intended outcome. They have become conditioned to hearing the "if-then connection" between transgressions and disaster, repentance and renewal. Members of Reverend Barber's congregation will warn you to listen carefully to understand the deeper biblical, historical, political, and moral and spiritual values being addressed in the text, tone, images, and admonitions of his sermons.

Prophetic sermons usually include some of the key features of the sermon Jesus preached at his hometown synagogue in Nazareth (Luke 4:16–21). It was based upon the scriptural tradition of his faith. There was clarity, concreteness, urgency, assurance of divine favor, and a declaration of God's action in the present moment. The nature of the sermon resulted in a "division of the house," a parliamentary procedure for requiring a public disclosure of which side of the issue the assembly participants were on. The outcome of the experience was that it created two groups of people—those like Jesus who were committed to being willing participants in the disclosed will of God and those who were in opposition to the divine mandate. Some received the message as "Good News" and others as an assault on their vested interests.

To those who consider God's will as the brightest hope for all creation, Barber's call to mourn is indeed a wish to have their spirits be in resonance with the heart of God. On the other hand, adversaries to the will of God will find it to be a warning of judgment and impending doom. Let us consider the contrasting scenarios.

We might call the first scenario "A Wish with Emerging Promise." To mourn is to feel or express sorrow. To lament. To grieve for someone who has died. To manifest the conventional signs of such grief. To make the low, continuous, sorrowing sound of a dove.

Many pastors overlook the part of the Christmas story about the Slaughter of the Innocents, when King Herod ordered the murder of all male infants in his effort to secure his throne against a child who might grow up to take it. But Reverend Barber, having been sensitized by contemporary slaughters of the innocent, could not close his ears or his heart to mothers across our land who weep like Rachel. Nor are the ears of God closed to those who mourn. And when God hears, help, in time, will surely come.

Prophetic preaching grows out of sensitivity to pathos in the heart of God and anguish in the experiences of God's children. When we are indifferent to the cries of the people and have lost touch with the sighs of God's heart, know that the prophetic spirit is in decline and our humanity is imperiled. Lest that happen, Barber reminds us of the quest for undisputed power and the deep suffering that attended Jesus's birth. How tragic that the traditional celebration of Christmas excludes one of the very reasons why Christmas needed to come.

Today, in the face of the brutal murder of children, racist attacks against people of color, the violation of the rights of the vulnerable and the elderly, and indifference to the plight of immigrants, it should seem natural to us "to grieve, to mourn." To be able to do so proves that one has not lost the capacity to respond to the misery of fellow human beings. That is good news in the light of the second beatitude, which says, "Blessed are those who mourn, for they shall be comforted" (Matthew 5:4). Moreover, the unrestrained barbarity of oppressive regimes has not escaped the watchful eye of our God. In due season, they who sow seeds of violence against the poor will reap the consequences of their ungodly deeds. The dove of the Spirit does not mourn in vain. The day of liberation is on the way. Yara Allen, a musicologist who travels with Reverend Dr. Barber, leads congregations all across this nation to sing, "Hold on just a little while longer; everything is gonna be all right." In so doing, she is echoing the psalmist who assures us that "weeping may linger for the night, but joy comes in the morning" (Psalm 30:5b). A prophet does not ask a tortured people to use Christmas as a time to ignore or deny their suffering or to try to cover up their pain with cheery Christmas carols. A prophet wishes them a *Mourning Christmas* with the audacious assurance that help is on the way. Their mourning and moaning have been heard and are provoking heaven and earth to a great day of deliverance. The preacher does not guarantee how soon, but when asked, "How long?" says confidently with prophetic patience, "Not long!"

The second scenario, on the other hand, we can call "A Warning of the Wrath of God." Because a prophetic sermon takes no delight in heaping fiery condemnation upon the heads of the unrighteous, but rather in moving their hearts to repentance, it does its best to alert them to calamities they would wish to avoid at all costs. The major problem is that many are not really convinced that there is a God who acts in history to restore justice, to address indignities against the poor, and to protect both the vulnerable and the environment against rapacious exploitation. Their gods of money and power have assured them that even if there were such a god, he or she has no jurisdiction in this Kingdom of Material Things. The Almighty Dollar and Absolute Power provide false protection for them against what they deem to be "fake threats" of divine retribution.

So, the preacher, out of love, sounds the alarm and proclaims as powerfully as possible that God the creator of the universe *is*, despite the claims of some to almost omnipotent power, invisible but powerful beyond our imagining; in love calls all things into the protective care of the beloved community; grants us freedom either to be in partnership or to resist; works against what works against justice and peace; does not forever withhold judgment and wrath; and will not rest until all are gathered into the unity of God's loving being.

Woe unto you who cannot hear these things. Prepare to mourn, all who risk the illusion of the nonexistence of the One who causes all things that are to be. Weep all who treat God's children as worthless things and trample upon the poor and needy. Gather your family, friends, colleagues, and business associates and confess to them that you have brought plagues and sorrows upon them because you dared to be an enemy of the God of truth, justice, peace, and compassion.

After doing all he could to invite the powerful to the mourner's bench of God's forgiving grace, Reverend Dr. Barber sets forth an eleven-point agenda by which we may be sure that we have made the righteous choice to be participants with God in helping to build the beloved community. He offers this as a moral compass and a prophetic plumb line by which to measure the righteousness of our commitments. When developing concrete proposals or lists of practical principles, Reverend Dr. Barber does not rely on his pet projects alone. As a member of a prophetic moral movement, he humbly draws wisdom from the collectivity of other seekers of righteousness. In our time, he is convinced that fusion politics is more likely to avoid the blind spots of partisan myopia due to differences in race, class, gender, education, ethnicity, or nationality. Discerning the path to justice for all is more certain when we all struggle together.

In an almost desperate attempt to make an airtight case for change, Reverend Barber calls on Dr. King and Coretta Scott King, on an MIT professor, the *New York Times*, sociological analyses, statistics, the prophet Isaiah, and the Apostle James. He even enlists the "mourning patriotism" of Langston Hughes and a song from a Broadway musical, "Make Them Hear You." One can always be sure that the preacher has tapped into the heart of his or her convictions when the message from deep in the soul bursts into song. If I had been there that day, I might have taken an ecstatic leap into eternity, singing:

No more mourning,
No more mourning,
No more mourning in vain.
Mary groaned when her son was born,
Mourning turned to joy that first Christmas morn.
Christ was born to comfort mourners and heal their pain.

THE REVEREND DR. JAMES FORBES is the president and founder of the Healing of the Nations Foundation, the national minister of the Drum Major Institute, and pastor emeritus of the Riverside Church of New York.

CHAPTER NINE

THE DANGER OF MISDIAGNOSING TERRORISM

MLK JR. BIRTHDAY CELEBRATION, JANUARY 17, 2016

Riverside Church, New York, New York

THE REVEREND DR. WILLIAM J. BARBER II

Gracious eternal God, thank you for this day that only you could make. Thank you for our minds yet being stayed on justice and our eyes yet being on the prize of liberty for all. Help us, hold us; we know that whenever you call men and women, whether it be Harriet Tubman or Martin King, William Lloyd Garrison or Rabbi Heschel, you take the risk of putting treasure in weak, frail, sometimes failing earthen vessels. But you do it that the excellency of the power might be of thee and not of us.

I speak to you today in the spirit of unity, because "we" is the most important word in the justice vocabulary. It is not what *I* can do or *you* can do alone, but what *we* can do when we work together and pray together. There is this text in the Book of Micah, chapter 2, around verse 5. In the Message Translation of the Bible, it reads like this: "God has had enough. God says, I've got some plans of my own: Disaster because of this interbreeding evil."

The prophetic texts of Judaism and the prophetic words of Jesus were among the favorites of Dr. King. You know, when Dr. King stood in this pulpit, he didn't mince his words. The texts that Dr. King loved were those two thousand texts in the Bible that spoke about justice and that challenged us to know, as a country, that we cannot ask for God's grace while we leave undone the weightier matters of the law: love and justice and mercy. For to do so in our public and political life is, at best, hypocritical, and at worst, heresy. The Bible talks about this more than anything else.

Over the last weeks, I've been reflecting on the meaning of Dr. King's life. I've got to stand tomorrow at Ebenezer, where he often preached. And I was drawn to this specific text from Micah because it's addressing something that we must address today. Terrorism, violence, and injustice were all around the people in Micah's day. But the people of Micah's day were misdiagnosing their problem.

Institutes of medicine say that when it comes to physical problems, diagnostic errors are often incredibly harmful to the patient; they may lead to a delay in treatment and even death. But you can also have social and political misdiagnosis. Now sources say that this text was prophesied in the context of increasing pressure and growing inequality because of the expanding Assyrian Empire in what we today would call the Middle East—Iraq or Iran. Certain political leaders of Micah's day and their paid state chaplains and prophets of Judah spoke about terror, violence, and injustice as something coming upon them from the outside. But God tells Micah, in essence, go declare unto them: you have misdiagnosed the problem.

Micah warns the towns of Judah of the coming disaster and the real problem. He says, your real enemy isn't Assyria. Your real enemy is what's happening inside of you. In 2:1–5, Micah denounces the appropriation of land and houses. This is a reference to the greed of the wealthy and the powerful that has resulted from the militarizing of the land. These wealthy landowners ensure that the fighting to come will affect the poor and not the wealthy, and that the poor will have to fight the wars that the wealthy create. That's what was going on.

Through Micah, God indicts those who lie awake at night devising new and creative ways to use the threat of terrorism and violence to steal the land and houses of others and increase the burdens of the weak without any moral restraint. My good friend and biblical scholar Dr. Liz Theoharis notes that when Micah emphasizes "plotting evil in their beds," it is an effort to emphasize the laziness and affluence of the rich and powerful and their plans to get everybody else to do the dirty work that they start. Micah states that these evildoers are basically rich and powerful, greedy political leaders who have little or nothing to do but to lie around in their beds thinking of ways to oppress others. And God says, I have had enough!

Then Micah renders one other diagnosis with an eye toward the preachers, the false religionists, and the so-called evangelicals of Judaism who promoted a heretical interpretation of faith that sought to be the chaplain of the empire, covering the devices of the wicked in the nation. Micah begins by saying that his opponents command him not to preach negative things, because Judah at the time held onto a certain exceptionalism that they thought God would never violate because they were the richest, the most powerful, the most militarized. But Micah responds with a sarcastic comment in verse 11: you want sermons that will tell you what you want to hear and how you can get anything you want from God—more money, more wine, you name it—and if somebody would do that, you would hire them on the spot as your preacher. But God says, I've had enough! And God is calling for a meeting, a revival. He's calling for real prophets to stand up and have a truth-telling meeting, a truth-telling revival, a holy convocation, because that's the only place where you can get a diagnosis straight when a nation has gone astray. And Micah knew then what we must know now, and that is that the danger of misdiagnosing terrorism, violence, and injustice necessitates a moral revival.

Like Micah, the legacy of Dr. King is one that refused to allow America to misdiagnose her real social sickness and political maladies. Historian Vincent Harding suggested an important sentiment about Dr. King: he was free. Free prophetically, Harding meant. After the passage of the 1964 Civil Rights Act and the 1965 Voting Rights Act, many preachers and politicians told Dr. King, "You've done enough for a black preacher; you've done enough. Just wait now, things will get better. You passed the Civil Rights Act, Voting Rights Act; just go on a lecture tour and get a good position somewhere." But on December 10, 1967, Dr. King, in a sermon titled "The Meaning of Hope," began with the prophet's mourning: "I'm worried about America." He said, I'm worried about a nation "sick with militarism"; I'm worried about a nation that still has fifty million poor people within its borders.

This was 1967. Something is wrong, he said. And he knew that we couldn't talk about it wrong. We couldn't misdiagnose it. And that's why he announced the Poor People's Campaign. He said, Let's go have a meeting in DC, so we can cut through the lies and cut through the deception. Earlier that year, right here, standing at a similar pulpit on April 4, 1967, one year exactly before a bullet tore open his throat and severed his spine in Memphis, he challenged America's misdiagnosis of the Vietnam War. Politicians and their state chaplains were saying that the Vietcong were the essence of America's problem, the great threat. And even many other civil rights leaders and activists were just going along with the misdiagnosis. Dr. King dared to render a second opinion, because he was free. But we don't hear a lot about it, do we? In the media, you won't hear a lot about it because of money's attempt to reduce Dr. King to a human relations specialist, rather than a prophet of God standing for human rights, justice, and dignity.

You see that this manipulation of his remembrance does not understand that we cannot have the dream of Dr. King—a radical, prophetic dream, not a daydream, not a nursery rhyme dream, but a prophet's dream—unless we are clear with our eyes wide open about the true nightmarish existence of terrorism, racism, violence, and inequality. The kind of hope and dream of Dr. King is, as Walter Brueggemann says in his book *Truth-Telling as Subversive Obedience*, "subversive imagination." It is dangerous truth-telling that will make empire devotees want you dead, because it grows out of a determined desire to render the right diagnosis. It is hope that is the refusal to accept the reading of reality that is the majority opinion. And we who are the heirs of Dr. King's vision can't allow society to mess up his remembrance. We must resist any attempt to tame his dream!

But as you know, just as many told Micah to shut up, so, too, did they try to silence Dr. King. After he preached at Riverside and challenged America, after he dared to talk about terrorism and violence on an international and national level, President Johnson revoked his standing invitation to the White House. The next day, 168 newspapers—even a couple of black newspapers—denounced him. Civil rights organizations walked away. The NAACP walked away. Labor walked away. Colleagues in ministry walked away. He became an unpopular figure after peaking at fourth in Gallup's Most Admired Man poll of 1964. By the end of '67, his name was nowhere mentioned. But we can't forget his legacy, nor what the poet Carl Wendell Hines Jr. says about our prophets in his poem "Now That He Is Safely Dead": "Now that he is safely dead, let us praise him, build monuments to his glory, sing hosannas to his name. Dead men make such convenient heroes, and besides, it's easier to build monuments than to build a better world."

And we cannot allow the same economic and political establishment Dr. King opposed in his lifetime to reframe his message and make it palatable for their own materialistic schemes today. And it's getting ridiculous. Evangelical students at Liberty University called me the other day to say that they are Christian evangelicals like me. Liberty University invited Donald Trump to be the MLK Day speaker, and some of the students see it as a hijacking of the dream!

In my own state of North Carolina, Governor Pat McCrory, who has engaged in modern-day nullification, signing the worst voter-suppression law in the country and denying Medicaid expansion, has made it public that he's showing up to a King Day event. But if King were alive, McCrory would be arresting him, just like he did us. My only prayer is that McCrory is going to the meeting tomorrow to repent for how he has violated the legacy of Dr. King.

Remember Jesus said to those in his days: You love the tombs of the prophets, but you do not love the prophets (Matthew 23:29). And in the Hebrew tradition, if you touched the tomb of a prophet, you were supposed to be made alive with the spirit of the prophet and not appeased by his or her memory. We have to remember Dr. King right! Rabbi Heschel said the prophet is an individual who says no to his society. And when he introduced Martin Luther King ten days before his death, Rabbi Heschel said speaking to a rabbinical assembly on March 25, 1968, "Martin Luther King Jr. is a voice, a vision, and a way, and the whole future of America will depend on the impact and influence of Dr. King." So, if we are to stand in the tradition of Dr. King, then we cannot allow America to misdiagnose her problem. And, yet, the news has been filled with pictures of death and killing and a form of terrorism and violence and injustice in San Bernardino, California. The evil of taking a life is vile and vicious, by ISIS or anyone else, anybody who's wanting to destroy life. And we must pray for the families. But as we look at this and the response of many, I hear a call from Dr. King and our ancestors to use our influence to speak truth in the midst of terror, violence, and injustice. I hear a call to challenge a fundamental misdiagnosis, because many are and will try to pimp and prostitute the deaths in San Bernardino for their own vicious political agenda.

Some, like hosts on Fox, use the death of these innocent people to push their accusations; their racist and fear-mongering agenda against President Obama, against immigrants, and against Muslims. One of these Fox talking heads said the greatest threat to national security ever is President Obama's interest in protecting Muslims rather than protecting America. Now, while the tradition of Dr. King would not agree with everything President Obama or any politician has said, that statement is ridiculous. Muslims *are* Americans.

Cornel West might call this the "niggerization" or the "othering" of certain people. And you know what that is? The definition of that word is not just simply the dishonoring and devaluing of black people, nor solely the economic exploitation and political disenfranchisement of black people. "Niggerization" is the wholesale attempt to impede democratization and to turn citizens into intimidated, fearful, and helpless subjects. Attacks on Muslims are used the same way that racists, past and present, have used fear-mongering against blacks. And this reveals, as writer and activist Phyllis Bennis and I discussed the other night, that America doesn't have a Muslim problem or even a terrorism problem as much as we have a racism problem and a xenophobia problem. Let's get the diagnosis right.

Let me push this further. Nothing is gained by pretending that there aren't terrible things to be afraid of. But we must be clear about the roots of terror. We cannot misdiagnose the malignancy of terror. It's not Islam. It's certainly not foreign. Terror has also been an American export, and we cannot hide behind blind, infallible notions of American exceptionalism to deny this. One of our nation's hymns, in the second verse, says, "America, America, God mend thine every flaw. Confirm thy soul in self-control, thy liberty in law."

Our misdiagnosis of terrorism and violence occurs when it is rooted in our heretical notion that some people don't matter as much as other people. The greatest terrorist attacks in history have American handprints all over them. The Middle Passage and centuries of slavery of millions of black human beings, followed by a hundred years of legalized Jim Crow, lynching, and terrorist race riots that killed thousands of black people from Springfield to Tulsa to Wilmington; church bombings, the assassinations of Martin, Malcolm, Medgar, Viola Liuzzo, James Reeb, Harriet Moore, et cetera, et cetera, et cetera. Let's not forget how our nation supported the terror of apartheid and divested only after massive protests, civil disobedience, and deaths. It was an embarrassment on the world stage.

Let us be clear about terrorism, violence, and injustice. Yes, San Bernardino was terrorism. But so was the Greensboro Massacre in the 1970s. So were the shootings at Mother Emanuel AME in 2015. So are the drone attacks on civilian homes in Afghanistan. So is the carpet-bombing of cities. Acts of domestic terrorism by persons like Timothy McVeigh have too often been called "bombings" but not "terrorism." The same is true of the terrorist takeover out west, where people have threatened to kill FBI agents. Let us wonder what the standoff would look like if they were black or Latino. Why was the killer who shot Muslim students in Chapel Hill not called a terrorist? Or the attacks on non-Christian places of worship? What about rogue, racist police shootings of unarmed blacks, children and adults, male and female, in Chicago and Charlotte and New York? Why in the shootings of Tamir Rice and Jonathan Ferrell was no one indicted so that the shooters' actions could be examined under the microscope of the courts? *This* is terrorism, violence, and injustice! We live in a time when we are going to have to use our influence to challenge the misguided misdiagnosis of terrorism, violence, and injustice. If violence means to hurt and abuse needlessly, we must redefine how we talk about it.

Civil rights matriarch Coretta Scott King helps us here. When asked about violence in the wake of her husband's assassination, she said poverty can produce a most deadly kind of violence. In this society, violence against poor people is routine. Starving a child is violent. Suppressing a culture is violence. Neglecting schoolchildren is violence. Refusing them public education is violence. Discrimination against a working person is violence. Ghetto housing is violence. Ignoring medical needs and health care is violence. Contempt for equality is violence. And even a lack of willpower to help humanity is a sick and sinister form of violence.

Like Micah, Martin, and Coretta, we must refuse the misdiagnosis. When we make invisible the hurt and the pains of the poor; it is a form of violence. Even in our political discourse we act like it's hard to just say "poor." We talk about the "middle class" and those attempting to work their way into the middle class. Some people are poor, and they're poor because of economic injustices that go on in this country.

Public policy can be violent. When we are the wealthiest and the poorest country in the world at the same time, that is a form of policy violence. When we use tax money to bail out companies where CEOs make 350 times more than their workers, but then we charge students interest on college loans, that's a form of policy violence. When Warren Buffett, himself a member of the super-rich, tells us that four hundred of the wealthiest Americans took home an hourly wage of $97,000, while we are refusing to pay living wages to 40 percent of all workers, 54 percent of black workers, and sixty-four million low-wage workers in total, that's a form of policy violence—especially when $15 is $5 lower than what the minimum wage would be if it had kept pace with inflation since 1968.

A study by Columbia University's Mailman School of Public Health tells us that more people die every year from poverty—two hundred fifty thousand—than from heart attacks, strokes, and lung cancer. That's a form of policy violence. When we know that rising income inequality breeds more inequality, and in turn translates into a waste of human talent, that's policy violence. It is violence when 1 percent of the US holds 39 percent of the country's wealth and 10 percent holds 74 percent, leaving the other 90 percent of us to fight over 26 percent of the wealth, according to a Federal Reserve report. Marian Wright Edelman tells us that it's a national moral disgrace that there are 14.7 million poor children in this country today, 6.5 million in extreme poverty, 150 years after the end of slavery. This number exceeds the combined population of twelve US states. Just an additional 2 percent of the federal government budget could eradicate 60 percent of this child poverty. Why don't we do it, even for our children? This is political, social, and policy violence.

Sixty years after *Brown v. Board of Education*, we have high poverty. Resegregated public schools are on the rise, while policies are funding privatized schools with public money. Teachers are being attacked relentlessly. And Supreme Court Justice Antonin Scalia said on the bench, when looking at a case involving affirmative action, that maybe it would be better for black students to go to a slower-track school where they would do well than to go to a highly selective college like the University of Texas. That's a form of political violence. So, if we're going to talk about violence and injustice, we must talk about *policy* violence, just like Micah, just like Martin, and just like Coretta.

When the NAACP can produce a report with the title *Born Suspect*, and when a sociologist can say that in America the prison is the most formative institution in the lives of poor black men, that's violence. When Michelle Alexander can call the crisis of mass incarceration "the New Jim Crow" and James H. Cone can call it "the Lynching Tree," that's violence. And the only way you can believe that 1.5 million black people ought to be in prison when we represent less than 12 percent of the population, and that we should be incarcerated at a rate nearly six times that of white people, is if you believe some form of a bell curve analogy that contends that blacks are just more immoral than other people. That's a form of violence.

Refusing to fix immigration in a land of immigrants is a form of political violence. Deporting rather than doing the right thing by people who have helped build this country is violence. Those who are doing this violence are immigrants themselves; if the rules they're proposing had been in effect earlier, their own grandmamma wouldn't have gotten in the country. They put immigrants out, but the people who hire them and pay them below the minimum wage in the first place are never arrested. That's a form of violence. The way some people want to treat immigrants reminds me of a lyric from a Bill Withers song: "Keep on using me 'til you use me up." That's what we do with immigrant laborers. We use 'em, use 'em, use 'em, 'til we use 'em up. That same thing was thought about black people after the profits of 250 years of slavery. They said, let's send them to Liberia. Many freed slaves said, the hell with that! We built this country; we're staying here!

If we're going to be a great nation, we can't afford to let this misdiagnosis go unchallenged.

Just as Micah was told by God to say to Judah, and Dr. King was told by God to say to America, it's time to call a meeting, a revival meeting of the soul, of the mind, and of the heart. We need a meeting today. And in this meeting we must dare, like the prophets, to connect love and justice in pulpits and in the public square. In this meeting we must challenge moral hypocrisy because the only antidote to these lies is a truth-telling meeting, a revival, a revolution of moral values that names violence in all of its forms, and then offers a vision for nonviolent transformation. In this meeting we must demand the right agenda. We must say: America, healing is available. Curing is available. You can be well, but you've got to do some things.

God says: Come together and focus again on my purposes. And when you do, Micah said God says: Look, you just have a meeting, and I'll be in the midst of it. I'll guide you. The prophets had a meeting. During the First Reconstruction following the violent Civil War, blacks and whites had a meeting. They came together. They came together to democratize southern legislatures. They changed the plantation economy. They expanded education, voting rights, economic power, and civil rights. Poor white farmers recognized the common cause with freed slaves. They had a meeting. They were called "fusion" coalitions. In the twentieth century, we had a Second Reconstruction. It was a meeting. Black and white, Christian and Jew, labor and civil rights activists, they joined together following the nonviolent struggles of Montgomery, *Brown v. Board of Education* in '54, the lunch counter sit-ins, the Freedom Rides, and they had a meeting—we had a Second Reconstruction. We saw legal victories, we saw the Civil Rights Act, the Voting Rights Act, Fair Housing Act. We saw economic expansion and Medicaid expansion. We need a Third Reconstruction. We need a third awakening. We need a third national revival. We need a meeting.

And, as I conclude, the forces of regression are scared of us having a meeting because they know how powerful we are when we get together. And they know that God will be in the midst. And that's why they're fighting it so hard. That's why they want the environmentalists to fight over there, and Black Lives Matter to fight over there, and Fight for $15 to fight over there, and the LGBTQ community to fight over there, and civil rights activists to fight over there. It's time to come together for a meeting.

That's what we say on Moral Mondays. It's about intersectionality. It's about coming together. So, from New York to North Carolina, from Mississippi to Manhattan, from the apartments in Harlem to homes in the South, we need a meeting of the heart. We need a meeting of the mind. We need a revival meeting, a justice meeting, a movement meeting, a revolution-of-values meeting. We need one of those meetings in which, as my grandmamma said, "something happens, and moves from heart to heart, and from breast to breast." And my friends, I know the power of having the right kind of meeting.

I'm telling you, when God is in the meeting, if we all get together, God will guide, God will move. I want you to know that when hands that once picked cotton join with Latino hands and have a meeting with progressive white hands, and have a meeting with labor hands, and have a meeting with Asian hands, and have a meeting with Native American hands, and have a meeting with poor hands, and wealthy hands, and gay hands, and straight hands—when we have a meeting and come together, our togetherness becomes the instrument of redemption. When we come together, we can make the right diagnosis. When we come together, we can declare this land is your land, and this land is my land. When we come together, we can ensure that all of God's children are respected and treated with dignity. When we come together, we can make sure that America lives out its promise: one nation under God, indivisible, with liberty and justice for all. When we get together, what a day!

Are there any Latinos in here? I need one to come to the pulpit. Is there anybody here who is LGBTQ? I need you to come to the pulpit. Is there anybody wealthy with a conscience? Come to the pulpit. Is there somebody poor? Come to the pulpit. Is there somebody that needs health care? Come to the pulpit. Is there a preacher here? Come to the pulpit. Is there anybody Jewish here? Come to the pulpit. Any Muslims here? Come to the pulpit. Any Black Lives Matter activists here? Come to the pulpit. Any labor here? Come to the pulpit. Come on! Any environmentalists? Come to the pulpit. Are there any teachers here? Come to the pulpit. Anybody who is Asian? Come to the pulpit. Any Native Americans? Come to the pulpit. America, we're coming! And when we all get together, what a day!

GROWING A LOCAL PEACE ECONOMY

JODIE EVANS

Cofounder CODEPINK: Women for Peace

Reverend Dr. Barber has brought back to our attention one of the most important and sadly distorted legacies of Reverend Dr. Martin Luther King Jr.: his profound ability to see that the struggle against violence and militarism is intractably linked to the struggle against imposed inequality and racism. King recognized that militarism in the United States was a root cause of the civil rights struggle and saw the domestic wounds of sustaining a global empire visible at the city-block level.

It was during a meeting in the Los Angeles neighborhood of Watts that I first understood the full brilliance of Dr. King's insights. Aqeela Sherrills, who had negotiated the peace treaty between the Crips and Bloods before the infamous Rodney King court verdict in 1992, invited me to one of his meetings with the gang members with whom he was working. I saw dozens of young men whose fathers had been fodder for the war in Vietnam. Afterward, the war came home and attacked their sons in the equally deadly forms of poverty, constant racism, and militarism. It resulted in an astonishing death toll in Watts and surrounding neighborhoods that history has already forgotten—twenty thousand lives over twenty years between approximately 1982 and 2002. This is more than the total lives lost in the resistances of Ireland and Palestine, yet it is hardly discussed within the context of Dr. King's three pillars of militarism, racism, and poverty.

Dr. King had turned much of his efforts in the critical year of 1967 toward the fight against poverty and the fight against the violence of the

US against the people of Vietnam. He would be sad to know that, fifty years later, nearly one in two people living in the United States are poor or low-income, according to the Census Bureau's Supplemental Poverty Measure; that 43 percent of our children live in families that struggle to feed, clothe, and house them; that sixty-four million workers make less than a living wage; and that there are more than ten million homeless.

Our foreign wars are also a domestic wrecking ball. This realization compelled me to fly across the country in the fall of 2002 when I learned that President George W. Bush was requesting that Congress fund a preemptive strike on the innocent people of Iraq. The brave and powerful words of Congresswoman Barbara Lee, the lone voice to stand up against the illegal and immoral attack on Afghanistan, captured the moment. As she would later recount, she channeled her moral compass, her conscience, and her God to make an historic call for peace as the US geared up for another disastrous war: "As we act let us not become the evil that we deplore." Like Congresswoman Lee, Dr. King knew that violence begets violence and that we need to pause, as there will be "no meaningful solution until some attempt is made to know [the perpetrators of violence] and hear their broken cries." ("Beyond Vietnam," April 4, 1967)

Militarism is at the root of the American experience. It is as American as apple pie. Genocide and slavery are America's earliest expressions of militarism. It is a common event in America to hide the ugliness of reality with stories created to seduce some of us out of confronting the darker origins that underpin our modern social order. These narratives offer false choices and pit us against one another and confuse us from seeing the immorality and insanity at the core of the structures we are at the mercy of. The reality behind our cultural covers is beyond stark: Walmart, one of the nation's largest employers, encourages its own underpaid workers to apply for food stamps, while the company's largest shareholders, the five Walton siblings, have as much wealth as the bottom 40 percent of the entire country, according to PolitiFact. The wages of the bottom 80 percent of earners have been flat or falling since 1973—a kind of economic pain suffered across all races of Americans who live at or below the poverty level.

In January 2017, Oxfam reported that eight men have as much wealth ($426 billion) as half of the world's population of seven billion. Even though the world produces enough food to feed 13.7 billion people, there are 1 billion hungry and malnourished, and another billion at the edge. This is an immoral act of intentional violence. We are facing a dual pandemic of poverty and militarization.

To speak or act critically toward the US empire, its military, and its police is to invite the full wrath of all the institutions of the elite (including its beloved "free and fair" media). Nat Turner, John Brown, Jeannette Rankin, Paul Robeson, Dr. King, Malcolm X, and Chelsea Manning, to name some of our country's brave voices for peace, deeply understood that the immorality and violence of the oppressor cannot be met with silence. Reverend Dr. Barber has reminded us that mention of empire is blasphemy and the penalty is political exile, demonization, and even death.

It was President Eisenhower who first brought to attention the rise of the "military-industrial complex." Today, this complex has become even bigger and more dangerous. First under George W. Bush and then under Barack Obama, ever greater portions of the military have been outsourced: both mercenary-style troops working for companies such as Blackwater/Constellis and hundreds of thousands of "consultants" working for companies such as Booz Allen Hamilton. The weapons manufacturers, such as Lockheed Martin and Raytheon, make billions from war and have hordes of lobbyists who pressure Congress to increase the already bloated Pentagon budget. These profit-making organizations, whose business mission is wide-scale murder and surveillance, are exempt from prosecution and moral accountability. The result is a perfect union of business, war, and the state.

The masters of war accomplish this by raising the fears of the people and promising to deliver safety and security. Real safety and security are achieved through mutual support and connection. As Dr. King said in his speech "Where Do We Go from Here?": "The call for a worldwide fellowship that lifts neighborly concern beyond one's tribe, race, class, and nation is in reality a call for an all-embracing and unconditional love for all people."

Dr. King was not confused by the appearance of false prophets. He saw that the millions butchered in Vietnam would obscure President Johnson's legacy on civil rights. The wholesale destruction of Libya, Syria, and Yemen, the resurrection of the nuclear weapons industry, and the militarization of Africa will define President Obama's and Secretary of State Hillary Clinton's legacies.

During our work to end war and militarism at CODEPINK, we traveled to Afghanistan, Iraq, Gaza, Pakistan, and Yemen. There we saw the same weapons and technology used abroad that are used to oppress the American people. I watched the immoral bombing of the people in Gaza in 2014, violence that was focused against the poorest of the poor. In those very same days I watched the *same* weapons used on a community of people grieving the loss of a brother, Mike Brown, shot down in cold blood in the middle of the street in Ferguson, Missouri. Outsourced military mercenaries in Iraq and outsourced prisons and prison guards in California were shipped in. In 2016, it was tanks aimed at us as we stood against the mining interests in Standing Rock, North Dakota. Domestic US police violence cannot be addressed without addressing the violence of the empire.

We live today in an era of historic globalization. The rise of ultraright nationalism, from Donald Trump to India's Modi and Turkey's Erdogan, should give all of us pause about taking the easy route by appealing to patriotism and accepting a simplistic concept of America. Dr. King's "I Have a Dream" speech deserves to be interpreted to include every child on our planet. Today, we all weep for the children of Yemen. We must therefore begin to refer to our family as the human family—beyond the already damaged idea of a world "family of nations."

Our future as a species is now dependent on a sick and damaged planet where only united global action will save us. A system that is defined by profits and greed is incompatible with our survival. We must now move beyond a commodity-based *economy* to a person- or relationship-based *society*. As Pope Francis told us in a July 30, 2016, press conference, capitalism is "terrorism against all of humanity."

Barber has reminded us that we must have a meeting at the American ballot box based on fusion principles. We must end our complicity and silence regarding the fact that the United States is still the greatest purveyor of violence in the world. We must humbly call for and attend new unions of the dispossessed in all countries: to end US militarism and end exploitation by US corporations. Now more than ever, to end evil we need fusion politics on a global level, true solidarity, and internationalism.

Our first steps begin with building local peace economies. We are called to create the conditions conducive to a moral life. When this is not happening, it is our call to speak out and courageously model what that looks like. Living morally liberates you; it separates you from the war economy and exposes the violent structures in society—it gives you the space to resist and change them.

We must divest ourselves, our time, our energy, our hearts, and our agreements from the war economy. Reverend Barber understands the power of the *peace economy*; the giving, sharing, caring, thriving, resilient, relational economy without which none of us would be alive. But the levers of power and culture want us to believe it is the war economy that keeps us safe and secure. The reality is that each of us supports each other in spite of the war economy.

Sharing and caring for one another: that is what nourishes our souls and lives. Those throughout history who call on us to see the bigger picture, to not be fooled by lies, are the shoulders on which we stand together as we walk out of the madness into the arms of love. History teaches us that only a fusion movement has any chance of success. Love, peace, and morality represent our best and last hope. It starts locally and ripples globally, as we are all connected. We must do this together.

JODIE EVANS is a peace, environmental, women's rights, and social justice activist. She is the cofounder of CODEPINK, which works to stop US military interventions overseas and promote diplomatic solutions. She has served in the administration of California governor Jerry Brown and ran his presidential campaigns. Evans has published two books, *Stop the Next War Now* and *Twilight of Empire*, and has produced several documentary films, including the Oscar- and Emmy-nominated *The Most Dangerous Man in America*, *The People Speak*, and the Oscar-nominated *The Square*. She sits on many boards, including those of 826LA, Rainforest Action Network, Institute for Policy Studies, and Global Girl Media, and is a member of the Popular Education Project. She is currently writing a book about divesting from the unjust, extractive war economy and building a just, sustainable peace economy.

CHAPTER TEN

YOU HAVE A RIGHT TO FIGHT FOR A LIVING WAGE

FIGHT FOR $15 NATIONAL CONVENTION, JULY 13, 2016

Richmond, Virginia

THE REVEREND DR. WILLIAM J. BARBER II

Brothers and sisters, I'm glad to be with you in Richmond today and I'm honored to join you in this national convention in this "Fight for $15." I don't come as somebody just here to speak. I have stood with you in the streets, in front of McDonald's and other places. I've joined you in jail because I believe this fight, and the fight for health care, and the fight for voting rights, and the fight against police brutality and violence are among the most important battles in our country today. This movement in many ways is as important as the Student Nonviolent Coordinating Committee movement was in the 1960s. Because right now you are helping to build a Third Reconstruction in America. I've been traveling all over the country with others leading The Revival: Time for a Moral Revolution of Values, and thousands have shown up. And in those thousands, Fight for $15 was always in the mix. Because Fight for $15 knows that the time for America to do right is right now.

Now it is fitting that we are gathered in the capital of the former Confederacy to face this nation's peculiar labor history. If you follow the James River from this city down to the sea, you will find the place where my African American ancestors first set foot on these shores. My African

American ancestors were brought here to work the land, to build this nation, but they were paid nothing for their labor. And after America's Civil War, when African Americans served in the southern legislatures for the first time, they built a movement with poor whites. Poor whites and Black people came together. They rewrote the constitutions of every southern state including North Carolina and Virginia. They banned slavery. They banned work without pay. They demanded equal protection under the law. And this wasn't in the 1960s; this was in the 1860s.

And in my home state, white and black preachers demanded that the new southern constitution include moral language. They wrote, "We hold these truths to be self-evident, that all persons are created equal, endowed by their creator, with certain inalienable rights, among which are life, liberty, the enjoyment of the fruit of your labor, and the pursuit of happiness." Because they knew labor without living wages was nothing but a pseudo form of slavery. And this has been the pattern in our history. We've never been what we should have been in America. But every step forward, every stride toward a more perfect union, has been the result of people like us coming together to push a moral agenda, an economic agenda, and a justice agenda. And that's why we have to resist those today who will try to divide us and try to tell us what's not possible, especially in the South. When we organize the South, we change the nation.

When Franklin Delano Roosevelt was in the presidency, his labor secretary, Frances Perkins, and businesses were telling him that if he raised the minimum wage the nation would lose jobs. The president's answer was, "No business which depends for existence on paying less than living wages to its workers has any right to continue in this country called America." (Statement on the National Industrial Recovery Act.) That was eighty-three years ago. Roosevelt stood up to the greedy corporate leaders in the South and in the North who wanted to block rights and living wages. And today, we must confront the lies and the myths. One lie is that the minimum wage is enough. The truth is, according to Policy Matters Ohio, in 2005, a minimum-wage paycheck brought less than it did in forty-nine of the past fifty years. Somebody ought to tell the truth. The truth is that living wages raise productivity, decrease turnover, and build jobs. And that's not just my opinion. That's hundreds of business leaders and leading economists. When you pay people more, it's good for workers, it's good for the economy, and it's good for America.

When you know this history, you'll understand why we are right to fight for $15 and a union. Every member of Fight for $15 ought to get Dr. King's 1964 book, *Why We Can't Wait*. He was clear about economic justice and civil rights. He looks hatred in the face and he said that we couldn't wait any longer to dismantle the systems of race, poverty, and black voter disenfranchisement. He said in that book that we needed, like Lincoln, to reach the better angels of our nation. He called on America to pass a Bill of Rights for the poor and the working poor. He called on America to fund a Marshall Plan to help poor folk in the urban cities and poor people in the mountains of Appalachia and poor people all over the South.

You know, a few weeks ago at the Democratic National Convention I talked about how we need a defibrillator to shock the heart of this nation. Dr. King demanded billions of dollars for a war on poverty rather than a war on poor people, because he knew we needed to shock this nation. Back then in his book *Why We Can't Wait*, he said, "While Negroes form the vast majority of America's disadvantaged, there are millions of poor whites who would also benefit from a massive bottom-up stimulus." And I say to my white brothers and sisters, we've got to stop being fooled now. There are eight million more white poor people than there are black people. There are five million more poor white people than there are Latinos. There are some people in the South and other parts of the country who want to keep white people, Black people, and Latino people away from each other, because they know what happens when we come together.

And I declare to you today, we must hear what Dr. King said. We can't wait. Hardworking people can't wait. Mothers trying to raise their children can't wait. Fast-food workers can't wait. Health-care workers can't wait. Airport workers can't wait. Restaurant workers can't wait. Minimum-wage workers can't wait. And even many of our good police that make less than a living wage can't wait either. It took us four hundred years to go from $0 to $7.25. We can't wait another four hundred years. In America, we've got to raise up. In a country where hundreds of thousands of people die every year from low wages and poverty, we've got to raise up now. According to the Institute for Global Labor and Human Rights, in a country where four hundred families make $97,000 per hour and corporate crooks get free bail-out money while we arrest people and put people in jail who are fighting for $15, we can't wait. We've got to raise up now. When unarmed black and brown children and men and women are shot down by rogue police who undermine the role of good police, we can't wait. We've got to raise up now. When the greedy attempt to buy elections through money and hostile takeovers, and legislatures are caught red-handed passing racist and discriminatory voting laws to suppress the vote and undermine the political power of black, brown, and white coalitions in the South—we've got to raise up now.

Do you realize that if you control fourteen southern states—North Carolina, South Carolina, Georgia, Florida, Tennessee, Alabama, Mississippi, Arkansas, Louisiana, Texas, Maryland, Virginia, Missouri, and Kentucky—you control twenty-eight seats in the US Senate? This means you need only twelve of the other thirty-six states to gain control of the Senate. You control 37 percent of the House of Representatives, which means you only need 14 percent more of the representatives from the other thirty-six states. The South controls 188 electoral college votes in fourteen states, which means if you divide black and brown and white people and take control of the fourteen southern states, you only need eighty-two electoral college votes from the other thirty-six states. I stopped by to say we can't wait. You're right; we have to fight now.

Now I know that somebody said we are wrong sometimes to lie in the street. We are wrong to do civil disobedience. We are not wrong.

It is wrong for politicians in the South to pit white workers against workers of color and against immigrants. It is wrong that when we win living wages in cities across the South like Birmingham, the state legislatures intervene and vote against those cities. In North Carolina, they pit the transgender community against the black community. These state legislators claim they are passing a bathroom bill, but actually the "bathroom bill" is full of antiworker legislation. It's full of labor discrimination. It's full of legislation that intends to block cities from raising the minimum wage. That bill needs to be flushed. So, my brothers and sisters, you are not wrong.

I am joined here today by a host of clergy from across the nation. You saw them this morning. We met afterward because raising wages is a moral issue. It's about right and wrong. And any claim to be a Christian evangelical that doesn't begin with a critique of systemic poverty and calling for economic justice is nothing but theological malpractice. It is a contemporary form of pharisaical hypocrisy. And it borders on a heretical interpretation of scriptures.

There are more scriptures in the Bible and other sacred texts about love, justice, fairness, the poor, and helping the least of these than there are on any other subject in all of religion. In the Qur'an, it says men shall have the benefit of what they earn. And women shall have the benefit of what they earn. In the Book of James, it says, "The wages of laborers who mowed your fields which you kept back by fraud, their pain is crying out and the Lord hears." In Leviticus it says, "You shall not oppress your neighbor or rob him or her of their wages." In Jeremiah it says, "Woe to him who builds his house by unrighteousness, and his upper rooms by injustice; who makes his neighbors work for nothing, and does not give them their wages." Timothy says, "You don't muzzle the ox, because the laborer deserves his wages." Malachi says, "I'm going to draw near to judgement. I will be swift witness against those who oppress the hired worker in his wages and hurt the widows and the immigrants and the children." Deuteronomy says, "You shall not oppress a hired servant who is poor and needy." Ezekiel says, "Your pride, your excess food, your prosperous ease—and you did not pay the poor what they deserve." Isaiah 10 says, "Woe unto those who legislate evil and rob the poor of their rights." Isaiah 58 says, "Loose the bands of wickedness." Translation in Hebrew: "Pay people what they deserve." And then, and then, your nation shall be called a repairer of the breach. You are right to raise up and declare that we can't wait any longer.

But as I close this convention today, there are going to be forces, my sisters and my brothers, that will always try to reject us. And as I look out on this crowd today, I know many of you, like me, have felt rejected. Why do we have to march so much and go to jail so much just to get folks to do right? Some of you out there, you've been rejected by some because of the color of your skin. I know it's so. Some of you have been rejected because of the work you do. And people make you feel like you don't matter. Some of you have been rejected because of where you're from. You weren't born in America. Some of you have been made to feel rejected because of who you love, because of your sexuality. Some of you have been made to feel rejected because of how you talk. Some of you have been made to feel rejected because you are raising children out of wedlock, or have a prison record, or there is something else that makes people want to reject you and push you back. But I've got good news for the rejected.

I come from a faith tradition, and the psalm says the stone that the builder rejected has become the chief cornerstone. In other words, the rejected have power. Power to come together. And when the stones that have been rejected come together, something powerful can happen. And I know the power of coming together. When the stones that the builders rejected get together, when we build and get together, when Fight for $15 and voting rights and Black Lives Matter and health care and clergy all get together, what a day of justice it will be.

FIGHTING TOGETHER
FOR $15 AND A UNION

MARY KAY HENRY

President, Service Employees International Union (SEIU)

For working people like Eric Winston, the call to action we hear in this sermon made sense right away. Eric was born and raised in Durham, North Carolina, and started working in restaurants when he was sixteen. Over the years he has cooked and served food in restaurants operated by corporations such as Waffle House, McDonald's, and Cracker Barrel. One afternoon, before the dinner rush at a Waffle House that Eric was working in, a woman from the Fight for $15 movement came in and ordered coffee. She struck up a conversation with a coworker that Eric overheard. She spoke about how people who work for massive fast-food corporations were organizing one-day strikes to call for a $15 wage floor and the freedom to form a union.

Eric, now thirty-seven, remembers that he was immediately intrigued. "When you do this kind of work, life is not easy," Eric says now. "You never have enough money to keep up. You know things have to change. But before I heard about the Fight for $15, I didn't have an idea of *how* things could change. The movement gave me hope. Learning about it gave me a vision for how change could be possible." He got involved. He went to meetings and talked with other people doing service work for wages that don't pay enough to allow them to afford basic needs like groceries, rent, or shoes for their kids. Later, he walked off the job three times during national strikes called by the working people of the Fight for $15 movement.

The strikes started in November 2012, when several hundred men and women who work at McDonald's and other fast-food restaurants in New York City coordinated the first walkout. From there, food-service workers in other parts of the country organized strikes as word spread and the call for $15 and a union touched a nerve.

When North Carolinians organized their first strikes, Reverend Barber was an early and critical ally. Eric talks about how Reverend Dr. Barber joined their picket lines, spoke about their fight, and was arrested alongside them in acts of nonviolent civil disobedience. Then Eric and other restaurant workers joined the Moral Monday actions, building a wider and more powerful sense of unity. "He touched my soul the first time I heard him speak," Eric says, recalling how Reverend Dr. Barber brought a deeply humane perspective to the fight for better work and more economic security. "It mattered so much to be reminded that in the world we live in we can't get by on our own. We're all in this together. We need each other."

Our generation of Americans is facing a serious crisis when it comes to the status of work. Large and profitable corporations are keeping wages as low as they possibly can, adding far too many jobs that don't pay people enough to live on. Working moms and dads are forced to live on the edge and rely on public assistance programs to make it week to week. When the economy does grow, the wealthiest at the top have been taking almost all of the gains for themselves, inflicting serious damage on families and communities across the country.

According to the National Employment Law Project, in 2015, 40 percent of all working Americans were paid less than $15 per hour. Lower wages make life even harder for working families of color and for women, who on average make less than white Americans and are more likely to work in low-paying jobs in retail, food service, and health care. The inadequate wage floor affects all Americans, even if you've never stepped foot in a restaurant kitchen. Because pay is so low, 52 percent of the families of fast-food workers need help from a public assistance program to keep themselves afloat. That costs American taxpayers $7 billion per year.

Jobs providing services, care, and education are the future of the economy. But currently, the way these jobs are designed makes it harder for people to get ahead, no matter how hard they work. Work schedules are often precarious and unpredictable, which of course means weekly incomes are too. Erratic scheduling makes it harder for people to get reliable childcare or attend school to learn a new skill. Many powerful corporations in the service economy do everything they can to avoid taking responsibility for the people whose work generates their profits. They dodge obligations by claiming that a subcontractor or franchisee is to blame for any problems with the job. They misclassify people as independent contractors to evade any role in providing access to health care or a retirement program.

One key reason why the economy is so out of balance is that wealthy elites have steadily decreased working Americans' bargaining power by attacking and weakening unions. As a result, a growing majority of working Americans don't have a collective voice through a union. And it's now much harder for working people to form new unions to gain a voice and get a seat at the table when decisions are made about their jobs and their government.

Keep in mind that the good-paying factory jobs that so many Americans understandably miss did not always pay well. There was a time when they looked a lot like today's service jobs: wages were low, jobs weren't secure, and workers' families lived in poverty. But by organizing and expanding strong unions, working Americans raised wages, created health-care and retirement benefits, and built the working middle class. Higher wages in manufacturing jobs rippled across the economy and pushed up pay levels in other sectors too.

Working Americans' collective strength in unions reached its peak in the middle of the last century. Since then, corporations have decided to break apart unions in the United States, aiming their first attacks on the unions organized by people working in private-sector jobs. While they were attacking unions, corporate CEOs and their political allies made an implicit promise. Supposedly, after unions were crushed, companies would be free to be more efficient and more profitable. This was supposed to generate more growth and make life better for all of us.

But that's not what happened. Instead, suppressing unions made it much easier for corporations to push the economy way out of balance. With nobody sitting across from them at a bargaining table it became all too easy for CEOs to take more and leave the rest of us with less. As more and more families sense that they keep falling behind, they also recognize that they are often ignored by our local and national leaders. When they watch CEOs and corporate elites escape accountability, working Americans no longer feel like they are equal citizens of our democracy. It should not be a surprise that growing numbers of working Americans come to believe that the people in power care mostly about helping the powerful.

The result can be resentment and fear. As hope for a secure future fades, voices of hatred and division rush in with what Reverend Dr. Barber has called the "powerful magic" of racism. We can't ignore the epidemic of pain and fear that's spread as corporations have moved or eliminated middle-class jobs, whether it was auto jobs in my own native Michigan, textile or furniture manufacturing jobs in North Carolina, or coal-mining jobs in Appalachia. Nor can we forget that Eric's ancestors were brought to our country against their will and were forced to do brutally tough work in cotton fields and tobacco plantations, generating spectacular wealth for a class of planter elites. Ever since, workers of color have faced an extra set of obstacles blocking their path, from that original sin of slavery, down through decisions to exclude black and brown working people from basic labor protections during the New Deal, and on through the continued disparities in access to education, fair criminal justice, and health care.

The struggle to win economic freedom alongside fully shared civil rights is not new. As Dr. King wrote in *Why We Can't Wait*, "Negroes must not only have" civil rights, "but they must also be absorbed into our economic system in such a manner that they can afford to exercise" those rights.

It is up to those of us who fight under the banner of the wide and growing Forward Together movement to march ahead together confidently. It's up to us to create an economy and a democracy that make a place for everyone, where we all have a say. We see this as a new chapter of a long story of the American struggle for freedom: both political freedom and the freedom from fear of eviction, from fear of having your kids go hungry, and from the grinding stress of living paycheck to paycheck.

Part of this new foundation should be a renewed commitment to broadly inclusive prosperity, with work that pays enough to sustain families. Raising wages fuels steady and balanced growth, powered by stronger purchasing power for ordinary families that provides more money to put back into their neighborhoods and help their communities thrive. By expanding and strengthening new kinds of organizations of, by, and for working people, we can counterbalance the enormous influence that wealthy elites have over our government and jobs. To accomplish these goals we need to draw lessons and inspiration from the fight that Reverend Dr. Barber has led, alongside his fellow North Carolinians, across their state. The fusion coalition that people in North Carolina assembled is something we need to replicate in states around the country.

Uniting people of all races, classes, faith traditions, and sexual orientations on issues where their concerns intersect meant that their fights became greater than the sum of their parts. Together, they are saying that they are sick and tired of being rejected. By sticking together they are showing that even the rejected can find their voice and make themselves heard. We need to learn the lessons of persistence, patience, and determination. The relentlessness of the Moral Monday movement allowed their collective voices to gain a hearing during an era when many people are disengaged from or disillusioned by the coverage of politics. That meant that by the time voters in North Carolina went to the polls in 2016, they had heard a clear and consistent story about how many divisive and biased policies Governor Pat McCrory had tried to impose on their state. By then, most Carolinians were ready to reject that agenda and McCrory. There are also lessons to learn from Eric Winston and the thousands of people of the Fight for $15 movement. They showed how taking a stand matters. Going on strike is not easy. It requires courage in the face of the fear of retaliation or losing a job. But the strikes grew and inspired working people across the country, increasing in momentum and numbers.

By the time Reverend Dr. Barber delivered this sermon in Richmond, the Fight for $15 had expanded far beyond fast-food cooks, cashiers, and counter workers. Home-care workers had joined. Early-childhood teachers had joined. Airport baggage handlers and wheelchair attendants had marched and gone on strike. Adjunct faculty at colleges and universities had organized unions to get their voices heard.

This action and unity has produced real change. Beginning in Seattle, citizen action produced answers from elected officials as major cities moved to boost their minimum wages to $15 per hour. Elected representatives in New York and California—states where 20 percent of America's workforce lives—responded to the call for a higher wage floor by also raising the minimum to $15. By one estimate, more than nineteen million working Americans have been able to boost their pay as a result of the Fight for $15 strikes. This meant that working families had $61.5 billion more in earned wages to invest in their futures. For the first time in a long time, real average wages started to trend upwards.

To sustain this progress, working people are finding new ways to stick together and stand up together. In New York, fast-food workers are moving to set up a new kind of worker-led organization. They want to win the freedom to directly contribute to their own advocacy organization by directing a portion of their paycheck to the group. They would gain the freedom to advocate for their common good, no matter who technically owns the restaurant where they work.

Another way that the Fight for $15 and union members will maintain progress in 2018 is by helping build the Poor People's Campaign: A National Call for Moral Revival, rededicating our determination to break down the barriers of systemic racism and poverty. We hope to use the power of organizing and action to push our fellow Americans to confront the moral damage inflicted on our country by policies that keep working people in poverty and withhold full and equal justice from people of color.

The people of the Fight for $15 movement are reminding all of us that a union is much more than a building or a letterhead—at its heart, a union is a movement of people fighting for one another. Because work has changed so much, with so many precarious jobs and with so many corporations trying to dodge responsibility for workers, our elected representatives need to sit down with working people to rewrite the rules to reestablish clear lines of responsibility in the new economy. With more and more young working people saying they support unions, momentum will grow to create new kinds of organizations of, by, and for working Americans. Eric Winston puts it this way: "Fifteen dollars will matter. It will help my kids. But without a union, it's not enough. We are people. We count. We need to be heard."

MARY KAY HENRY is international president of the two-million-member Service Employees International Union (SEIU), and her leadership is rooted in a deep-seated belief that when individuals join together they can make the impossible possible. Under her leadership, SEIU has won major victories to improve working families' lives by strengthening and uniting health-care, property-services, and public-sector workers with other working people across the United States and Canada, including Puerto Rico.

CHAPTER ELEVEN

BOTHERED AND BAPTIZED BY THE BLOOD

MARCH 6, 2016 IN HONOR OF THE
51st ANNIVERSARY OF BLOODY SUNDAY

All Souls Church, Washington, DC

THE REVEREND DR. WILLIAM J. BARBER II

In the eleventh and twelfth chapters of the Book of Hebrews, in the Message translation, it says:

There were those who under torture refused to give in. And refused to go free, preferring something better, resurrection. Others braved abuse and whips and yes, chains and dungeons.

We have stories of those who were stoned, sawed into, murdered in cold blood. Stories of vagrants wandering around the earth in animal skins—homeless, friendless, powerless, and the world didn't deserve them. They were making their way as best they could on the cruel edges of the world. In this all-out match against sin, others have suffered far worse than you, to say nothing of what Jesus went through. All of that bloodshed, so don't feel sorry for yourselves. For no matter what you are facing you have not yet suffered unto blood. This morning I want to talk about being bothered and baptized by the blood.

Paul found himself having to preach to a people who had seen a Tea Party takeover. Well, I'm in the wrong century, but they had seen the takeover of people who specialized in hate and hurting others, who had great victories on the backs of the poor and marginalized. Now, the people he was talking to had seen victories as well, but they were facing new challenges. Things were rising up that they thought had already been taken care of, and some of them began to say, "You know, back then in the '60s—I mean, the first century—we stood up, we fought, but now we got a little something and our jobs and our 401(k)s and our nice houses and our nice pray sections in church, and, you know, we are going to just accept what is, take what we can get. In fact, we might even decide to just turn back all of this movement stuff. It's not really worth it as long as we can have a nice place to come on Sunday or Saturday and get us a little peace."

And to this sentiment, Paul said, "Wait a minute—don't forget how you got here. For you to be here, in this church, some people were whipped, cut, murdered, and ruined financially, but they kept pressing on and made it the best way they could by faith. Those before you were in an all-out war against sin, and they suffered unto blood; they shed blood. And you have not suffered unto blood yet, because you are still in the land of the living." Paul also said, "You should be bothered when you see domination taking over."

Indeed, we should be bothered by the national disgrace that we are the wealthiest nation in the world and the poorest nation in the world at the same time. We ought to be bothered by that. We ought to be bothered by the fact that the gaps between the rich and the poor are greater, and we know that God made this world sufficient for all of us.

We ought to be bothered when we see people blame President Obama and others, and say that poverty is his fault, when the fact of the matter is that since the end of the 1960s, we have had a war on the poor. We've stopped even calling the poor's name. Even those who call themselves liberal progressives use those same cute phrases and say we are trying to work to help those who are trying to make their way into the middle class. But some people are not just trying to make their way into the middle class. They are trying to save what Jesus rode into Jerusalem on and it rhymes with "class."

We should be bothered in a nation that gives banks free money but raises the interest rate on college loans. We should be bothered by people who take corporate welfare but do not want to give the poor welfare when welfare is in the constitution—"promote the general welfare." And we are locking people up for fighting for $15 while corporate crooks are going free.

We should be bothered when we know that twenty-four states denied Medicaid expansion simply because they do not like having a black man in the White House. It doesn't make any sense either, because Medicaid expansion would provide jobs; it would cover the sick, the working poor, including veterans. Eight million poor, working people do not have health care today because governors and legislators all over the country, mostly in the South and Southwest, deny Medicaid expansion. Thirty thousand people are dying every year, not because it was their time to die but because a governor or legislator would not give them health care.

We ought to be bothered when bad police are trying to convict and assassinate unarmed black men and women, boys and girls, on the spot, sometimes in less than two seconds. We ought to be bothered that a heretical brand of religion is claiming that Christianity is antigay, antiabortion, and yet proprayer. Well, down home we used to say, "Yes, I know Jesus; yes, I know Jesus, and I know Jesus for myself." I can't find anywhere where Jesus was an advocate of hate and meanness. The Jesus I know made love and justice and the poor the center of God's attention. We ought to be bothered that many pulpits are bought and turned into current-day false prophets and protectors of systems of exploitation. We must be bothered where pulpits and churches have become the chaplain of the empire rather than prophets of the nation.

We should be bothered that politicians create distractions and insults because they know the media and the American public will lean into that and turn off our interpretive analysis, while at the same time they are saying, "I will give you war, I'll take your health care, I'll refuse living wages, I'll resist immigrants, I'll outlaw your sexuality, I'll take your money, I'll privatize your schools, I'll control women's health, I'll destroy the environment, I'll practice voodoo economics." Just because you smile and find cute, poetic ways to say meanness doesn't mean you're not mean. Assassins smile.

We ought to be bothered. But I couldn't come here, one day before March 7, the anniversary of Bloody Sunday, and not say that what should bother us, perhaps most, in a voting democracy, is that we are seeing the worst attacks on voter rights and worst voter suppression since the 1800s. In a democracy, this kind of attack on voting rights, where extremists are cheating to stay in office because they know if everybody votes they cannot win in the public square, is a sin. Now, I know your universities don't like to use that word too much, but you better hold on to it, because every now and then you need to call something what it is. It is sin.

The great Prophet Isaiah, who my Jewish friends lift up, has a word in chapter 10, verses 1 and 3, and it says it like this: "Woe unto you that legislate evil and rob the poor of their rights." Paul said, "It is sin when you break up and hurt community." It is immoral, and we should be bothered enough to fight back.

And it's time for America to have a grown-up conversation about race. Race is not just when you call me the n-word. And it's not just a conversation for the extremists. Liberals and progressives, too, need to have a conversation about race. Not too long ago I met a strange reality. I met a racist gay person who was celebrating the Supreme Court doing what they did on marriage but who was OK with the court deciding against voting rights. That's a trick. This should bother us.

The First Reconstruction of the 1800s was stopped through a direct attack on voting rights. First thing black and white people working together in the First Reconstruction did was change voting rights. They deconstructed the deconstruction of the racist Redemption Movement, which had put in poll taxes, grandfather clauses, and literacy tests. The Second Reconstruction ended with an all-out attack on voting. It was called the Southern Strategy. George Wallace used it. Strom Thurmond used it. Barry Goldwater used it. Ronald Reagan used it. George Herbert Walker Bush used it. Richard Nixon used it. They all called the Voting Rights Act the worst legislation against states' rights. They all supported racial gerrymandering and second primaries. They all worked to suppress and shift and stifle the power of the vote.

And now here we are in the adolescent stages of a Third Reconstruction that has been signaled by mass movements breaking out all over the place: Moral Monday, Raise Up 15, Black Lives Matter, immigrant rights. This has been signaled by the demographic shift that suggests that if 30 percent of the unregistered black voters in the South register and connect with Latinos and progressive whites, the Southern Strategy will be broken. No longer will any person be able to control the 160 electoral votes in the former thirteen slave states or control the governorships.

At this very moment, when we have the power to build a Third Reconstruction, we also have the power to see fusion politics between blacks and whites and young and old and gay and straight and labor and all persons who are concerned about America. At the very moment that we have an opportunity like we've never seen, we are also seeing the worst attacks on voting rights since the nineteenth century.

Attacks: the *Shelby* decision, June 25, 2013, when the Supreme Court ruled 5 to 4 to gut the Voting Rights Act; and January 21, 2010, when *Citizens United* was decided. After *Shelby*, we had an avalanche of retrograde changes in thirty-two states, and all of those states are where the black and the brown vote was rising. North Carolina was the worst. They knew that 70 percent of African Americans use the first week of early voting, so they cut that. They knew that 41 percent of African Americans use same-day registration, so they ended same-day registration, out-of-precinct voting, and straight-ticket voting.

We're seeing apartheid redistricting. Stacking, packing, and bleaching black voters not just to keep black folks out of office but to undermine the ability of blacks, whites, and Latinos to elect candidates of their choice. In fact, here is the new trick down south: they are actually redistricting to give black people an extra black senator or an extra black House member so that they can dilute the black vote in other districts where blacks and whites might get together and elect progressive candidates.

And all this has happened while the Congress has carried on a more-than-975-day filibuster. After June 25, 2013, it was the duty, according to the Fifteenth Amendment of the Constitution, to fix the Voting Rights Act. For over 975 days, they have engaged in what Dr. King called "interposition and nullification." Strom Thurmond didn't filibuster the '64 Civil Rights Act but for thirty-six hours. Here we are today, and Loretta Lynch, the first black woman attorney general, has less power than the attorney general of the United States had on August 7, 1965, when the Voting Rights Act was first passed. She has no preclearance power to nullify state laws that restrict voting rights.

Here we are today, when people can get elected through unconstitutional laws and get seated and sworn into office and pass legislation, and we are only able to challenge that after the fact. It takes two, three, four, sometimes more years to challenge. The attack on voting rights is systemic—systematic racism and classism at its worst in this democracy.

And my friends, it is not just a black issue. The attack on voting rights is an attack on public education because the same people who are against public education are against voting rights. It's an attack on health care. It's an attack on workers' rights. It's an attack on women's rights. It's an attack on LGBTQ rights. It's an attack on immigrants' rights. And we should all be bothered.

In any other country where people fought for the right to vote, there would be a mass movement in the street, especially in the nation's capital. Those of you in DC who know about taxation without representation, you should be organizing march-ins and sit-ins in the Capitol every day. We should be fighting down south, and you should be fighting up here. It's our moral calling, because we should be bothered by the blood.

But we should also do it because we have been baptized by the blood. Our foreparents knew that the fight for justice and equal protection under the law and voting rights was a righteous cause, a moral calling. They didn't march as Democrats and Republicans. Go read the record. Look at the pictures. They didn't have partisan signage. They marched as saints of God. They marched as all souls. They marched as children of the universe. They marched as moral agents in a mean world willing to die for the cause.

And to see the Supreme Court undo the Voting Rights Act, and to see the Congress refuse to fix it, and to see some of us willing to just settle for whatever they will give us, is sin. It's a form of sin, a form of apathy. It's like watching somebody go down to your grandmamma's grave, dig it up, open the casket, throw the bones out on the floor, just stomp all over, and you just sit there. Every right we have won was baptized in blood. That's why, during the movement in the '60s when blood had been shed, preachers like Dr. King would take the podium at funerals to interpret the blood. They would give a prophetic interpretation of the death so that even though the people were hurting and they were bothered by the blood, they would also decide to be baptized in the blood, so that they would leave the funeral and stand and give their lives for the cause.

That's why, at the funeral of James Reeb and the funeral of Jimmie Lee Jackson, Dr. King posed this question, "Who killed them?" Then he said that they were not killed just by a few ignorant men. What killed James Reeb and Jimmie Lee Jackson was an irrelevant church, an indifferent clergy, an irresponsible political system, a corrupt law enforcement hierarchy, a timid federal government, and an uncommitted Negro population. Then he said, in essence to honor the blood, "Let us leave the ivory towers of learning and storm the bastions of segregation."

Do you remember when Dr. King preached that sermon for those four little girls? And nothing is more horrible. I was just there last week, marching on the Birmingham state office building. I walked into the basement where the bomb went off and blew up those four little girls. I was there in the Sixteenth Street Baptist Church, organizing. That day, Dr. King said, though they died viciously, they died nobly. They are the martyred heroines of a holy crusade for freedom and dignity. So, this afternoon, in a real sense, they have something to say to each of us in their death. They have something to say to every minister of the gospel who remains silent behind the safe security of stained-glass windows. They have something to say to every politician who has fed his or her constituents with the stale bread of hatred and the spoiled meat of racism. They have something to say to all of us. The practice, the hypocrisy of racism. They have something to say, yes, even to every Negro who has passively accepted the evil system of segregation.

Their blood is speaking, and it says to us, black and white alike, that we must substitute courage for caution. We must be concerned not merely about who murdered those four little girls but about the system and the way of life and the philosophy that produced their murder, their death. Their blood says that we must work passionately and unrelentingly for the American dream. I stopped by this sacred space. This pulpit, built by John Quincy Adams, who once said vote your principles, no matter what the majority does—I stopped by to say that we need this spirit again. We need to recognize our baptism in the blood.

How dare the Tea Party, with its spiked tea, trample on our voting rights. How dare the Koch brothers and others spend pornographic and lewd amounts of money to attack voting rights, years after the Voting Rights Act was signed and after blood on the bridge and Bloody Sunday. How dare they use their money to finance political power to desecrate the very heart of our democracy. How dare they desecrate the graves and the memory and the blood of the martyrs. We must resist this sin. Too many people have died. Too many people have suffered. Too many people have bled. And there's too much power in the blood. When asked tomorrow, "Why do you remember Bloody Sunday, fifty-one years ago?" we answer that we remember it so that we can recommit and reconsecrate ourselves back to the movement. We remember it because we've not yet resisted unto death, but everything we have, somebody died for. We remember it, and we will do something now to say they didn't die in vain. We will not let what was won be taken away.

America will be America again. We will restore our mighty dream. We will never give up on the right to vote. Justice yesterday, today, and tomorrow is our better crop. Because there is power in the blood, and if it didn't stop them then, we can stand now.

They stood on Bloody Sunday; not just any Sunday, but Bloody Sunday, where bodies were put on the line, so that the body of our politics in America could be changed to guarantee the protection of the voting right. For a long time I didn't understand why some folk got killed and others stood up. My Jewish friends had to help me with that. I had to read the Old Testament, and the Old Testament tells you. You see the shedding of blood was shown on TV cameras all over the world, and instead of running from Alabama, they ran to Alabama.

People came from everywhere and decided to make a stand, and the blood of the martyrs fueled the pen of history with the ink that would be used by a former segregationist named Lyndon Baines Johnson to sign the Voting Rights Act, cosponsored by a Republican and a Democrat. How? How did the blood do that? It was the blood that shamed the nation and forced people to do the justice that they had said they would never do. Well, in the Old Testament scripture, it says there's life in the blood. There's life in the blood. There's life in the blood.

And that's where Moral Mondays came from, really, if I were to tell you the truth. Moral Mondays happened within the first fifty days of 2013. Our legislature cut 500,000 people's Medicaid; they cut 900,000 people's earned-income tax credit so they could give fourteen families a tax break. They cut 180,000 people's unemployment. They took a billion dollars from education, made North Carolina worse than Mississippi, but when they filed the bill the week of Bloody Sunday to roll back voting rights, we began to say, if they are going to crucify the sick, and crucify the poor, and crucify the hurting, and crucify children, and then crucify voting rights, every crucifixion needs a nonviolent, suffering witness that will stand up against it.

So, my friends, I'm bothered and I'm baptized in the blood. Let us remember that every privilege we have came through the blood of the slaughter. Every voting right has come through the blood of the slaughter. Every opportunity has come through the blood. Every taste of freedom has come through the blood. Every ounce of equality has come through the blood. The Voting Rights Act was signed in blood. And when you mess with it, because it's a blood document, it ought to bring us to life. It ought to stir our souls.

The Bible says that life is in the blood. James Reeb said, one time, that we can never take a break or vacation. I'm going back down south. I came here this morning, tired, but to make a plea to my northern friends in DC. Just like the abolitionists of old, we need you to stand up. James Reeb, when he left here, came down south. We need you to take up the cause.

There ought to be a protest in the nation's capital. Maybe it ought to be led by All Souls. Can I give an altar call? Since they killed Viola Liuzzo, one of yours. Since they killed James Reeb, one of yours. Since y'all got this great band that can march it right on down there, maybe All Souls ought to start a movement leading friends to Speaker of the House Paul Ryan's office and Senate Majority Leader Mitch McConnell's office. Maybe you oughtta sit in, let them arrest you. Tell them, you're not here as a Democrat. You're not here as a Republican. You're here because you've been baptized in the blood. You're here as people of faith, and you're not going to let them take away what people died for. Let us remember the blood so that we'll work to beat back these extremists. Let us remember the blood so that we will not only commemorate, because I'm tired of commemorating the past. We need to recommit ourselves to the past.

There's wonder-working power in the blood. The martyrs gave their lives because there's power in the blood. Love is greater than hate because there's power in the blood. Justice is better than injustice because there's power in the blood. Right is better than wrong because there's power in the blood. Compassion is better than corruption because there's power in the blood. Giving, heaven's way, is better than the greed of this world because there's power in the blood.

We can't let racism have the last say. Don't ya hear the blood crying? Ain't no turning back now. Hallelujah.

CHEATING TO WIN ELECTIONS IS A SIN

PENDA D. HAIR

Cofounder and Director, Forward Justice

The vision for a multiracial, morally centered US political movement held and promoted by Reverend Barber is breathtaking. The goal is nothing less than a radical transformation of American politics to align our laws and public policy decisions with "our deepest moral principles." Centering politics on these moral principles, instead of on the personality of candidates or current partisan fault lines, will bring Americans together into a powerful "fusion" coalition led by people of color, joined by whites committed to making antiracism front and center. In this vision, an electorate committed to deep, antiracist moral values will demand through the ballot box that laws and public policies serve the general welfare, particularly the needs of the poor, rather than interests of the rich and powerful. A powerful movement that promotes antiracism and antipoverty policies and opposes extreme militarism will take power through nonviolent means, including peaceful protest, preaching, teaching, and voting.

Not only is this transformation of electoral power possible, it is under way, led by voters of color, whose numbers are growing, joining with progressive whites, including supporters of labor rights, LGBTQ rights, environmental protection, gender equality, and immigrant justice. In his sermon at All Soul's Church in Washington, DC, in March 2016—on the eve of the fifty-first anniversary of Selma's "Bloody Sunday"—Barber hails the current era as the "adolescent stage" of a Third

Reconstruction, "signaled by mass movements breaking out all over the place: Moral Monday; Raise Up 15; Black Lives Matter." When fully realized, the Third Reconstruction will produce laws and public policies to support a Beloved Community where all can thrive.

Barber's call for the Third Reconstruction harkens back to King's vision of a moral electorate requiring legislation for the common good. After more than fifty years following the enactment of the Voting Rights Act, Barber believes the demographics of the electorate and the power of a moral framing of policy issues make this the time to bring King's vision to reality. He envisions an electoral majority and a base of people nationally and in the states that is organized and committed to progressive principles derived from the world's great faiths and other sources of moral wisdom.

In the context of this transformative vision, it is not surprising that Barber views voting as a moral right and responsibility. Democracy, when truly open to all people, provides a path for ordinary folks to gain power. Without money, military might, or other existing power, elections are the best hope for the poor and oppressed to have a chance of overcoming the suppression wrought by those with riches and those driven by greed.

Barber not only preaches this vision, but before vaulting onto the national stage, he spent decades in North Carolina demonstrating that it can become our reality. After winning election as president of the North Carolina State Conference of the NAACP in 2006, the coalition made voting rights an urgent NAACP priority and helped convince the North Carolina General Assembly in 2007 to enact same-day registration, which allows voters to register and vote on the same day during early voting, and to expand the early-voting period, among other voter-protective measures.

In 2008, Barack Obama carried North Carolina by 13,692 votes, demonstrating that a multiracial, fusion coalition could win statewide elections. This was the first time since Jimmy Carter in 1976 that a Democratic candidate for president had won the state's electoral votes.

After 2008, progressive strategists started dreaming of a durable progressive voting coalition— termed the "rising American electorate" or the "Obama coalition," among other labels—that could capture the presidency and win a majority in Congress and many state legislatures. Researchers and activists noted that demographic change was making voters of color, who statistically identify as progressive on most issues, a larger share of the electorate both nationally and in many states. While progressives rejoiced, the Obama victory sent shockwaves through the racially polarizing, white-dominated modern-day Republican Party. In North Carolina, for example, 94 percent of GOP voters in 2016 were white, according to the University of North Carolina's Carolina Population Center. As Jack Hawke, in the *Carolina Journal* of the John Locke Foundation, writes, "Former Governor McCrory's campaign manager acknowledged this growing new electorate produced when he credited McCrory's 2008 loss to the Obama campaign's focus on turning out African Americans and youth using early voting."

As North Carolina illustrates, the possibility of a radical shift in political power as the result of a larger and reenergized progressive voting base led by people of color was not lost on the Republican Party. After the Southern Strategy took hold, the party of Lincoln had become a party of white people. It stood at a fork, with two paths to continued viability. It could try to attract more people of color and other centrist and left-leaning voters by changing its regressive policy positions and try to address directly issues of racism and coded race-baiting within the party. Or it could cement its minority status by holding onto regressive, racist positions while "cheating" to win elections. The years since the 2008 Obama victory leave no doubt that the modern-day Republican Party leadership chose the latter option, primarily using three strategies: (1) motivating its majority white base by inciting racial tensions and creating fear of the ascending nonwhite majority; (2) making it disproportionately harder for people of color, young people, and the poor to vote ("voter suppression"); and (3) gerrymandering voting districts to reduce the ability of people of color and voters who are members of the Democratic Party to elect candidates in proportion to their numbers.

Barber's Bloody Sunday sermon focused on two forms of cheating by extremists seeking to stay in office through undemocratic schemes. If not overcome, these forms of widespread cheating may be able to thwart the will of the progressive majority for decades. This iteration of time-old schemes by a regressive bloc to hold onto power through cheating and trickery threatens the Third Reconstruction, just as violence and trickery defeated the first two Reconstruction periods. In Barber's theological view, cheating the voting majority of the chance to elect officials who will adopt a morally centered public policy is not just illegal; it "is sin."

A renewed, aggressive push for voter-suppression measures—obstacles disproportionately placed in the way of certain groups of voters, most notably people of color—emerged in the aftermath of the 2008 election of President Obama, particularly in states controlled by the Republican Party. These measures include obstacles to voter registration; oppressive voter ID requirements; reductions in early-voting opportunities; elimination of opportunities to register and vote on the same day during early voting (same-day registration); illegal purges of registered voters from the voter rolls; disenfranchisement of people with felony convictions; and requiring documentary proof of citizenship to register and vote.

Since 2008, twenty-two states have enacted new statewide voter-suppression laws, and in 2017 at least ninety-nine additional bills proposing such measures were introduced in thirty-one states, according to the Brennan Center for Justice. For example, Pennsylvania in 2012 enacted a photo-ID requirement that the Republican state House majority leader admitted was passed to "allow" Mitt Romney to carry the state in the 2012 presidential election (Romney lost the state to Obama). Mississippi, Texas, Wisconsin, and Arkansas were among the states that enacted extremely strict voter ID laws between 2008 and 2013, while Ohio and Florida cut back on early voting, and Arizona and Kansas pioneered requirements that voters produce documentary proof of citizenship prior to registering or voting.

Several of these measures have been barred by the courts. Nonetheless, voter-suppression measures have gone into effect in many states and their fate in other states is still to be decided in the courts. There can be no doubt that voter suppression has impacted recent electoral outcomes and that the threat of expanding voter suppression is real. For example, in 2016, Wisconsin required a type of photo ID that was extremely difficult to obtain and that three hundred thousand registered Wisconsin voters did not possess. Donald Trump prevailed over Hillary Clinton in Wisconsin by 22,748 votes.

Cheating to win elections was made easier by the 2013 Supreme Court ruling in *Shelby County v. Holder*. That case blocked enforcement of Section 5 of the Voting Rights Act, which since 1965 had required jurisdictions with particularly egregious voting rights records to obtain approval ("preclearance") from the US Department of Justice or a three-judge federal court prior to making changes to their voting practices. A divided court ruled that the act's formula to identify egregious voting-rights states and localities was outdated and thus unconstitutional. But as Justice Ruth Bader Ginsburg, writing for the four dissenting justices, put it, "Throwing out preclearance when it has worked and is continuing to work to stop discriminatory changes is like throwing away your umbrella in a rainstorm because you are not getting wet." At the time of the *Shelby* decision, fifteen states were covered by Section 5 in whole or part, and nine of those were southern states from the former Confederacy: Alabama, Florida (five counties), Georgia, Louisiana, Mississippi, North Carolina (forty counties), South Carolina, Texas, and Virginia. Of those fifteen states, ten have enacted or begun enforcing previously enacted voter-suppression measures, including seven of the formerly covered southern states.

Prior to *Shelby*, the requirement that covered jurisdictions prove that voting changes were nondiscriminatory prevented much of the South from implementing new voter-suppression measures. But *Shelby* threw the door wide open, and legislatures in formerly covered southern states raced to adopt measures making it harder for people of color to vote. Within hours of the *Shelby* decision, Texas attorney general Greg Abbott announced the immediate activation of the state's oppressive voter ID law—a law that had been found discriminatory and blocked by both the US Department of Justice (DOJ) and a three-judge federal court. Mississippi similarly quickly announced activation of its voter ID law that had been pending review by the DOJ.

House Bill 589, which has been popularly called North Carolina's "monster" voter suppression law, illustrates the ugly connection between race and partisan politics. African American registration and turnout surged in North Carolina between 2000 and 2012, in part because improvements in voting methods made the ballot more accessible for those who suffered from the state's sordid history of racial discrimination. African Americans used the state's seventeen days of early voting at a much higher rate than whites, and African Americans used the first week of early voting in particular more heavily than whites. African American disproportionately benefited from same-day registration as compared to whites. African Americans voted out of precinct at higher rates than whites and thus benefitted more from the partial counting of those ballots. African American youth used preregistration at higher rates than whites. African Americans in the state are so strongly affiliated with the Democratic Party that their race is a better predictor of voting Democratic than party registration, as was commented on in *NC NAACP v. McCrory*.

Immediately after the *Shelby* decision, the *New York Times* reported that the Republican chair of the powerful North Carolina Senate Rules Committee announced that the "headache" of preclearance had been removed and the legislature could move forward with the "full bill." The "full bill" eliminated precisely the voting methods used more heavily by African Americans: same-day registration, partial counting of out-of-precinct ballots, and preregistration of sixteen- and seventeen-year-olds. It also cut the first week of early voting and required voters to show specific types of photo ID that many African Americans did not have.

After three years of litigation, the United States Court of Appeals for the Fourth Circuit found that HB 589 was enacted with the intent of suppressing the votes of African Americans. The court found that "the General Assembly enacted legislation restricting all—and only—practices disproportionately used by African Americans." Indeed, the state admitted at trial that it reduced early voting because counties with Sunday voting in 2014 were "disproportionately black" and "disproportionately Democratic." The court saw this "as close to a smoking gun as we are likely to see in modern times[;] the State's very justification for a challenged statute hinges *explicitly* on race—specifically its concern that African Americans, who had overwhelmingly voted for Democrats, had too much access to the franchise." Concluding that the General Assembly "target[ed] African Americans with almost surgical precision" and "impose[d] cures for problems that did not exist," the court struck down North Carolina's racially discriminatory voter ID law and reinstated critical avenues for ballot access including same-day registration during early voting, the safeguard of out-of-precinct voting on election day, preregistration of sixteen- and seventeen-year-olds, and the first week of early voting.

In several southern states, including Alabama, North Carolina, and Virginia, district drawers intentionally used race as the predominant factor in creating districting plans that advantage GOP candidates. As Barber's Bloody Sunday sermon notes, they did this by "packing" African American voters into a small number of districts, "bleaching" the surrounding districts. African American voters were "wasted" in districts where their candidate of choice could otherwise win with a much lower percentage of African American district residents. These "apartheid districts" deprived African American voters of a voice in surrounding districts, where their presence, when combined with progressive Latinos, whites, and other allies, could have tipped the balance from a regressive to a progressive representative. The Supreme Court recently held that such racial-packing strategies had been used to draw congressional and state legislative districts in North Carolina and in at least one congressional district in Virginia and invalidated those "apartheid districts" as unconstitutional.

While the Supreme Court has invalidated intentional apartheid districts, the REDMAP strategy used by the Republican Party in the 2010 redistricting cycle purportedly used partisan data, rather than race, in many states to give Republicans an advantage in winning congressional and state legislative elections. Using massive amounts of dark money for misleading campaign ads, Republican operatives ousted enough state legislators to increase the party's majority control of both houses from fourteen states to twenty-six, while Democrats' majority control of both houses fell from twenty-seven states to sixteen. This control over state legislatures, in addition to gains in governorships, gave Republicans substantial power over the post-2010 redistricting nationwide. With highly sophisticated technology and data, they drew extremely oddly shaped districts (with descriptive names such as the "lollipop swirls" and the "hanging claw") that allowed Republican candidates to win vastly more seats than the number of Republican votes would suggest should be mathematically possible. For example, in Pennsylvania, Republicans won thirteen of eighteen US House seats in 2012, even though Democratic congressional candidates attracted almost one hundred thousand more votes statewide. Similar lopsided results occurred in both congressional and state legislative elections across numerous states. The strong affiliation of voters of color with the Democratic Party makes such blatant partisan power grabs also a question of racial equity.

Racial fearmongering and cheating through rigged districts and voter suppression allowed regressive, open supporters of white supremacy to sweep into vast political power at the national and state levels in 2016. Despite these overwhelming victories, supporters of white supremacy and regressive policies are not a majority of the US electorate, as shown by the popular votes won by Hillary Clinton and by progressive congressional candidates. And in North Carolina, because of the Forward Together Moral Monday Movement led by Barber, the state partially bucked the regressive coup. Former governor Pat McCrory, who oversaw the extremist assault on the poor, the environment, LGBTQ rights, women's rights, immigrant rights, and voting rights was the central target of the Moral Monday protests since 2013 and was ultimately defeated in his 2016 bid for reelection. In 2016, North Carolina voters also elected a progressive attorney general, secretary of state, and auditor, as well as an African American state supreme court justice.

Although Reverend Barber's 2016 Bloody Sunday sermon did not anticipate the sweeping electoral victories of the white minority later that year, its message is timeless and continues to provide a roadmap for building the Third Reconstruction. The incredible body of movement work that Barber has led reveals strategies that work to combat voter suppression. The Moral Monday Movement's organizing around the lawsuit challenging the "monster" voter suppression law shows that protecting voting rights is a moral, fusion issue that will motivate voters to exercise the right to vote. The struggle must be waged on multiple levels, including in Congress, state legislatures, the airwaves, the street, and the courts. In Congress, the strategies of the Moral Movement have been used to spotlight Congress's sinful stalling and inaction on the Voting Rights Act and to demand that it address the devastating consequences of the *Shelby* decision and restore the Voting Rights Act. Dr. Barber's work also demonstrates the importance of focusing on the South, which national progressives have largely neglected for decades, but which holds 160 of 538 electoral votes and 138 of 435 US House seats, as well as the highest concentrations of people of color of any region in the country. Recent elections in Virginia and Alabama, where voters of color propelled progressives to victory, confirm Reverend Barber's wisdom in pointing south. To succeed, progressives must confront issues of race directly, rather than focusing solely on class. As Barber says, "You cannot understand America's class problem without hooking it to America's race problem," and "America needs to have a grown-up conversation about race." Finally, Barber's work emphasizes the strength, resolve, and wisdom that today's activists can draw from the martyrs of the past, who gave their lives to secure voting rights and civil rights for us all.

———————————————

PENDA D. HAIR is the legal director and cofounder of Forward Justice. For the past three years, she has led the legal team for the North Carolina NAACP in a landmark voting rights case, *North Carolina NAACP v. McCrory*. She is the former director of the Washington, DC, office of the NAACP Legal Defense and Educational Fund, and is the founder and former codirector of the Advancement Project.

CHAPTER TWELVE

STANDING DOWN
IS NOT AN OPTION

WATCH NIGHT SERVICE, DECEMBER 31, 2016

Metropolitan AME Church, Washington, DC

THE REVEREND DR. WILLIAM J. BARBER II

We come now to the close of a year that has proven that we as a nation have a heart problem, and somebody's got to be willing to go all the way until there is a transformation. When America is weighed in the balance of God's desire for love and justice, we are found wanting. We've seen again this year a theme which recurs too often in the American story, that we go forward only to step backwards, that every stride toward freedom is met by a backlash of hate and fear. Here in the twenty-first century, racism and economic fear still too often conjure a powerful magic that compels this nation to seek safety in hating the other and security in the false nativism that has failed us before and will fail us again.

Long before any Russian computer hack, the American electoral process was compromised by racism and fear. The Southern Strategy's divide-and-conquer tactics touched something deep within our social DNA, a fundamental fear that is ever seeking to come forth and masquerade as a normal condition. One of the most underreported stories of 2016 is that America experienced its first federal election in half a century without the full protections of the Voting Rights Act. We had twenty-five debates during the presidential primaries and the general election, and not a single question was asked about fixing the Voting

Rights Act. In Hebrew, your voice is your vote and your vote is your voice. It's the same word. It's a troubling reality that so many do not have their vote and their voice still today.

Fourteen states had new voting restrictions in place for the first time, including swing states, in the 2016 presidential election. On Election Day, there were 868 fewer polling places in states with a long history of voter discrimination, like Arizona, Texas, and North Carolina, affecting millions of voters. Yet it has received almost no coverage. In my own state of North Carolina, as journalist Joan Walsh reported in the *Nation* on November 7, 2016, black turnout decreased 16 percent in the first week of early voting, because while we won a case in court against the worst voter suppression, they only did what they had to do. That meant they've kept open 158 fewer early-voting places in the 40 most heavily black counties. So, we cannot, my friends, understand 2016 without turning back the pages of campaign history, to the Redemption Movement of the 1870s that selected Rutherford B. Hayes, who took the presidency without winning the popular vote and turned back the gains of Reconstruction. We must understand the 2016 election in relationship to Barry Goldwater's campaign in 1964, George Wallace's campaign and Richard Nixon's election in 1968, and even Ronald Reagan's campaign in 1980, which was laced with the language of hate and bigotry, including the decision to launch his run for office in Philadelphia, Mississippi, the site of the murders of Chaney, Goodman, and Schwerner.

My sisters and brothers, let us be very clear, this is nothing unprecedented in the American experience. I'm talking about elections, Donald Trump, and this current Southern Strategy. His appeal to the lesser angels of our nature, and the appeal of so many to those lesser angels, is as American as apple pie. And let us be also equally clear: this is not just about a president. It is about an entire web of money and influence that has been working to tie up democracy in America and in other countries around the world. Even as the divide between the rich and poor is at the widest in our nation's history, our electorate is growing more diverse every year, and oligarchs know they cannot hold onto power in truly democratic elections.

So, we are witnessing an all-out assault, foreign and domestic, on the very heart of our democracy. And this is not simply about the preservation of a government conceived of by human beings. It is really fundamentally about the well-being of creation and the survival of the creatures who bear God's very image. We live in a moment when millions desperately need a government and a society with a heart. Millions of Americans need health care. My own baby girl, who just graduated with two degrees from North Carolina Central, is afraid, and I see it in her eyes, because she has a preexisting condition. She developed a brain disorder when she was a year and a half old. She says, "Daddy, what is it? Do they want us to die? I'm just twenty-two years old. And the man that operated on me is Ben Carson [the US secretary of housing and urban development], and now he's fighting to cut programs that protects his own patients."

We live in an America where many still need living wages and protection from xenophobia, immigration resentment, systemic racism, homophobia, religious bigotry, and climate destruction. Too many are crying and too many are dying. And, so, this is about whether a government for the people and by the people will in fact serve the people. It is about whether we as a people can reconstruct the heart of our democracy. And we've been clear, as I've traveled with the Reverend Dr. James Forbes Jr. and the Reverend Dr. Liz Theoharis and Sister Traci Blackmon and our Jewish and Muslim friends to twenty-two states in less than eight months on a moral revival tour, that our faith in constitutional traditions points us toward some fundamental moral values. Protecting and expanding voting rights, ending voter suppression, ending unconstitutional gerrymandering, pursuing women's rights and immigrant rights and LGBTQ rights and labor rights, religious freedom rights and equal protection under the law, are all things that we can find embedded in our moral and religious values.

If God lets the sun shine on the just and the unjust, then how dare somebody in government think they have the ability to take away someone's equal protection under the law. Policies that are prolabor, antipoverty, and antiracist are moral matters. A moral agenda builds up an economic democracy through full employment, living wages, and the alleviation of disparate unemployment. A moral agenda finds a just transition away from fossil fuels. A moral agenda ensures affordable housing, direct cash transfers, and other safety-net support for families struggling to get by—those who are not just poor, but as my grandma used to say, "po'." A moral agenda has fair policies for immigrants and critiques of warmongering, where people are talking more about nuclear weapons than about negotiation. It is a moral matter that we have equality in education by ensuring that every child receives a high-quality, well-funded, constitutionally guaranteed, and diverse public education, as well as access to community colleges and universities. A moral agenda includes health care for all, expands Medicaid in every state, ensures access to Medicare and Social Security, and then moves toward a universal, transparent, and equitable health-care system. How dare any politicians get free health care because the people elected them and then stop the people that elected them from having the same thing. A moral agenda protects women's health and ensures fairness in the criminal justice system by addressing continuing inequalities for black, brown, and poor white people. And a moral agenda fights the proliferation of guns. The unholy hold the NRA has on our body politic is immoral.

And so, we wrote to Mr. Trump, saying, "We do not believe these ideas are left and right, they are right and wrong. That's the struggle." And we said, "While we know no human being is perfect, we wish to speak to you about these moral issues, because far too much is at stake for you to succumb to the worst demons that try to hijack our democracy." We said to him we would not meet with him at the towers, but if he so chose we could meet in a house of worship. The role of moral leaders is not to make politicians of any party comfortable but to challenge them and critique them, because some things we stand for no matter who's in office. And I want to tell you that when that letter went live tonight, nearly three thousand clergy in America have signed onto it.

The Spirit is telling us that we must build a movement that declares standing down is not an option. Not by power, not by might, but by the Spirit we must bring poor people together—black, white, Latino, Christian, Muslim, Jewish, gay, lesbian, straight, trans, people of faith, people who may not be of faith but who believe in a moral universe, civil rights and labor—around a moral revival and a Poor People's Campaign. It will be a moral fusion movement like Pentecost, a movement that can see that there is a difference between the darkness of the tomb and the darkness of the womb. It will be a movement that says, "We will not allow our poor black brother's body to swing and it not get our attention." It will be a movement where Muslims can join with Jews and we can all hold ourselves together. And, so, this is our resolution. This is our resolve. We are going forward together and not taking one step back.

Our resolve is like that of William Lloyd Garrison. In the first issue of the abolitionist newspaper *The Liberator*, Garrison, a white preacher, wrote, "I do not wish to think, or speak, or write with moderation. I am in earnest. I will not equivocate. Ask a woman whose child is in a burning house to be moderate? I will not be moderate. I will not retreat a single inch and I will be heard." Like Garrison, we cannot stand down. Like Frederick Douglass, who said in 1886 on the twenty-fourth anniversary of the Emancipation Proclamation, "Where justice is denied, where poverty is enforced, where ignorance prevails, and where any one class is made to feel that society is in organized conspiracy to oppress, to rob, and degrade them, neither persons nor property will be safe," we cannot stand down. Like Ella Baker, the great freedom fighter of the twentieth century, who said, "In order for us as poor and oppressed people to become a part of a society that is meaningful, the system under which we now exist has to be radically changed. It means facing a system that does not lend itself to your needs, and devising means by which you can change that system," we cannot stand down.

Like the poet Jayne Cortez, who said, "If we don't fight, if we don't resist, if we don't organize and unify, and get the power to control our lives, then we will wear the exaggerated look of submission, the bizarre look of suicide, the dehumanized look of fear, and the decomposed look of repression forever," we cannot stand down. With Dr. King, we must confess and testify, "There comes a time when silence is betrayal, and there comes a time that we must stand flat-footed and declare eternal dissatisfaction with poverty, racism, materialism, and militarism." There comes a time when we must say like Jesus, "Woe unto those who engage in religious practices but leave the weightier matters of love and justice and mercy and faith undone." There comes a time, like the apostle Paul in his letter to the Hebrews, when we must proclaim, "We are not of those who shrink back to destruction. But we are those who persevere unto the salvation of the soul, because faith is the substance of things hoped for and the evidence of things not seen."

In fact, as we welcome the new year, let me remind you that there was a time when there were three millennial boys: one of them was in the moral movement of his day, the other was in the movement for black lives of his day, and the other was in the Fight for 15 movement of his day. The names that the enemy gave them were Shadrach, Meshach, and Abednego. Y'all know what I'm talking about. And they were dealing with this king who was a narcissist. He believed his own press reports. They tell me he loved to build towers. And nobody had ever seen a tower like Nebuchadnezzar's towers. He loved to cover his towers in gold. He loved to make them shine. And he loved to have meetings in the towers. And he loved people to bow down and worship him at the towers.

Nebuchadnezzar told these Hebrew boys that if they didn't bow down, he'd throw them in the fire. But what he didn't know was that those boys had a fire in them already. Those boys had refused to eat the king's meat or drink the king's wine at Mar-a-Lago—I mean, at Babylon. And rather than get drunk with the wine of the world and forget those that came before them, the boys had a fire in them, because they kept alive the stories of the deliverance from Egypt. They had a fire in them, because they remembered how Samson stood up against the Philistines. They didn't believe the press. They didn't believe the tweets that the king kept putting out. While the king was tweeting, they were singing the songs of Zion, and they were renewing their spirit.

And the king and his men didn't know it, but every age has a moral movement. Shadrach, Meshach, and Abednego were part of a moral movement, and they didn't stand down. Instead they said, "Even if God doesn't change things right now, we're going to be a witness that standing down is not an option." And because they didn't, they changed the king. They changed the climate. They changed the consciousness. They changed the fire. When they went in, the fire was seven times hotter, but when they came out they didn't even have the smell of smoke on them. They brought about a moral revolution because they would not stand down.

And I've stopped by on January 1, 2017, to say that I believe in the power of a moral movement. I believe that standing down is not an option. I've read about it in my Bible. I've seen it in American history. My faith informs me. But I want you to know that it's not hypothetical because I've experienced it over the last three or four years. We started fighting with Moral Mondays down in North Carolina. They said it wouldn't matter because extremists had all the power. They told us to bow down and wait until the next election. Extremists took control of all three branches of government, and they weren't backing down an inch. But we stood together for three long years. We went in the fire together. We marched together. We prayed together. We went to jail together. We registered voters together. We went to the legislature together. We sued in court together. And this year in the face of all this other Trumpism, we saw a change down in the South, down in North Carolina, because somebody refused to stand down.

So, I stopped by to tell you that Nebuchadnezzar would not have fought so hard to get these boys to bow if he didn't know the power they would have if they stood together. I need you to turn to your neighbor and say, "Neighbor, Nebuchadnezzar is scared of you. That's why he's trying to get you to bow. He knows that if you stand, it'll be all right." There's strength in our standing. I stopped by to tell you we may be headed into some fiery times, but bowing down is not an option. Falling down is not an option. Looking down is not an option. Standing down is not an option. We have to go into the new year standing up. We can't bow until justice comes. We can't bow until mercy comes. We can't bow until the glory comes. Now one day we'll be able to bow, when every heel is made low and the rough places are made smooth, and the crooked places are made straight and the glory of the Lord is revealed. I'm bowing then, but until then, until then, until then bowing is not an option. Standing down is not an option. Stand! And when you've done all that you know how to do, stand.

How many of you want to be a part of a real Poor People's Campaign: A National Call for Moral Revival? How many of you know we have to stand in every state capitol and we have to stand in Washington, DC? How many of you know it's time to audit America? How many of you know this is bigger than Democrat versus Republican? How many of you understand it's our turn?

Some progressives called me the other day and said, "Reverend Dr. Barber, it don't do no good. We've tried." I said, "Wait a minute, son. See, your history is wrong. Today would be the thirty-first day of the standing in the Montgomery bus boycott movement." They said, "I been to a rally." I said, "That's the problem. This ain't a microwave moment. This is an in-the-fire moment." I pretty much guarantee you we're gonna get thrown in the fire, but if you go in bowed down, you lose your power. But if you go in standing—and my Jewish, my Muslim, and my Christian friends can agree with me—somebody will walk in that fire with you. Somebody called in Jehovah. Somebody may have said it was Allah. Somebody else said it was a preexistence of Jesus. But whoever it was, when you stand, you're guaranteed divine assistance. All I want you to do is hold hands standing, because this is what we're gonna have to do. This is our time, y'all.

And so we're here, Lord, at the dawning of the new year. We haven't seen it, but you met us on the threshold. Use our souls, God, to stand up in this world, to stand up in this nation. Use us to stand up in our consciousness and give others the courage to do so. Stand us up with the courage to audit this nation that we might correct, help be a part of correcting. Enable us to stand not for the poor but with the poor and with the broken. And now, God, even where we sometimes are weak, and sometimes we limp, don't give us grace, let us recognize the grace you've already given us that which is sufficient. Now, God, give us wisdom while we're standing. Speak to us. Show us the way that we might stand and be good soldiers at the end of our journey, that you might give us the crown of life. Thank you now, in the name of the God we serve—many ways, many names—but one God. In that name we pray, amen.

A MORAL AGENDA FOR MERCY AND JUSTICE

THE REVEREND DR. KATHARINE RHODES HENDERSON

President, Auburn Theological Seminary

Five years ago, Auburn Seminary and its partners gathered together eighty faith-rooted justice leaders in Nashville, Tennessee, to ask these questions: "Is there a multifaith movement for justice? Could we, who come from widely diverse backgrounds and belief systems, suspend the things that divide us—from the petty to the political, from practice and ritual to the lofty theological—long enough to listen to the still small voice of the divine calling us to do the work of justice, mercy, and love together? Could we join in support of a common set of principles and policies that would govern our shared life?" The questions were in part rhetorical because many of us felt that we were already helping to midwife and bring such a movement to life. Yet sometimes the very act of naming something can help people to know what they are seeing right before their eyes.

Here's what I saw on New Year's Eve. The Watch Night Service 2016 was one incarnation of the multifaith movement for justice. It was a celebration of the work of Reverend Dr. Barber and his organization, the Repairers of the Breach, over a decade in the making, as well as the work of many others, woven together in a web of connection. The night represented a major inflection point, marking all the labor that had come before, which had been hard enough, but also leaning into the new challenge represented by the election of Donald Trump as president of the United States.

What I witnessed that night was a resounding answer to the questions we posed at a retreat planned by Auburn Seminary, Mountain Top, a vision of the pluralist, inclusive, loving United States we aspire to build together—an intergenerational holy mash-up of Christian leaders, a rabbi, an imam, and Valarie Kaur, a young Sikh leader who was "anointed" that night with the respect and recognition by all the seasoned leaders gathered, and whose speech with the words "What if this darkness is not the darkness of the tomb but the darkness of the womb?" has been watched by over forty million viewers online. We also heard witnesses from the front lines, women fighting for a living wage, for water fresh enough to quench the thirst of their children without making them sick; and testimonies from immigrants fearing the onslaught of US Immigration and Customs Enforcement agents leading to deportation and exile from this country, their home.

We were brought together under the banner of a centuries' old Watch Night tradition, well known in the black church but new to some of us. I looked it up on Wikipedia to learn that it recalls the New Year's Eve of 1862, when American slaves gathered in anticipation of the news that President Abraham Lincoln had signed the Emancipation Proclamation. On this Watch Night, what many of us felt was that, despite leaving family, friends, and the usual New Year's Eve revelry behind, we found ourselves in exactly the place we were supposed to be, a foretaste of the world God intends. What we did on this night was to celebrate the web of mutuality and faith that connects us while gathering strength for the difficult journey to come. Few in the congregation on Watch Night 2016 felt that we were on the eve of a new emancipation.

On this Watch Night, Reverend Dr. Barber was the last of several who spoke, not so much to provide a crescendo to the evening, as if the rest of us who spoke were the lead-up acts at a rock concert, but more to give space in this new movement moment to others from different traditions and newer generations, including women and others whose voices often go unheard. Although Barber was shaped and formed in a black church tradition and the civil rights movement of the 1960s that may have privileged a male voice with a certain kind of authority, he is helping to lead a flexible fusion movement that presupposes a multiplicity of voices and actors, especially emerging ones, working together. It means sometimes leading from the front and sometimes from behind; sometimes speaking and sometimes keeping silent.

The content of Barber's Watch Night sermon likewise is deeply inclusive. It expresses the anguish not just of a select privileged few but of a comprehensive list of the many who are under siege. It is not an ode to political correctness or identity politics, both of which have become tropes to discredit resistance to forces that seek to divide us, but a lament of biblical proportions about a whole nation losing its way. Listen to the vast array of assaults on the heart of democracy that he enumerates: voting laws specifically designed to disenfranchise large parts of the population; economic greed and racist structures that keep some in permanent situations of poverty without a living wage; the destruction of the planet and the well-being of creation; the dismantling of access to health care, especially women's; a criminal justice system that is anything but just; Islamophobia and bigotry of all kinds, including against LGBTQ folks, against whom, for some, God and the Bible are not enough to stave off the fear of "the other" and must be supplemented with guns.

For Barber, these "preexisting conditions" are the sum total of what the multifaith movement for justice must address through a moral agenda—not the "moralistic agenda" of the Moral Majority or the Religious Right, focused on singular issues like abortion or sexuality—but a comprehensive intersectional agenda that addresses connected problems and demands equally connected solutions. As Barber himself says, the moral agenda flows not from the perspective of the political left or right, but from a deep conviction of right and wrong. This was the kind of moral argument Congressman Joseph Kennedy III made in March 2017 as he spoke out against the repeal of the Affordable Care Act and against House Speaker Paul Ryan's statement that eliminating the program was "an act of mercy."

Said Congressman Kennedy, "With all due respect to our speaker, he and I must have read different scripture. . . . The one I read calls on us to feed the hungry, to clothe the naked, to shelter the homeless, and to comfort the sick. It reminds us that we are judged not by how we treat the powerful, but how we care for the least among us. There is no mercy in a system that makes health care a luxury. There is no mercy in a country that turns their back on those most in need of protection: the elderly, the poor, the sick, and the suffering. There is no mercy in a cold shoulder to the mentally ill. This is not an 'act of mercy.' It is an act of malice."

Barber's words on Watch Night anticipated Kennedy's moving speech. They also echoed the voices of the Hebrew prophets, outlining what is at stake for us as a culture. You can almost hear in his words the prophet Isaiah: "Is this not the fast that I choose to loose the bonds of injustice, to let the oppressed go free and to break every yoke?"

But in another sense, Barber represents a different kind of prophecy, what theologian Cathleen Kaveny might describe as "prophecy without contempt." I might call it the feminine prophetic because, instead of railing against the sin and the sinful, Barber quickly moves to an invitation, an open call to a big tent, to all those willing to stand up and be counted, reminding us that "standing down is not an option" and that "silence is betrayal." In content, tone, and action, Barber embodies and models a new kind of prophecy. He offers a summary of his mode of prophetic leadership in his book *The Third Reconstruction*, writing: "This is not a story about me. The most important word in the justice vocabulary is always 'we.'" Barber's words at the Watch Night service were prescient. The challenge of the Trump era has been as bad as (and worse than) we might have imagined. We have watched the ascendency not of leaders who listen and act with mercy but of "strong men" who dream backwards with nostalgia to a mythic time of nationalism, economic and militaristic might, and the firm stronghold of a certain brand of Christian white male supremacy.

On November 8, 2016, a vision for the America of the 1950s won. A moral agenda in the White House is eclipsed by the ascendency of an agenda not of mercy, but of malice, evil in its execution. A license for violence and bigotry has been issued by those in power such that an off-duty cop can physically, verbally, and emotionally abuse a thirteen-year-old African American child in public and then pull out a gun and shoot at him; children in classrooms are in tears for fear of a parent's deportation; Jewish cemeteries are desecrated and swastikas appear on subways and the doors of churches; and Muslims are terrorized here in America and in many cases banned from entering the country at all.

But others are heeding Barber's call to stand up, as did Shadrach, Meshach, and Abednego, the brave millennial trio in the Book of Daniel, rather than bowing down to the tyrannical strongman Nebuchadnezzar. In our day, too, people are learning that when they stand up together and remain faithful, the flames of the fiery furnace will not consume them but will strengthen their resolve. They are learning that, in resistance, resilience can be found.

Barber's words at the turn of a new year ushered in what many are calling a multifaith movement for justice, a fusion movement of people of faith and no faith, who are coming together to march, to strategize, to advocate, petition, sing, and pray. Each element on the continuum of this movement may be imperfect in planning and execution, as many are quick to point out. But each effort is powerful nonetheless as leaders and everyday folk stand up not for what is left or right, but for what is right as opposed to what is wrong. Some in this movement are veterans of resistance; others are brand new to the struggle and just waking up. As my friend and colleague Dr. Prabhjot Singh put it truthfully and wryly: "I (and my fellow Sikhs) have been in the tundra for a long time; now I just have more company."

There are the million-plus women and men, young and old, who marched globally during the Women's March on Washington wearing pink pussy hats that communicated a resounding message: "Peace is loud!" There was International Women's Day, variously celebrated with a work stoppage by women as well as additional marches. Almost a thousand churches, synagogues, and mosques, as well as mayors and regular citizens, have organized sanctuary spaces. Rabbis across the country gathered to protest the Muslim ban, and Muslims reached out with financial support as allies to Jews as cemeteries were desecrated or faced bomb threats. Although the official Standing Rock protest was defeated and its encampment destroyed, its supporters took their voices and feet to Washington, DC, to fight on. Beyond these specific examples, it may also be that Americans as a whole are becoming more inclusive and compassionate. A poll released by the Public Religion Research Institute on attitudes toward transgender Americans, religious liberty, and perceptions of discrimination facing Muslims and immigrants suggests that "in every instance, it shows that the majority of Americans are increasingly welcoming of the rich diversity that makes America great." As the Reverend Paul Raushenbush writes on Auburn Theological Seminary's blog, the efforts exerted by regressive forces "on issues of immigration, LGBT rights, women's rights and racism do not reflect the growing consensus about the just and inclusive America that the majority is dreaming of."

People are learning the lesson of the prophetic "we" embodied by Shadrach, Meshach, and Abednego's concerted action: the strength that comes from going into the fiery furnace together. This is also the lesson of the biblical heroine Esther, who stood up to Haman and saved her people, for she had been born to take action precisely for "such a time as this." People are learning what Valarie Kaur's grandfather taught her from the Sikh tradition, words to which she returns when the going gets rough: "The hot winds cannot harm me; I am sheltered by the divine." And following the words of Jesus himself: "Whatever you do to the least of these, you do to me."

Reverend Dr. Barber, like other modern-day prophets and citizen activists, provides a vision for this world that is "groaning in travail," an alternative moral vision to decry the cruelty of this moment. The kind of dreaming backwards offered by the current administration requires a powerful counter effort to dream forward toward a future of an inclusive America that honors and acts on the dignity and difference of all people and offers a homeland where "none shall make them afraid." This moral vision offers a healing antidote to the often soulless, one-dimensional, and transactional world of progressive politics. Ours is an inclusive vision for 2050, when America will be a minority-majority country, as we give birth to a new world whose contours we are only beginning to see.

The traditions of those who are part of the multifaith movement for justice offer inspiration in the form of countless stories of those who stood up against all odds to create a more humane, loving, and just reality, bringing their stones, large and small, to the pile. Our spiritual traditions offer language that can inspire hope, frame public issues in fresh new ways, and nourish future generations.

People of faith and moral courage are upstanders in the struggle for justice over the long haul, beyond any election season. Nothing is lost. The spirit and wisdom of past liberation struggles—involving civil rights, anti-apartheid efforts, feminism, HIV/AIDS, economic justice, sanctuary—continue to influence and inspire this moment, as do more current endeavors around the Movement for Black Lives and Occupy.

There are those who are hungry for a word of hope, and Reverend Dr. Barber brought a unique prophetic vision of an inclusive America on Watch Night, just as he did at the 2016 Democratic National Convention when he asked the crowd: "Is there a heart in the house? Is there a heart in America? Is there a heart for the poor? Then, stand up. Vote together. Organize together. Fight for the heart of this nation." And so we shall.

THE REVEREND DR. KATHARINE RHODES HENDERSON is president of Auburn Seminary. Author of *God's Troublemakers: How Women of Faith*

Are Changing the World (2006), Henderson is an internationally known speaker and has been featured in the *Washington Post*, the *New York Times*, and *USA Today* and on MSNBC, NPR, and elsewhere. Henderson is currently writing her second book, on how modern-day prophets are shaping a just America.

CHAPTER THIRTEEN

THE NEED TO KNOW WHO WE ARE IN TIMES LIKE THESE

JANUARY 13, 2017

Washington Hebrew Congregation, Washington, DC,
in Celebration of Martin Luther King Jr. Day

THE REVEREND DR. WILLIAM J. BARBER II

Gracious God who holds us, helps us, sustains us, once again surprise us and allow a flawed, weak, and failing part of your creation, lips of clay with lips of clay, to somehow, by your grace, speak words of life. Amen. Shalom. As-salamu alaykum.

There are two passages of scripture I want to read tonight. The first is in the Torah, Numbers 13, but I want to read it in the Message translation of the Bible since my Hebrew is not quite up to par.

"When Moses sent them off to scout out Canaan, he said go up through the Negev and then into the hill country, look the land over and see what it is like. Assess the people. Are they strong or weak? Are they few or many?"

And verse 27 says,

"We went to the land to which you sent us and oh my, it flows with milk and honey, just look at this fruit. The only thing is that the people who live there are fierce. Their cities are huge, and their towers are well fortified. And worse yet we saw descendants of the giant Anach. Amalekites are spread out over there, the Hittites, the Jebusites, the Amorites, they all hold the high country. And the Canaanites are established on the Mediterranean Sea and along the Jordan."

Now Caleb interrupted and called for silence before Moses and said, "Let us go up and take the land now. We can do it." But the others said, "We can't attack those people, because they're stronger than we are. They spread scary rumors with their tweets; I mean they spread scary rumors among the people of Israel." They said, "We scouted out the land from one end to the other. It's a land that swallows people whole. Everybody we saw was huge. Why, we even saw the Nephilim giants; the Anach giants come from Nephilim. Alongside them we felt like grasshoppers, and they looked down on us as if we were grasshoppers."

The second passage comes from Hebrews, in the New Testament, chapter 10, verse 38: "Now, the just shall live by faith, but if any man draw back, my soul shall have no pleasure in him. But we are not of those who draw back unto destruction, but we are those who persevere unto the salvation of the soul. Now faith is the substance of things hoped for, and the evidence of things not seen."

Tonight, I want to have a conversation with you about the need to know who we are in times like these. Coming here tonight in this historical moment where political strongmen all over the world, even here in the United States, are parading and boasting and bullying around, I felt a Holy Spirit draw me to these two texts, one from the Torah and one from the New Testament.

In the first, the people of Israel are on the edge of the Promised Land after having lived through four hundred years of slavery, after Pharaoh's reign and after the Red Sea. The prophet Moses sends twelve into the land to investigate what God had promised them. And oh, what a land full of possibility, pregnant with plenty for all. So, the twelve spies come back and say, "Let's go in and possess that which the Lord has shown us." But ten said, "That's not all that's in the land. There's some giants there. There's some problems there. There's some big ones there. There's some strongmen in the land." And in their mind, they say, "These strongmen, you know they live in these towers. High, fortified walls. They live in these towers. They live in walled communities.

They've got all these generals around them. They look invincible. And they've surrounded themselves with the military."

Now we may have gone in as men of Israel, but when we saw their walls, towers, fortifications, raw power, ruthlessness, and their willingness to do anything to hold onto power, we saw ourselves as grasshoppers. Only two, Caleb and Joshua, dared to register a minority report. They dared to remember what God had already brought them through, the strongmen that God had already overcome, and the walls that God had already taken them through. Only Caleb and Joshua, especially Caleb, remembered who his people were in these tense times and said, "Let's go in! We can possess the land."

Now the second text is Paul, a Jewish son now an apostle of Jesus Christ, and he's writing to the Hebrew church that's under pressure from Caesar and Herod, the Roman strongmen of his day. He writes to people whose very presence challenges the meanness and might of Rome and the strongmen of the first century AD. He writes to a people who believe in love and justice and mercy and compassion, and who find themselves about to succumb to the pressures around them, about to turn back. And Paul writes to them and says, "Wait a minute. We are not of them who shrink back unto destruction, but we are them who persevere until the salvation of the soul, and now faith is the substance of things hopeful."

And then Paul reaches back to the Old Testament heroes of the faith and he begins to call the roll. We call it the hallmark. He says not to forget who you come from—by faith Abraham, by faith Isaac, by faith Jacob, by faith Joseph, by faith Moses, who when he was born was hidden for three months by his parents because they saw he was a proper child and they were not afraid of the king's commandment. By faith Moses, who when he had come to years, refused to be called the son of Pharaoh's daughter. By faith he chose to suffer affliction with the people of God rather than enjoy the pleasures of sin. For season by faith, you know who you come from? You come from people like Gideon and Barack and Samson and Jephthah and Rahab and David and Samuel. Through faith, they subdued kingdoms and brought righteousness and obtained promises and stopped the mouths of lions. By faith they quenched the violence of fire and escaped the edge of the sword. Out of their weakness they were made strong, waxed valiant in the fight, and turned to fight the armies of the alien. By faith, women received their dead raised to life again. Others were tortured, not accepting deliverance, that they might obtain a better resurrection. By faith others had trials of cruel mockings and scourgings, moreover of bonds and imprisonment. By faith they were stones, they were sown asunder. They were tempted. They were slain with the sword. They wandered the valley in goatskins and sheepskins destitute, afflicted, and tormented. Of whom the world is not worthy, you know who you are, then you will not shrink back unto destruction. Paul knew that when you know who you are, despite how the times try to change you, you remain who you are.

Now I want to raise these texts tonight, because properly defining oneself and one's nature and one's calling is a critical, philosophical, theological discipline that has penetrating and practical implications; particularly when one is in crisis, facing seasons of challenge or confronting threats which seek to take your identity or redefine who you are. Knowing who you are is critical to your sanity and your abilities to sustain a fight back when you are facing what theologian Paul Tillich called "the very threat of non-being" and "nonexistence" in his book *The Courage to Be.* This is how our slave foreparents made it through slavery. Oh, yes, they were called everything but children of God by the oppressive slave masters and the system of slavery, but somehow, deep down in their spiritual DNA, they were still able to sing, "Before I be a slave, I'll be buried in my grave and I'll go home to my Lord and I'll be free." They knew they were not slaves no matter what title the world put on them. They knew they were not cattle or chattel. They knew they were creations of God, and therefore, because they knew who they were, they did not have to accept the definition of those who sought to oppress them.

Now to be sure, my brothers and sisters, we've always had to fight to maintain a proper sense of self, because America has always struggled with knowing who she is. America has had a kind of split personality, at times a political and social schizophrenia, a great gulf between what she dreams to be and what she is in reality. If you are crazy, America will run you crazier. Have y'all heard the second verse of that song? "America, America, God mend thine every flaw." America has defined herself as we the people, a nation whose noble statement of identity says, "We know these truths to be self-evident, that all persons are created equal, endowed by their Creator with certain unalienable rights, among which are life, liberty, and the pursuit of happiness." America has said that establishment of justice is the first principle of our nation, and yet Dr. King critiqued this nation he loved so much and said in his speech "Where Do We Go from Here?," at the eleventh annual Southern Christian Leadership Conference convention in Atlanta, "Let us be dissatisfied until America will no longer have a high blood pressure of creeds and an anemia of deeds." "America never was America to me," Langston Hughes wrote. "And yet I swear this oath—America will be!"

America, yes there has been progress, even an African American president named Barack Hussein Obama, whose father was a black man from Kenya and whose mother was a white woman from Kansas. He was not the Wizard of Oz. He was the president of these United States. But even at his farewell speech, he had to note that America still struggles with her anemic, schizophrenic condition. Her defining documents say one thing, but we still see misery, inequality, death, systemic racism, and injustice that undercuts our moral character and treats so many in ungodly ways. So, we have a nation that is great but yet has great struggles, with what she says she is in words too often juxtaposed with what she is in action. For those of us who want so much for her to live out the true meanings of her creed, to move this nation closer to where her words and deeds match, we must know who we are and who we're called to be—because crazy can't help crazy.

We who have great hopes for this nation cannot afford to be schizo-phrenic in knowing who we are and in knowing the calling to justice which defines us. And that's what made Martin Luther King so pow-erful. He wasn't perfect. He had his flaws and struggles. He was barely twenty-six when the zeitgeist tracked him down in Montgomery because of the actions of a shero named Rosa who knew who she was, who knew she was more than only a seamstress and more than a back-of-the-bus rider. He was just thirty-nine when he was murdered. He was young, but he was so clear about who he was and who his people were. It wasn't al-ways so. Don't think that somehow Martin Luther King came out of the womb as he was. He didn't go to Montgomery to stay. His plan was to go down to Montgomery and pastor an uppity church where some of the folk taught over at Alabama State, staying just five years before com-ing back to Atlanta to teach at Morehouse College. He could've gone to any church in the North, where pulpits much bigger than Dexter Avenue had called him. But he returned to the South.

Then, one night, after a vicious phone call threatened to kill him, his wife, and his baby, King got up, prayed, and asked God to release him. He didn't always know who he was. God, you better get me out of this. He was troubled by fear and trepidation. He said in his own words he was "ready to give up." And then he heard God. He'd heard his daddy talk about a personal God. But then he met God for himself, not inside of a synagogue, not inside of a church, not inside of a march but over a cup of coffee with his mind pulling him this way and that way, teeter-ing between two opinions. He heard God say, "Martin, let me tell you who you are. Stand up for freedom. Stand up for justice and I'll be with you." And this defining moment was the source of his determination. It told him who he was.

When the people of Israel faced all of the trouble in the Promised Land, Caleb told them who they were. And when the Hebrew people wanted to turn back, Paul told them who they were. These texts were among some of King's most favored. Sometimes when a house would be bombed and people would be worried, he would say, "We are not of those who shrink back unto destruction." These are texts that reminded him that we must maintain a sense of who we are and ask God to keep us. And it's important for us to do that now because we have messed up the memory of Dr. King. Oh God, corporations sponsor free breakfasts in his honor and people come to the King celebration that he wouldn't even attend if he was alive. Martin was not some easygoing human-relations specialist. He was a determined prophet, defined by God to fight against the forces of destruction for the soul of this nation.

We who dare to own King's name are called to challenge economic injustice and poverty. In a sermon in 1956 called "Paul's Letter to American Christians," King preached about the danger that America will misuse capitalism. He writes, "I still contend that money can be the root of all evil. It can cause one to live a life of gross materialism." This is seven years before the march on Washington. Those who say Martin Luther King didn't deal with economics until 196-whatever need to hush and read. In that sermon at Dexter, he talked about how the 1 percent was ruling over the 99 percent. This was fifty years before Occupy. He talked about how bad it is when 1 percent of the population controls 40 percent of the wealth. And he said, "America, if you keep claiming to be a nation of faith, you have to solve this problem." And then, eleven years later, 1967, in his last speech before the Southern Christian Leadership Conference convention, he said, if our nation can spend millions on fighting unjust wars and billions to put a man on the moon, "our nation can spend billions of dollars to put God's children on their own two feet right here on earth." That's Dr. King. And then he said, "Let us be dissatisfied until the tragic walls that separate the outer city of wealth and comfort and the inner city of poverty and despair shall be crushed." And, then, two weeks before he was killed, he said, "America may very well go to hell." That's Dr. King. I thought I wouldn't get too many amens on that, 'cause he said America may well go to hell if she does not deal with the issue of child poverty, adult poverty, and economic and racial injustice. In fact, it's actually wrong to just talk about "I Have a Dream" because what most folk don't know is that's the hoop.

Black preachers know what I'm talking about. "I Have a Dream" is the closing. King had preached the first seventeen minutes about the nightmare that, one hundred years after abolition, the Negro is still not free. He hadn't planned to close with the dream, but gospel singer Mahalia Jackson was there, and she knew you can't leave them there. In fact, I heard that even said advisors told Dr. King, "Don't you go out there preaching like this in front of all these people. You be more professorial; don't you close with that 'I have a dream' like you did in Rocky Mountain, North Carolina, and Detroit, Michigan." But Mahalia Jackson heard him and she said, "Doc, tell 'em about the dream!"

And I'm telling you, Dr. King would say to us today, "We are called." Touch your neighbor and say, "We are called to address economic injustice and poverty." We are only eight years from the greatest recession since the Great Depression, or I should say we're only eight years from when America decided to acknowledge the Great Recession—a whole lot of people had been in recession thirty years before America decided to acknowledge it. Indeed, many people have been in a permanent recession. We have fourteen million poor children in this country. One hundred fifty years after the signing of the Thirteenth Amendment ending slavery, people are still enslaved by poverty. More than two hundred fifty thousand people die every year from poverty—more people die from poverty than die from heart attacks and strokes and cancer. We see a presidential cabinet of billionaires and a mean-spirited Congress where one man named Paul Ryan has even said that feeding a hungry child a free lunch robs them of their soul. And they want to deny raising the minimum wage yet give corporate welfare and tax cuts to the greedy.

Now, with the free health care that they get only because the people elected them, they want to repeal health care for the very people that elected them. What kind of morality is that? They refused to expand Medicaid in twenty-two states—most of them in the South—simply because they didn't like a black man in the White House, continuing to pit poor white and black people against each other. Since June 2013, eight million people a year have gone without Medicaid expansion, according to the *New York Times*. This means that about forty thousand people a year have died. And they didn't die because God called them home. They didn't die because it was their time. In fact, a group of preachers, imams, and rabbis in North Carolina declared a couple years ago that if anybody in our synagogue, church, or mosque died because of a lack of health care, we were not going to lie and say God called them home. We were going to call the media in, just like Emmett Till's mama did, open the casket, and say, "That's what happens when governments and legislatures do not care about the people."

You see, my friends, Dr. King would dare us to tell the truth. Truth is, America is a welfare nation. It was free labor in slavery that built this nation, created its economy, and made it prosperous. America took this welfare. You want to talk about welfare? It was the former slave owners that were the first ones to receive welfare. After the Civil War, they wanted help from the federal government, even though they had violated the Constitution. But they wanted help. They didn't want to give the former slaves forty acres and a mule. You talk about welfare. When Franklin Delano Roosevelt's Aid to Dependent Children was first developed, black women couldn't get it. People in agrarian and domestic service couldn't get it. In fact, 50 percent of white women couldn't get it. Same thing with Social Security. Assistance in public housing was first given to white people. And it's still true today that there are more white people on food stamps than Latinos and African Americans. But the real issue is not who gets welfare in the first place. The issue is why, in the wealthiest nation in the world, people still need it.

People are hungry, homeless, out of work, and out of doors, and in this context if folk need it, what is wrong with welfare? It's in the Constitution. It says, "Promote the general welfare." What's wrong with less than a penny out of every federal dollar going to help people have food, school, and heat? We give corporate welfare to banks when they mess up! We give them our money to play schemes. We give welfare to corporations that on a percentage basis pay less in taxes than secretaries and janitors who work for them. I remember that when Mitt Romney was running for president he said corporations were people. Well, I thought people were people. Rather than treating a corporation like a person, why don't we treat people like people? What's wrong with welfare? In fact, and some of the great theologians in this pulpit may correct me, but the God I serve is pro welfare. The God I serve is pro helping people. Somewhere I read that Jesus had compassion for folk and that he fed five thousand. Somewhere I read Jesus set up free health clinics everywhere he went. He gave universal health care all over Israel and never charged a leper a copay. Somewhere I read in the Old Testament that God would send cornbread and barbecue quail to the refugees that were coming out of Egypt. Somewhere I read in Isaiah that God said, "Woe unto those that make unjust laws that rob the poor of their rights and make women and children their prey." I heard Jesus in his last sermon— he was kind of paraphrasing, he was riffing like the rappers, he was sampling from the Old Testament—he said, "When I was hungry, did you feed me? When I was naked, did you clothe me?" He was pulling that out of Deuteronomy.

And we must know that we are called. Dr. King wanted us to know that. We, not somebody else. We who are alive are called to address the issue of poverty. And the truth of the matter is, my brothers and sisters, we keep committing attention violence against the poor. Politicians talk about the rich and the middle class but will not say the word "poor." How can you not say the word poor? Forty million to one hundred forty million people are struggling through poverty, depending on how you measure it, and most of them are children. How can you not at least say the word poor? Poor. For the poor, we must have investment in the most hurting communities, and infrastructure development, education equality, living wages, and health care. For the poor, we must have a green economy. For the poor, we must move away from militarism so we can have a real war on poverty that we fight until it's over, because the war on poverty was the shortest war we ever fought. We left the field. We must decide it's a crime that poverty exists, not that the poor are criminals. Poor. Can't we say the word poor? Poor. Poor. Poor.

The second thing we must know is that here in the twenty-first century, racism and economic fear still too often conjure a powerful magic, which compels this nation to seek safety in hating the other and security in the false nativism that has failed us before and will fail us again. We are called. Dr. King is not getting out of the grave. I'm not being funny here. I'm being real serious. We can't have more commemoration services to just talk about what he did. We are called to address racism. Because, my brothers and sisters, long before any Russian computer hack, the American electoral process was compromised by racism and fear. The Southern Strategy's divide-and-conquer tactics touched something deep in our DNA, a fundamental fear—racism—that is ever seeking to come forth and masquerade as normal. When we right now are on the verge of appointing an attorney general who has a contempt for the Fourteenth Amendment, the Fifteenth Amendment, and the Voting Rights Act he will be required to enforce, we are called to address racism.

Racism is not just "I don't like them because they're black." I mean, that's the kind of racism of David Duke and the Klan. But systemic racism is when one of the most underreported stories of 2016 is that in America, during the first federal election in fifty years without the full protection of the Voting Rights Act, we had twenty-five debates during the presidential primaries and general election and neither party dealt with voting rights. I'm walking in the tradition of Dr. King now, so you know I have to criticize both parties. We didn't have one hour on voting rights. We didn't have one hour on poverty. Not one hour on how many people would really be impacted with the removal of health care. Fourteen states had new voting restrictions in place for the first time in 2016, adding to the other twenty-some states that had put others in place.

Nell Painter, professor emeritus of American History at Princeton, wrote an article in the *New York Times* before the election, and said of Trump, "Here is the iconography of a tragic, traditionally American call and response. The call: a challenge to the status quo of white people on top. The response: outbreaks of meanness. . . . Trump is so obviously unsuited for the job of president of the United States, but he is suited to answer this call [of reclamation]."

Jamelle Bouie told us in *Slate* how Trump was elected: "It's not just anger over jobs and immigration. White voters, many of them that voted for him, hoped that Trump would restore the racial hierarchy upended by Obama." He writes, "Obama's election was about change, but for a lot of people the change felt like inversion of the hierarchy. And when you couple that with broad decline in incomes and living standards caused by the Great Recession, it seemed to signal the end of a hierarchy that has always placed certain folk on top." And Robin DiAngelo, a professor of multicultural education, described the phenomenon [in an essay] as white fragility, "a state in which even a minimum amount of racial stress becomes intolerable, triggering a range of defensive moves." As a result, she writes, "The reactionary wave that swept across America in November is not an anomaly in our history. It is instead an all-too-familiar pattern in the long struggle for American reconstruction." Anybody who watched and saw that red band running from North Carolina all the way across into some of the Rust Belt places needs to know something about the deconstruction of Reconstruction in the 1800s, the Mississippi Plan, the Rutherford B. Hayes Compromise. You have to know something about when Woodrow Wilson, long before Stephen Bannon was in the White House, screened *The Birth of a Nation* in the White House in 1915 to signal the end of Reconstruction. You have to know something about how, in 1883, the Civil Rights Act of 1875 was replaced by a Supreme Court that came about because of the deconstruction of Reconstruction. And that's why at the March on Washington, Dr. King said, "One hundred years later." He was being sadly sarcastic. He was saying, "I thought we dealt with this in 1875, and here we are still dealing with it in 1963."

You can't understand what's going on without going back and looking at how when President Harry Truman embraced the civil rights movement, southern Democrats formed their own segregationist states' rights Dixie Party in 1948. And when *Brown v. Board of Education* was decided, in 1954, there was a reaction to that. The first riots broke out in Boston, not in the South. Then there was the killing of Emmett Till. And then you saw the Second Reconstruction of the Civil Rights Act, the Voting Rights Act, the Fair Housing Act, the War on Poverty, and Medicare and Medicaid. But then there was a backlash as soon as African Americans and brown people began to receive the benefits that others had already received. As activist and writer Tim Wise said, "These programs were racialized." So, Richard Nixon runs the "law and order" campaign of 1968, which was an intentional effort to manufacture a solid South by appealing to racial hate and fear without using racial language. His adviser Kevin Phillips described the Southern Strategy: "We can win if we can find a way to make people as mad as George Wallace makes them without the same language. So we won't use the n-word anymore, we'll use words like tax cuts and entitlement reform and law and order."

And that's what's been used, funded by oligarchs who use this division to elect candidates who will embrace the false notion of "trickle-down economics" underneath their race-card politics, lining the pockets of the wealthy by fooling working-class white people into thinking that their real enemy is black people and brown people. But when you're poor and you can't pay your light bills, we're all black in the dark.

So, in this moment, part of what we have to do, rabbis, is help America face these questions: What is it that causes many poor whites—the 2017 census reports there are nearly eighteen million whites that are poor, eight million more poor whites than black, and five million more than Latinos—to vote against the very programs that they need? What makes poor whites vote for a candidate who promises them they'll be against the LGBT community, against abortion, and for prayer in the schools, but then they don't read further and see that those same candidates are against living wages and health care? What myth will make you vote for somebody who's going to take your health care? Two-thirds of the people who are losing their health care are poor white people—some of the very people that voted for Trump. What myth makes somebody think that allowing your schools to be resegregated is somehow going to help your children? What myth makes you think that privatizing schools with public money is the way to go when your poor, white child still can't go anyway? What makes somebody say Black Lives Matter is extreme when a jury in Charleston, South Carolina, can't convict a police officer who they watched shoot a black man in the back? I mean, what myth is so powerful that it keeps working-class, poor white people from building a multiracial coalition together? The truth is, if we registered 30 percent of the unregistered African Americans in the South, and they connected with working-class and poor white people and working-class and poor Latinos, we could change the South. And if you change the South, you change the nation. What myth makes Republicans and Democrats not want to talk about race?

In fact, I want you to get to my friend Senator Bernie Sanders and tell him it's not going to work to just talk about economics and not talk about race. Because in America you can't talk about race without talking about economics, and you can't talk about economics without talking about race. It's a mistake to ask how we are going to reach working-class white people. No, the question is how we are going to reach everybody—white, black, and Latino. And if you do not deal with the idolatry of race in America and how it connects to everything else that we deal with, then we cannot have the kind of radical revolution of values that Dr. King talked about. But Dr. King said there are three things you have to address simultaneously: racism, classism, and militarism. And you can't ever unhook that unholy trinity. A grown-up conversation about race is the only hope for this democracy. It's one that we must lead. What trumps common sense? Racism is a mythology. It is a mythology so powerful that it causes people who need each other to allow certain people to divide them with fear and othering.

During the Watch Night service on January 1, 2017, we announced three things. We called for all moral people to stand up. We said that we will conduct a race, poverty, and class audit of the last fifty years. And we said that we believe it's time for a national Moral Revival, a Poor

People's Campaign all over this country and in the nation's capital to change the narrative and force this country to deal with the issue of race and poverty. That is the only way. Dr. King said it's the only thing—when you can get poor blacks and whites and others to come together. And we must speak truth as to who we are, because an entire web of money and influence has been working to tie up the American democracy. Even as the divide between the rich and the poor is the widest in our nation's history, our electorate is growing more diverse. Wealthy oligarchs know that they cannot hold onto power in truly democratic elections, so we are witnessing an all-out assault, foreign and domestic. That's why I want us to pray for Congressman John Lewis, because he dared to question the legitimacy of this election. And there are gonna be a lot of folk that are going to jump all over him and say, "John, you just need to be nice and go along to get along." But John didn't get his head beat down on that Edmund Pettus Bridge to be nice and get along. There comes a time you have to tell the truth. There comes a time when being silent is actually a betrayal of all that you claim you believe.

My friends, this moment is not simply about the preservation of a government conceived by human beings. Because when immigrant communities face harassment, exploitation at work, and the threat of mass deportation; when our Muslim and refugee sisters and brothers hear serious discussions about registration systems that remind us of the papers that black people were required to have during slavery; when we hear there are efforts every day trying to pit the Jewish child against the Palestinian child and the Palestinian child against the Jewish child, we know we must work to make this moment fundamentally about the well-being of creation itself and the survival of those creatures who bear God's image. Us.

And so, in this moment, it's about whether we as a people can reconstruct the heart of our democracy. We, right now, are being called to speak with and for the weak and the voiceless. In 1967, in "The Trumpet of Conscience," Dr. King said, "The dispossessed of this nation—the poor, both white and Negro—live in a cruelly unjust society. They must organize a revolution against the injustice, not against the lives of their fellow citizens, but against the structures through which the society is refusing to take means which have been called for, and which are at hand, to lift the load of oppression and poverty." This was the voice of our hero in the last year of his life. This was his revolutionary spirit moving on behalf of the poor and on behalf of the nation. And this, my friends, is our calling.

We must know who we are in times like these. We must raise our voices. We must use our feet to march for justice and shape the conscience of our state. We must use our hand to mark the ballot. I have a sneaking suspicion that we are going to have to do some civil disobedience inside the US Capitol. It can no longer be seen as off limits to the legitimate discontent of the people of this nation. We must use our pulpits to sound the alarm. We must turn loose our lawyers to fight in the courts. And we the faithful must be reminded that we are not called to be the servants of the state but the conscience of the state. We are called to be the moral guardians of communities. And in times like these we must remember that we are called to a prophetic witness. Our challenge is to know that this popular, private, soul-saving, society-ducking, afraid-to-take-a-stand, chickenhearted, for-me-only promulgation of the faith is not faith at all. God demands that we stand for justice. God demands by the Spirit that we care for the brokenhearted, the captive, the blind, and the unaccepted.

The Torah tells us that we are not grasshoppers. The Bible tells us that we are not supposed to turn back and give in to destruction. We are not supposed to give in to destructive politicians, to destructive economics, or to destructive injustices. They cannot have the last word on our watch. No, we are called by our faith to push forward and persevere unto the saving of the soul, unto the saving of this nation, unto the saving of our communities, unto the saving of our children, and unto the saving of our integrity. Our faith is an action faith. Faith is the substance of things hoped for and the evidence of things not seen. By faith in God we have the courage to be. By faith we go from strength to strength. By faith, plans to kill us make us alive. By faith, we go through trouble and never let trouble overwhelm us. By faith, we never give up believing. By faith, we never let sorrow immobilize us. We never let pain invalidate us. We never let challenges turn us. We never let danger defeat us. By faith in the face of frontal attacks on our rights, we are called to change situations and not simply to accept them. We are called to stand up and not to bow down. By faith in God, difficulties lead to deliverance, and challenges lead to celebration, and handicapped people participate in holy miracles, because faith in God is more powerful than any concern, more powerful than any foe, more powerful than any problem.

Yes, these are tough times. The mean and the greedy are cocky on every side. They want us to have pity on billionaires and inflict more pain on the poor. We have more knowledge and more technology, more information available to do justice and love mercy than ever before, and at the same time we have more resistance to right than we've ever seen. Never before in recent history have we seen so much money being spent in resistance to the cause of equality. The money being spent to go backwards is lewd, it is pornographic, it's blatant, and it's arrogant.

Yes, these are troubling times, but by faith we don't give in to evil. Faith stands up to Pharaoh. Faith speaks truth to power. I wish I had a witness here. Faith takes on the giants. Faith refuses to accept sinister situations. Faith refuses to be a slave to other folks' oppression. Faith refuses to be chattel property of injustice. Faith and moving forward is the only way to save our souls and the soul of this nation. Faith is knowing that when God helps you, there is no challenge that can't be met. There's no mountain that can't be climbed. There's no valley that can't be crossed. There's no enemy that can't be defeated. There's no darkness that can't be overcome. There's no pressure that can't be pushed through. There's no political power that can't be overturned. There's no challenge that can't be survived. There's no war of the spirit that can't be subdued. Faith.

My God, I feel something right now. Seems like I hear the Mississippi Mass Choir singing "Hold on to Your Faith": "The things we have to suffer bring tears to our eyes, yet we're holding onto our faith. Satan is busy stirring up the wrath, gathering stones to block my path. Our enemies inflicting all the hurt they can by throwing their rocks and hiding their hand. You dig one ditch, you better dig two, for the trap you set for me just might be for you. God put it in our heart and you can't take it. Our souls on fire and your word can't harm it. We're working, we're toiling, we're hoping, we're praying, we're waiting, we're watching, we're fasting, we're believing, we're marching, and we're holding on to our faith."

We must hold on. Too many challenges abound. Hold on. Too many injustices are real. Hold on. Too much inequality exists. Hold on. We are not those who shrink back unto destruction. We must persevere. We must hold on to our faith and declare before God and this nation called America, when it comes to our rights ordained by God and guaranteed by the Constitution, we will never lose faith. We will never, never, never turn back. One election can't turn us back. A loudmouth can't turn us back. George Wallace couldn't turn us back. Bull Connor didn't turn us back. Our faith might get bruised and battered. Our hope for this nation to live out what it's said it's gonna be might get challenged. We might get discouraged, but we'll never lose faith.

If I was home in my little country church I'd say we may endure for a night but joy will still come in the morning. We might have some dark Fridays of crucifixion, socially and politically. But if we don't lose our faith, dark Fridays turn into Resurrection Sunday mornings. We shall overcome. We shall survive. Justice will win. Truth will live. The lion will lie down with the lamb. Crooked places will be straightened out. Rough places will be made smooth. God's glory and God's power will be seen. Sounds like I hear the Lord saying, "Stand up and be counted."

Modern-day racists must not know who we are. The Tea Party must not know who we are. We are the sons and daughters of Martin. We are the sons and daughters of Rabbi Heschel. We are the sons and daughters of Rosa Parks, Dorothy Day, Harriet Tubman, Frederick Douglass, and William Lloyd Garrison. We are the sons and daughters of

Abraham and Sarah and Muhammad and Moses and Jesus and Mary. We were born for right now, and we who believe in freedom will not rest. By faith we've already made it through four hundred years of slavery. By faith we've already made it through Jim Crow. By faith we've already made it through the Holocaust. By faith we've already seen our leader assassinated, but instead of killing the dream they killed the dreamer. The dream still lives on. We ought to sing that song that Dr. King sang and quoted at the end of the march from Selma to Montgomery: "Mine eyes have seen the glory of the coming of the Lord. He is trampling out the vengeance where the grapes of wrath are stored. He hath loosed the fateful lightning of His terrible sword. His truth is marching on. He has sounded forth the trumpet that shall never sound retreat. He is sifting out the hearts of men before His judgment seat. Oh, be swift, my soul, to answer Him. Be jubilant my feet. Our God is marching on. Glory, Glory, Hallelujah."

Glory. Let's march together, glory. Let's stand together, glory. Let's save the soul of America, glory. Glory, glory, glory, glory, glory, glory, glory, hallelujah. His truth.

LYRICAL CONNECTIONS: THE MUSIC AND MESSAGE OF THE MOVEMENT

YARA ALLEN

Director of Cultural Arts, Repairers of the Breach;
Movement Song Leader and Theomusicologist

I heard Mahalia Jackson's voice early in life. I was around five or six, and my parents played her vinyl recordings on our record player. I knew her voice before I knew her name. My paternal grandmother hummed her songs as she dusted the furniture in her home. By the time I was old enough to understand who she was, she was gone. I learned her story over the years and came to appreciate her personal struggles, sacrifices, and contributions.

Filling the role as song leader in the Forward Together Moral Movement, as I often do, I see this amazing woman and her importance through a more personal lens. I understand the gravity of her role when I'm called on to feel the weight of the moment and move it with song. I hear her music with a new, personal interpretation and connect with this portion of Reverend Dr. Barber's sermon by referring to my own experiences. As he prepares to speak and I am called on to sing, I get that it's not mere formality, but a clearing of a channel to assist him in moving in the fullness of his prophetic gifts. I thoroughly understand that it is a role of support on the most spiritual level. Appropriately so, before I sing, I invite the ancestors to hold the notes, lyrics, and spirit with which the song is delivered and I trust that Mother Mahalia is leading the way.

In Reverend Dr. Barber's sermon "The Need to Know Who We Are in Times Like These," I understand Mahalia's call to Dr. King to "Tell them about the dream!" She knew the messenger, she knew the message, she understood the dream, and she was aware of the spirit of that moment. Preachers often sing their sermons, especially in the African American church, and Dr. King mastered this technique, as does Reverend Dr. Barber with his melodic delivery often rolling into a powerful call-and-response refrain. During the "I Have a Dream" speech in Washington, DC, Mahalia understood Dr. King's need to sing and the people's need to hear his song in such a pivotal moment. It's a connection that I believe to be imperative between messenger and minstrel.

Because of personal encounters with racism early in life, I was seared with a resolve to fight injustice. As time progressed, I gravitated toward the arts, but I could not shake the need to fight, so I wrote poetry that channeled my righteous anger into the arts. I became active in the community by writing plays, presenting poetry, speaking publicly, and singing. As I became more aware of the issues that threatened the well-being of North Carolinians, I immersed myself in social justice work. I connected with a North Carolina–based organization, Black Workers for Justice, and began singing in a cultural ensemble that carried the message of truth and justice. This work moved me into a position with the Center for Community Change, which gave me the opportunity to engage in community building in eastern North Carolina. During this time, I also helped to mentor teens who were preparing to step into life as independent young adults.

I had been following the annual Moral March and HKonJ People's Assemblies under the leadership of Reverend Dr. Barber since its second year. The message of the movement resonated strongly with my experiences and my desire to engage in social justice with a deeper level of commitment. After a few years, I was asked, along with my sister Sauuda Eshe, to sing for the annual people's assembly, and every year since we have helped to lift the music. Along the way, we have collaborated with other justice-loving singers and musicians. Eventually, I began working with the North Carolina NAACP as field secretary for the eastern North Carolina branches and cultural arts convener. My work in eastern North Carolina took me back to many of the same counties and communities that I organized in while employed with Center for Community Change. The work was intense but so were the challenges that we faced. I am currently with Repairers of the Breach, still organizing, teaching the history and importance of music in a moral, fusion movement, throwing my "life against the system" (as described by Bernice Reagon) and still hoping that, someday, there will be enough hands on the arc bending it toward justice that injustice will simply surrender!

Traveling with Reverend Dr. Barber has been surreal, grounding, eye-opening, and affirming. In 2014, I was called on to travel by plane with him to Washington, DC. I had an extreme phobia of flying. On the day of our departure, he was reassuring but firm as we approached the plane via the corridor. I cried, shook uncontrollably, and even stopped several times along the way. Tears streamed down my cheeks onto the carpet and I heard Reverend Barber behind me saying, "Yara, you can cry, you can shake, you can sing, but you have to keep moving! We have work to do! You have work to do, and you can't do it without flying." He was both tough and understanding, reassuring me that it would be all right. He offered support all the way and, eventually, we boarded. As we flew, I felt the fear melt away from my bones. I knew it was time to work and that this was the release that my spirit needed to fulfill what I was meant to do. Since then, I've traveled the country with Reverend Barber, teaching, singing, and organizing.

Music is as important to current movements as it was in past movements. Not only does music help to regulate the pulse of our moral outcry, but it provides the family of movement builders a space to create, to bond, to be inspired, encouraged, and comforted. It offers a space for celebration and contemplation. In current movements, we still follow the time-tested tradition of strategizing, protesting, civil disobedience, and post-release community gathering. In each of these phases of moral outcry, music is implemented for various purposes and outcomes. Music, then and now, offers encouragement, focus, support, comfort, expression of celebration, consolation for disappointment, and resolve. We must never forsake the songs of our ancestors because their spirits reside within those familiar tunes that escorted our grandparents through troubled waters with an undying hope for change. In a metaphorical sense, many of these tunes are covered with the blood of those who suffered brutality and even death. To forsake the songs that have brought us through the suffering is to forsake the memory and sacrifices of those who suffered.

Today, we've broadened the movement arts to include various forms of poetry, visual arts, theater, dance, and more. We've even gone digital with the arts, which means we can reach, inform, and influence even more people today than we did in movements past. It is imperative that we employ every creative vehicle available to spread the message of resistance and hope. We can create a new narrative in favor of justice by using a variety of platforms to speak truth to power! We must work to put lyrics, physical movements, and paint to the pain that is sweeping the nation because of legislative oppression.

If it's true that art is everywhere, then we have the potential to change the songs and flip the scripts so that people hear, see, and feel messages of resistance and hope. We still need the Negro spirituals, the civil rights chants and songs, old-school blues and folk songs, but we need them to intersect with positive hip-hop, pop, neosoul, and inspirational music. We need theater to intersect with spoken word and spoken word with dance and dance with visual arts. This intersectionality of the arts lifting the moral outcry against injustice will seal the deal on a broad-scale fusion movement. In the words of Reverend Barber, "When we all get together, what a day! What a day! What a day!"

YARA ALLEN is the director of cultural arts for Repairers of the Breach and a movement theomusicologist. She is a visiting artist at Auburn Theological Seminary and the codirector of music and movement cultural arts for the Poor People's Campaign: A National Call for Moral Revival.

CHAPTER FOURTEEN

WE SHALL NOT BE MOVED!

2017 NATIONAL NAACP CONVENTION, JULY 28, 2017

Baltimore Convention Center, Baltimore, Maryland

THE REVEREND DR. WILLIAM J. BARBER II

The apostle Paul wrote, "Be steadfast, immovable, always abounding in the work of the Lord" and then, "Do that knowing that your labor is not in vain." There is—what we say in theology—a *Sitz im Leben* to every scripture, a context to every text. The context of that text is that the early Christians found themselves under attack. There was a narcissistic egomaniac sitting on the throne who loved to build towers and put his name on them. This may sound familiar, but I'm talking about the first century.

Caesar wanted everyone to bow down to him. Caesar declared that he alone could make Rome and all of her provinces great; that he and he alone could fix things. Caesar lived in his own alternative world with his own alternative facts. Caesar loved to text—I mean chisel out messages. He wanted everyone to worship him. He did not want these people around who followed God, who understood that to follow God was to love justice and to love love and to love mercy and to love truth. He wanted to strike them down. He wanted to move them out of the way. In fact, he had participated in the assassination and the cruel crucifixion of their leader who carried their dream. But against the backdrop of Caesar's narcissism, his attacks, his injustices, his downright craziness, Paul tells the faithful, "Be steadfast, immovable, always abounding in the work of the Lord."

Nearly a hundred years ago, 1918, right here in America, at the end of World War I, a racist narcissist occupied the White House. He played *The Birth of a Nation* in the White House. He was a president of a college and a governor of a state, but political office and education don't keep you from being a racist. He worked to turn back desegregation. He glorified the Klan. The NAACP was barely nine years old, but it was in that time that W. E. B. Du Bois wrote these words to Woodrow Wilson and the nation in the May 1919 article "Returning Soldiers" in the NAACP magazine the *Crisis*, which he'd cofounded: "We are returning from war! We return from the slavery of uniform which the world's madness demanded us to don to the freedom of civil garb. We stand again to look America squarely in the face. We sing, 'This country of ours, despite all its better souls have done and dreamed, is yet a shameful land.'" He said this country lynches. He said this country disenfranchises its own citizens.

"This is the country to which we 'soldiers of democracy' return. This is the fatherland for which we fought! But it was our fatherland. It was right for us to fight. . . . But by the God of heaven, we are cowards . . . if now that that war is over, we do not marshal every ounce of our brain and brawn to fight a sterner, longer, more unbending battle against the forces of hell in our own land."

So let it be known, America: "We return. We return from fighting. We return fighting. And we will not be moved."

You see, my friends, whether it is Paul in the first century, Du Bois in the twentieth century, or Leon W. Russell and Derrick Johnson in the NAACP in the twenty-first century, there is a time when we must plant our feet, stiffen our spines, gird up our faith, and declare we are immovable. The word "immovable" not only means "we won't move," the word immovable actually means "we can't move." You hear what I'm saying? The word "immovable" means there's something down on the inside that won't allow us to move even if we wanted to.

We are in some difficult times in America right now. From the White House to the Congress to the state houses there are narcissistic egomaniacs holding power. And it's not just Donald Trump. Trump is a symptom of a deeper moral malady. And Trump is not new. He's as American as apple pie. Nell Painter says about the American democratic process, we have a call for justice and then a call for injustice and many times they happen simultaneously. There are those who want to make America great again by taking America back again. And that's not just a slogan of a president. That is literally seen in the bills and legislation coming through Congress. And in this process, they want the NAACP, the Rainbow, and anyone else who dares challenge them to move out of the way.

But we come to Baltimore—I see some cameras back there—to say to them and to say to America: If you want us to move, then stop killing all our men and women, girls and boys. Stop profiling and punishing and stop the shooting to death and choking to death by rogue cops who hide behind badges in order to hide their racism and get off scot-free.

If you want us to move, tell those states—those thirty-three states that are passing and trying to pass racial voter-suppression laws—to stop. Tell them that long before Russia ever hacked our political system, racism had already done it. Tell them that we see the nine hundred fewer sites to vote in the black community and the hundreds of thousands of votes that were suppressed in the last election. Tell them that we understand that twenty-two states that passed voter-suppression laws represent forty-four senators and 51 percent of the United States Congress and 54 percent of all African American voters. Tell them that case after case has proven intentional and surgical racism. Tell them that if you want us to move, stop appointing attorney generals who are against voting rights. If you want us to move, then stop blocking full restoration of the Voting Rights Act for over 1,450 days. If you want us to move, then stop setting up phony voter integrity commissions and stop racist redistricting.

If you want us to move, tell politicians who got health care from public money to stop trying to take health care from nearly thirty million people. Tell them to stop passing policies that are nothing more than political murder because thousands will die. Millions like my daughter will lose coverage because of a preexisting condition.

If you want us to move, tell those politicians that are sold out to greed and want to give $700 billion back to greedy corporations—you want us to move? Tell them to stop. We haven't seen this kind of transfer of wealth since the wealth that was transferred on the backs of slaves. According to the Economic History Association Encyclopedia, in 1860, the receipt price for every slave in America was $3.6 billion; $700 billion is 190 times more than the receipt price of slaves in 1860.

If you want us to stop, if you want us to move, then stop denying poor workers $15 and a union while four hundred families make an average of $97,000 an hour. If you want us to move, then stop poisoning our water in poor, especially black communities. If you're mad as hell at Syria's Assad, you ought to be mad as hell at the politicians in Michigan and other states and other cities around the country who are passing laws that oppress people.

You want us to move? Stop talking to us about the mythology of black crime. America has a criminal history and a violent history. If you're going to talk to us about black crime, talk to us about the Wall Street criminals that never get charged.

If you want us to move, stop attacking our immigrant brothers and sisters. Stop attacking our Muslim brothers and sisters. Stop using our gay and lesbian and trans brothers and sisters as a scapegoat for your underhanded morality. You want us to move? Stop feeding the prison-industrial complex and give our public schools what they deserve to educate our children.

If you want us to move, then stop these modern-day false prophets from going into the White House and praying for the president and encouraging him to keep on doing what he's doing and never remind him and others that the Bible says, "Let justice roll down like waters, and righteousness like a mighty stream." "Woe unto them who legislate evil and rob the poor of their rights." Never say that the Bible says to every nation, "When I was hungry, did you feed me? When I was naked, did you clothe me? When I was sick, did you visit me?"

If you want us to move, then stop texting lies, stop telling lies, stop turning people against each other with lies! Because until you stop, we can't move. There you go. Too much is at stake. Too many martyrs have died. Too many tears have been cried. In the face of slavery, Harriet Tubman and Frederick Douglass didn't move. In the face of Jim Crow, Harry T. Moore, Medgar Evers, Rosa Parks, Martin Luther King, Abraham Heschel, and Ella Baker didn't move, and neither can we. We've got to stand, and when we've done all we can do, stand anyhow.

We must declare in this season, like a tree planted by the water, we shall not be moved. Moving is not in our DNA. Moving is not in our vocabulary. The Lord is our shepherd. We've been made to endure for a night, but joy comes in the morning. No weapon formed against us shall prosper. As long as there's life in our body, we shall not be moved. The race is not given to the swiftest, to the strongest, but to they that endure to the end. Do I have a witness?

We shall not move. The God we serve can part Red Seas, can make alive valleys of dry bones, can bring down Goliath with one stone. The God we serve can get up from three-day-old graves. We shall not be moved! Tell Trump, tell Paul Ryan, tell Mitch McConnell, tell the extremists, tell the courts, tell the racists: we shall not be moved! We're not moving from the streets! From the courts! We're not moving from the ballot box! I wish I had a witness, God! God has made us immovable. Like a tree planted aside the waters, we shall not be moved! Grab your neighbor by the hand and say, "Neighbor, stand!" Stand! Stand! Like a tree planted by the waters—We! Shall! Not! Be! Moved! Glory!

LISTENING TO THE HEART AND HURT OF THE PEOPLE

CHARMEINE FLETCHER

Executive Assistant, Repairers of the Breach

I have had the privilege of serving as the executive assistant for the Reverend Dr. Barber for more than twelve years. In this role, I've also had the distinct privilege of typing and retyping most of the manuscripts for his sermons. This has meant an erratic schedule. He does not always get inspiration during the normal eight-to-five workday. He reads constantly. He writes on note pads and sends text messages and email at any and every moment.

Though many themes recur throughout his sermons, Reverend Barber always tries to hear the particular hopes, dreams, and needs of the audiences he is addressing. Recently, we were in Baltimore for the 108th national convention of the NAACP, a critical convention because new leadership had taken the helm: an interim president and a new board chair. This convention occurred six months into the Trump administration as the very core issues the NAACP has fought to address throughout its existence were threatened by each decision, policy, and appointment. Adding to the historic nature of the moment, Barber had just been consecrated as a bishop by the College of Affirming Bishops and Bishop Yvette Flunder, an openly lesbian pastor and internationally known leader. He left the consecration in New Orleans to fly to Baltimore. I watched as he struggled even on the plane with exactly how to speak to the convention. In fact, he told me he had not written a word yet and could not decide on a launching or landing place. I knew what this meant. Reverend Dr. Barber once explained to me that writing a sermon was like flying a plane: you have to know how to take off and where to land before you can map out a flight plan.

They had titled his fifteen-minute spot at the convention "Immovable." When we arrived in Baltimore, Rev. Dr. Barber spent two days walking and talking and praying and sometimes crying with the people. He listened to those gathered at the convention. At one point, we said to him that we needed him to move along and not spend so much time with the people. To this he said, "I'm listening for the heart of God by listening to the heart and hurt of the people." He told us that Ezekiel spent seven days lying among the people before he was licensed to preach. Jesus spent thirty years in the ghetto before he preached a sermon.

Late Monday night he asked me to take dictation and help finish the transcript that he would use for that speech on Tuesday morning at 10 a.m. We finished around 3:30 a.m.

Then that morning I heard him deliver "We Shall Not Be Moved." I was moved, even though I had typed it. He added impromptu pieces that were not in the original. What thrills me about Reverend Barber's preaching is his commitment to always lift up, no matter where, his faithfulness to the context of the text. He has often said to me that it is a necessity—not to simply take a text and make a pretext but to be faithful to the text.

In the audience, I noticed that because he had listened to the people, the people were listening to him. In this oratorical moment that became a community, he was even able to ad lib and articulate how the community felt. He challenged a statement by Deputy Attorney General Rod Rosenstein at the convention about gang crime and crime in the black community by pointing out that he'd had nothing to say about the criminal acts of Wall Street and the social political crimes being committed by Attorney General Jeff Sessions through his attacks on voting rights and refusal to fully support efforts against police brutality.

It was as though he was not really speaking to them from a platform but was among them. Even as he challenged those in the audience, it seemed to come from a friend, a fellow colleague in the struggle, not a leader for them but *with* them. Some of them were waving their hands, some crying, some shouting, some sitting silently but with a deep intensity. They seemed to be hearing from him a way forward.

This was grounded in the kind of commitment we have to make even in the darkest and most difficult times. Several of the people he admires—like former NAACP CEO Kweisi Mfume and the Reverend Jesse Jackson—others stood to join Reverend Barber as he preached until a call and response, known in the black church and in the prophetic readings of the Bible, had taken full effect.

As I've seen time and time again, community was formed through oratory where the preacher and the people became one. That community became hopeful in the midst of despair. This was not the kind of hope that ignores the pain and ugliness but the kind of hope that says to wicked and mean power structures, no matter what you do, we shall not be moved.

By the time the sermon was over, the whole audience was declaring it, the people on the stages were declaring it, and everyone understood that even if the battle is a long one, the first battle is the battle with our own selves. It is a commitment to say to the forces of injustice that we will not be moved from our mission of love, justice, mercy, and standing up for what is right. We must stand and not be moved.

CHARMEINE NYOKO FLETCHER is the executive administrator and scheduler for Repairers of the Breach. She has served as Reverend Barber's executive assistant for more than twelve years and travels extensively across the country and abroad doing logistics for the movement. She served ten years as a social worker for the North Carolina Department of Social Services and is a decorated retired veteran who served twenty years in the United States Air Force. Charmeine lives her life as a servant in the ministry, following the biblical scriptures of Jesus Christ.

ACKNOWLEDGMENTS

We owe deep gratitude to everyone who has contributed to the book and, more important, the Forward Together Moral Mondays Movement, the Moral Revival: Time for a Revolution of Values, the Poor People's Campaign: A National Call for Moral Value, and the moral movement for justice growing and spreading across the country and world. We thank the contributors to the book; their responses show the necessity of coming together with a moral agenda that unites living wages with LGBTQ rights and environmental issues, unites housing and homelessness to the calamity of voter suppression and systemic racism. For help preparing and editing the manuscript, we thank Daniel Jones, Noam Sandweiss Back, and particularly Dr. Colleen Wessel-McCoy, as well as a team of transcribers including Lindsey Jordan, Nancy Taylor, Julio Torres, Quantez Pressley, and others. We also want to acknowledge Inga Skippings and Carter Wright for their help on chapter 10 responses. We thank the amazing team at Beacon Press, especially our editor, Will Myers, and the director, Helene Atwan. And to our families, colleagues in the struggle, and loved ones, thank you for your commitment and clarity. Indeed, we who believe in freedom cannot rest until it comes.